BECKETT, DERRIDA, AND THE EVENT OF LITERATURE

Cultural Memory
in
the
Present

Mieke Bal and Hent de Vries, Editors

BECKETT, DERRIDA, AND THE EVENT OF LITERATURE

Asja Szafraniec

STANFORD UNIVERSITY PRESS
STANFORD, CALIFORNIA
2007

Stanford University Press
Stanford, California

©2007 by the Board of Trustees of the Leland Stanford Junior University.
All rights reserved.

No part of this book may be reproduced or transmitted in any form or by any means, electronic or mechanical, including photocopying and recording, or in any information storage or retrieval system without the prior written permission of Stanford University Press.

Library of Congress Cataloging-in-Publication Data

Szafraniec, Asja.
 Beckett, Derrida, and the event of literature / Asja Szafraniec.
   p. cm. — (cultural memory in the present)
 ISBN 978-0-8047-5456-9 (cloth : alk. paper) — ISBN 978-0-8047-5457-6 (pbk. : alk. paper)
  1. Beckett, Samuel, 1906–1989—Criticism and interpretation. 2. Derrida, Jacques. 3. Literature—History and criticism—Theory, etc. 4. Authorship—Psychological aspects. 5. Literature—Philosophy. 6. Deconstruction.
 I. Title.
PR6003.E282z8375 2007
848'.91409—dc22   2007004809

Typeset by Westchester Book Group in 11/13.5 Garamond

For my parents

Contents

	Acknowledgments	xi
	Introduction	1
1.	The Question of Literature	27
2.	A Singular Odyssey	55
3.	Beckett, Derrida, and the Ordinary	71
4.	Beckett's "Exhausted" Archives	92
5.	Singular Points of Transaction (I): The Subject	118
6.	Singular Points of Transaction (II): "What Are Poets For?" The Authority of Literature	140
7.	Singular Points of Transaction (III): "Wanting in Inanity." Negativity, Language, and "God" in Beckett	161
	Concluding Remarks	183
	Notes	193
	Bibliography	231
	Index	241

Acknowledgments

Part of this book was written during my stay at the Department of Comparative Literature at SUNY Buffalo. I would like to thank Rodolphe Gasché for his invitation and continued support. At different stages of writing the manuscript my colleagues from both the Department of Philosophy of the University of Amsterdam and the Amsterdam School of Cultural Analysis read and commented on parts of it: Mieke Bal, Christel van Boheemen, Paola Marrati, Burcht Pranger, Ruth Sonderegger, and Martin Stokhof, and, on his leave from Barnard College, Peter Connor. Other colleagues gave me what I perhaps valued most: their friendship. Among these, I would especially like to mention Dorota Mokrosinska; Yolande Jansen; my roommate, Frank Rebel; and Marie-Aude Baronian. Richard Moore helped me prepare the manuscript in more ways than one, not only turning out to be a wonderful editor but also coming up with invaluable critiques and advice. Finally, I would like to thank Erik for sharing his inner peace with me in times of turmoil.

My deepest thanks are to Hent de Vries for his unfailing encouragement and advice. Without him this book would not have been written.

An earlier version of a section of this book has already appeared in print. Chapter 7 was published in 2005 in *European Joyce Studies Annual* (Amsterdam: Rodopi, 2005). I gratefully acknowledge the editor's permission to use that material here.

Introduction

> L'ouverture de la modernité n'est rien d'autre que l'ouverture de la pensée à l'événement en tant que tel, à la vérité de l'événement outre tout avènement de sens.
> —Nancy

"That Wasn't Possible for Me with Beckett": Derrida's Unmet Challenge

If it seems to us productive to bring together writers and thinkers who draw on similar intellectual traditions, this is not merely on hermeneutic grounds—because it helps us to understand their work, to fill in, by cross-reference, the lacunae where an underlying thought has been taken for granted. Rather, by staging an imaginary dialogue between two authors, we want to become alert to issues that, endemic to the thought of one, might form a challenge to the thought of the other. This work started as the search for such a challenge to the thought of Jacques Derrida: a challenge that might be found in literature and that would put to the test his ideas about the latter—not a small task considering that Derrida to a large extent owes his fame to his remarkably insightful interpretations of literary works. The idea of confronting Derrida's understanding of literature with the work of Samuel Beckett was born the moment I read Derrida's response to an interview question about Beckett posed by Derek Attridge (who was relaying it on behalf of one of his students). I quote this question and Derrida's response to it in its entirety.

D.A. Let me move on to some specific authors and texts. In an interview you once mentioned Samuel Beckett along with other writers whose texts "make the limits of our language tremble." As far as I'm aware, you've never written on Beckett: is this a future project, or are there reasons why you have observed this silence?

J.D. Very rapidly. This is an author to whom I feel very close, or to whom I would like to feel myself very close; but also too close. Precisely because of this proximity, it is too hard for me, too easy and too hard. I have perhaps avoided him a bit because of this identification. Too hard also because he writes—in my language, in a language which is his up to a point, mine up to a point (for both of us it is a "differently" foreign language)—texts which are both too close to me and too distant for me even to be able to "respond" to them. How could I write in French in the wake of or "with" someone who does operations on this language which seem to me so strong and so necessary, but which must remain idiomatic? How could I write, sign, countersign performatively texts which "respond" to Beckett? How could I avoid the platitude of a supposed academic metalanguage? It is very hard. You will perhaps say to me that for other foreign authors like Kafka, Celan, or Joyce, I attempted it. Yes, at least attempted. Let's not speak of the result. I had a kind of excuse or alibi: I write in French, from time to time I quote the German or the English, and the two writings, the "performative signatures," are not only incommensurable in general, that goes without saying, but above all without a "common language," at least in the ordinary sense of the term. Given that Beckett writes in a particular French, it would be necessary, in order to "respond" to his oeuvre, to attempt writing performances that are impossible for me (apart from a few stammering [and thus oral] tries in some seminars devoted to Beckett in the last few years). I was able to risk linguistic compromises with Artaud, who also has his way of loving and violating, or lovingly violating a certain French language of its language. But in Artaud (who is paradoxically more distant, more foreign for me than Beckett) there are texts which have permitted me writing transactions. Whatever one thinks of their success or failure, I have given myself up to them and published them. That wasn't possible for me with Beckett, whom I will thus have "avoided" as though I had always already read him and understood him too well.[1]

In what way could the work of Beckett fall beyond the scope of literature as understood by Derrida? (It should be noted that Beckett was not unfamiliar with the work of Derrida; in his *L'amitié de Beckett,* André

Bernold mentions that he discussed the work of Derrida at length with Beckett in the early to mid-1980s.)[2] The two reasons Derrida gives for his incapacity to respond to Beckett seem unsatisfactory. First he blames his sense of being in excessive proximity to (and even his "identification" with) Beckett. In fact, Derrida says it was easier to write on Artaud, whom Derrida experienced as "paradoxically, more distant, more foreign" than Beckett. Yet this appears less paradoxical than it might seem when we consider that a strategy pursued by Derrida when commenting on many texts is to demonstrate an inherent naïveté, or at least an unexpected ambiguity at work in a given text. (This is after all considered to be a deconstructive gesture par excellence: the demonstration of the impossibility of permanently excluding the excluded, the demonstration of its return, often even as the necessary presupposition.) When writing on Celan, Derrida questions the possibility of a unique event; when writing on Artaud, he dismantles his naïve desire for absolute presence on the stage; and when writing on Blanchot, he works to show how his writing on death is actually a triumph of life. Obviously, Derrida cannot do this with respect to a text that stands in absolute proximity to his thought without sabotaging his own philosophical enterprise. However, this in itself does not preclude any possibility of comment; after all, Derrida could uphold a work that is remarkably close to his own enterprise as paradigmatic of his own ideas, as happened in the case of his essay on Kafka's "Before the Law." The excessive proximity thus not providing a sufficient explanation, Derrida ventures an additional reason for the difficulty he experiences in commenting on Beckett: the shared language. Contrary to what common sense might lead us to expect, shared language is a disadvantage in Derrida's project of commenting on literary works. Derrida treats his operating in a language other than that of the work upon which he is commenting as an alibi (in its literal sense, "elsewhere"), necessary to preserve untouched the idiom of the other work; there must be no "common language" between the two.

It is not at all clear why this rule of incommensurability, of "no common language," seems to be so pertinent to Derrida, who after all managed to comment on Mallarmé, Genet, Blanchot, and Flaubert, and in the same breath admits to being capable of "linguistic compromises" with Artaud. The interviewer himself does not seem to be thoroughly satisfied with this answer and presses on:

D.A. Is there a sense in which Beckett's writing is already so "deconstructive," or "self-deconstructive," that there is not much left to do?

J.D. No doubt that's true. A certain nihilism is both interior to metaphysics (the final fulfillment of metaphysics, Heidegger would say) and then, already, beyond. With Beckett in particular, the two possibilities are in the greatest possible proximity and competition. He is nihilist and he is not nihilist. Above all, this question should not be treated as a philosophical problem outside or above the texts. When I found myself, with students, reading some Beckett texts, I would take three lines, I would spend two hours on them, then I would give up because it would not have been possible, or honest, or even interesting, to extract a few "significant" lines from a Beckett text. The composition, the rhetoric, the construction and the rhythm of his works, even the ones that seem the most "decomposed," that's what "remains" finally the most "interesting," that's the work, that's the signature, this remainder which remains when the thematics is exhausted (and also exhausted, by others, for a long time now, in other modes).

With Joyce, I was able to pretend to isolate two words (*He war* or *yes, yes*); with Celan, one foreign word (*Shibboleth*); with Blanchot, one word and two homonyms (*pas*).[3]

Only in this second response do we get a glimpse of what it might be that permits Derrida's "writing transactions" with Artaud but makes them impossible with Beckett. Derrida confesses that, whereas he did manage to "isolate" significant words in Joyce, Celan, and Blanchot, he attempted in vain to extract "significant lines" from Beckett. The attempt described here fits perfectly with Derrida's conception of literature as an economical use of language, permitting one to say everything by means of encoding, to set up an archive in a minimal space: a word, a date so "economically" powerful that it would be able to gather in itself the maximum of possible figures, references, and meanings. ("The economy of literature sometimes seems to me more powerful than that of other types of discourse," says Derrida in the same interview.) This economical motif—the gathering of a multiplicity of meanings in a singular trait—constitutes half of Derrida's conception of literature (the other half being the reflection of the literary work on its own universality), the whole presenting itself as an interaction of the singular and the universal. If we are to accept Derrida's response as having an explanatory value, then we must assume that it was not possible for Derrida to make "transactions" with Beckett because his texts failed to provide an economically potent and thus "significant" word, date, or phrase; in other words, because they failed to provide the singular moment that would elicit a pertinent response from Derrida's machinery of thought.

One could object that Derrida's not writing on Beckett was a matter of a temporary lack of opportunity, to which only his premature death has given a status of permanence. Suffice it to say that during his philosophical career, Derrida was on various occasions asked to appear at conferences devoted to Beckett and always declined, giving similar reasons. In 1994, Derrida was invited to contribute to "Beckett in France"—a special edition of the *Journal of Beckett Studies*—and again turned down the invitation, writing courteously that he was unable "not only but in particular because of my inability to write something that Beckett would deserve."[4] It would have been difficult to find a more attractive opportunity to experiment with Beckett. This edition, which started with the idea of a special issue on Gilles Deleuze and Beckett, soon evolved into a presentation of a broader spectrum of very innovative approaches to Beckett, including a contribution by Badiou. Consequently, Derrida's refusal seems to suggest that when he gave up on the idea of writing on Beckett, he did so for good.

However, my concern is not merely to establish the reasons that might hinder Derrida in his attempts to give a reading of Beckett. I am interested in what this impediment says about literature, and in what way this could present itself as a challenge to Derrida's concept of literature. With this question, the present work would like to align itself with other Beckett studies interested in the relation of Beckett's work to philosophy (including contributions by Adorno, Blanchot, Butler, Connor, Deleuze, Hill, Locatelli; for a more extensive list, see Anthony Uhlmann[5]), and with those discussions of Derrida that pertain to his interest in the philosophy of literature. More generally, by both discussing Derrida's approach to literature and addressing some recent philosophical interpretations of Beckett, I would like to contribute to the discourse that investigates the relationship between philosophy and literature.

Derrida's statements on Beckett in the interview with Derek Attridge provoked in one Beckett critic an almost vehement response under the sweeping title "At Beckett's Grave (or Why Jacques Derrida Has Given Up on Writing in the Direction of Beckett—for the Moment)." In this manifesto-like comment that argues for "reestablish[ing] the sense of an authorial and human presence in [Beckett's] works,"[6] and regretfully announces that "we obviously lack clearly worked out methodologies for dealing with Beckett's art," the author ends up accusing New Criticism, and Derrida with it, of "totalizing claims which . . . sweepingly proclaim the death of the author." (Incidentally, this critic is also the author of the chapter "Beckett and the Philosophers" in the prestigious *Cambridge Companion to Beckett* [1994].) Whereas it is true that the complex issue of the author in Beckett is largely unresolved, nothing is less true than the implication that Derrida takes the idea of the "death of the author" for granted. His *Parages* in particular testifies to the contrary (and might even turn out to be helpful to the discussion of authorial issues in Beckett). "Survivre," the title of one of the essays included in *Parages*, stands, among other things, for the paradoxical survival of the author. Not to mention that in *Signsponge*, Derrida speaks emphatically of "that death or omission of the author of which, as is certainly the case, too much of a case has been made" ("cette mort ou omission de l'auteur dont on fait, c'est le cas de le dire, trop grand cas").[7] This is indicative of the number of misunderstandings and unresolved issues that we will encounter in the Beckett-Derrida domain.

Beckett and the Philosophers

Let us consider what Beckett scholars address as the "vexed but fundamental question of Beckett's relationship to the philosophers."[8] Most at stake is the nature of Beckett's quite original experiment and its meaning for philosophy, rather than Beckett's philosophical erudition, the traces of which emerge with a certain regularity in his work. (Guelinx, Descartes, Spinoza, Schopenhauer, Heidegger, and Wittgenstein—the latter despite Beckett's explicit denial of any familiarity with his work—are perhaps the names of philosophers most often cited in connection with Beckett.) Only that explains the numerous philosophical readings of Beckett's oeuvre: readings, that is, either by philosophers, through philosophy (focusing on problems recognized as philosophical), or for philosophy (providing a starting point for philosophical inquiry). Some of those contributions are very short or function as part of a larger argument, but they have been influential enough to merit mention nevertheless. Among those who wrote on Beckett in the early years, between the fifties and the seventies, were Bataille, Blanchot, Cavell, Adorno, Kristeva, Cixous, and Foucault (who referred to Beckett in the opening lines of his influential essay "What Is an Author?").[9] The eighties brought responses from Deleuze, Nussbaum, Ricoeur, and Lyotard.[10] That decade also brought numerous publications devoted to exploring relations between Beckett and particular philosophers (Beckett and Schopenhauer, Beckett and Nietzsche, Beckett and Heidegger, and Beckett and Baudrillard).[11] In the nineties, Badiou and Deleuze gave intriguing interpretations of Beckett, and Blanchot published a further short text. Beckett scholars and literary critics also realized that they could not circumvent the philosophical issues in Beckett's work: Perloff wrote on Beckett and Wittgenstein; Uhlmann wrote on Beckett and the "post-structuralists" (especially Foucault); and, quite recently, Richard Lane edited a book gathering contributions on Beckett and philosophers from Nietzsche to Badiou.[12]

With her *Wittgenstein's Ladder: Poetic Language and the Strangeness of the Ordinary*, literary critic Marjorie Perloff pleaded for a more analytic approach, trying to counteract the otherwise overwhelmingly "continental" (with the exception of Cavell's essay) reception of Beckett's work. Her book has been received as a turning away from so-called "theory"—the word that for Perloff is almost synonymous with Derrida—toward the anti-theory that she associates with a Wittgensteinian mode of investigation.

Finally, next to the continental-analytic debate, a case apart among the philosophical approaches to Beckett is the work of Alain Badiou, at odds with "all three of the great currents of twentieth-century philosophy—the analytic philosophy descended from logical positivism and the later Wittgenstein, the hermeneutics variously inspired by Dilthey, Heidegger, and Gadamer, and the poststructuralism developed by Derrida and Lyotard."[13] I leave aside the question of whether it makes sense to adhere to the strict division between the hermeneutic and "poststructuralist" strands of continental thought; what this citation makes clear is the purported radical otherness of Badiou's approach. Indifferent to the anti-Platonic crusade of recent continental thought, Badiou takes Plato (his particular reading of Plato, that is) as his example and a guiding hand. Badiou charges Heidegger and most contemporary French thinkers—including Derrida—with the "fetishism of literature":[14] "since Nietzsche, all philosophers claim to be poets, they all envy poets, they are wishful poets or approximate poets, or acknowledged poets, as we see with Heidegger, but also with Derrida or Lacoue-Labarthe."[15] He then sets out to free philosophy from what he sees as its subservience to literature, without however renouncing an interest in literature. One of Badiou's examples being Beckett, I will inquire to what extent Beckett's work can be seen as instrumental to Badiou's project of a critique of the relationship between philosophy (and Derridean philosophy in particular) and literature.

The Relationship between Philosophy and Literature

"You are not a serious philosopher! If you continue, you will be placed in a department of . . . literature,"[16] cautions an imaginary opponent in Derrida's *Monolingualism of the Other*. The apparently excessive importance he attaches to the potential of literature to question philosophical discourse often awakens in Derrida scholars the urge to shelter his image from such "obscure" areas as the literary. They find it necessary to separate his thought from this aspect of his interests, to treat him as becomes a "serious philosopher," to protect him, against his own choices and interests, from what he himself, amused, addresses as the risk of being relegated to a "department of rhetoric or literature."

This warning, or risk, can only be intimidating if "a serious philosopher" experiences it as a menace. And, indeed, many a self-respecting philosopher takes the threat of being relegated to a department of literature very seriously. It is one thing to admire literature, having the alibi of operating in a distinct region of philosophical discourse; it is another to be exiled from that region to a discipline that has as its task the understanding and explanation of literature. For, the "serious philosopher" will say, it is a discipline in which rhetoric is stronger than sustained argument; a discipline that deals with the practically lawless, since its singular law eludes us. And if we agree that it is lawless, does that mean it's open equally to everyone, or is entrance arbitrary and whimsical? But can philosophy do without the examination of literature? The controversial relationship between philosophy and literature is known to have oscillated between such dramatically opposite positions as Plato's suggestion to banish the poets from the ideal state and Richard Rorty's perception of philosophy as a genre of literature. The controversy is by no means recent: one of the very early desires of philosophy was to make literature disappear—Plato's *Republic* testifies to this.[17] As Stanley Cavell points out, this famous banishment of poetry from the ideal city is, significantly, not a banishment from what Socrates calls "our city of words"—that is, from discourse itself.[18] Quite the contrary. Nonetheless, the impact of that ancient condemnation of poetry is, rightly or wrongly, still felt. The often-heard complaint from the departments of aesthetics is that, after Plato,

[t]he history of philosophy has alternated between the analytical effort to ephemeralize and hence defuse art, or, to allow a degree of validity to art by treating it as doing what philosophy itself does, only uncouthly.[19]

It is not only Plato that is being addressed here. Kant, too, is a target on the grounds that his notion of "purposiveness without a purpose"[20] refuses art any bearing on life, and also Hegel, for presenting art as "philosophy in one of its self-alienated forms, thirsting for clarity as to its own nature." In other words, Hegel may be taken as attempting to demonstrate that "art is philosophy in its embryonic form."[21]

Yet, particularly in the case of Hegel, such an interpretation lends itself to being modified in a significant way. What if literature were like a thorn in philosophy's side from the very beginning, forcing it to develop a whole defense mechanism, a mechanism that we now consider to be the essence of philosophy? The status of literature would no longer be merely that of simple historical precedence (by virtue of which art is now overtaken by the philosophy for which it paved the way). Its priority would now be that of a transcendental kind. To understand literature would be for philosophy to understand its own forgotten and feared premises. One corollary of such a shift in perception would be not only that literature can function as a field of philosophical inquiry but also that philosophy needs to examine its own relation to literature.

There is yet another way of looking at the relationship between philosophy and literature—not in terms of philosophy's responding to the crisis caused by literature (this is how we could interpret Plato's concern with the "demoralizing" effects of literature) but, conversely, in terms of literature's responding to the crisis in philosophy. That the literature of early German Romanticism did respond to such a crisis is uncontested; the works of that period may be seen as the product of the first significant rapprochement between philosophy and literature. The authors of *The Literary Absolute* pressed this argument one step further. For them, Romanticism (and, in particular, Friedrich Schlegel's attempt to elaborate a concept of the "fragment," published in 1798–1800 in the journal *Athenaeum*) would not even be comprehensible if not seen "in its proper and unique articulation with the philosophical."[22] Jena Romanticism, as it is called now, is of importance to us because it can be treated as the origin of the modern notion of literature that at the same time is inextricably linked to philosophy. Nancy and Lacoue-Labarthe's reading of the *Athenaeum* "Fragments" shows literature to have originated as a response to a philosophical crisis. This crisis starts with Kant's struggle with the presentability of "ideas," a project that he pursued implicitly throughout the three *Critiques*.[23] Only if the (unrepresentable) idea of freedom can somehow take shape can the Kantian *cogito* be seen as something more than merely an "empty form" or a "pure logical necessity," and hence as a subject capable not only of the "spontaneity of understanding" but also of autonomous moral actions. The last *Critique,* with its overt purpose of building a bridge between the first two, offered a hint of a solution in the shape of the aesthetic ideas: the possibility of the staging (*Darstellung*) of the "never substantial 'substance' of the 'subject'" by means of the *Beautiful*."[24] Thus, Kant sought to demonstrate the possibility of an artistic self-production of the free subject. But this delegated the responsibility for the unity of the philosophical system to art: a crisis. In virtue of its having originated as a response to this crisis—a response that philosophy itself elicited—the received concept of literature must to an extent be philosophical.

These two examples, one of philosophy establishing itself in a gesture of self-defense against literature, and the other of the modern notion of literature establishing itself in response to philosophy, show that philosophy and literature, rather than competing with each other, have from the beginning been engaged in a productive exchange. Heidegger later pushed this idea to the extreme, claiming that as much as the task of the poet is quasi-philosophical, the task of the philosopher is quasi-poetic. While all thinking is *dichtend* (inventive), not all of it is *dichterisch* (poetic), nor is it *denkerisch* (thoughtful). But authentically innovative thinking should be *denkerisch-dichterisch,* both thoughtful and poetic. This postulate became especially relevant after the *Kehre,* which required a transformation of language from propositional to poetic; it was, after all—as Heidegger himself acknowledged in the "Letter on Humanism"—the problem of language that made him interrupt the itinerary he set with *Being and Time*. In Heidegger's eyes, only "poietic" language was able to present an alternative to the metaphysical language of *Being and Time*, and to succeed in saying "Being *as* Time," in its historicity (*Seynsgeschichtlichkeit*).[25]

How does one embark on a project concerning the relationship between literature and philosophy? To approach it by defining the two domains (i.e., by determining their essential qualities) would be self-defeating, considering that even if we assume that it is possible to pinpoint the qualities that are essential for philosophical discourse (e.g., sustained argument, clarity of exposition), this is not possible for literature, since what the latter seeks to attain is precisely to overcome and exceed its own essence. At least a certain kind of literature, conceived as a continuous experiment, seeks to attain this. Furthermore, philosophers can be seen as experimenting with literary means of expression in their works in a way that is inseparable from the "properly" philosophical argument. Stanley Cavell has repeatedly argued as much with respect to Wittgenstein's later work (in his 1962 essay "The Availability of Wittgenstein's Later Philosophy" and in his 1996 essay "The *Investigations*' Everyday Aesthetics of Itself").

Seen in this way, the description of literature as trying to overcome its own essence does not hold for all that is commonly taken to belong to the category of literature, but both more and less than that. At stake here are the texts that, in Derrida's words, "make the limits of our language tremble," which include works as different as Joyce's *Ulysses*, St. John's *Apocalypse*, and Plato's *Phaedo*—not all that commonly passes for literature but also not only that. The works named here belong to three different canons and not accidentally so, because for Derrida, the dividing line between philosophy and literature does not pass between sets of works commonly associated with those discourses but cuts through each individual work. The rethinking of the dividing line in terms of "another criterion . . . can and must destroy the great ensembles that give us Plato, Descartes, Kant, Hegel on one side, and Homer, Shakespeare, Goethe on the other. . . . The relation to language is different in *each* case."[26] We are urged by Derrida to consider each work's relationship to natural language as singular, independently of whether or not it belongs to the canon of literature or philosophy.

If we look more closely we shall find a Platonic literature that is not the literature of Hegel, and a Shakespearean philosophy that is not the philosophy of Dante, Goethe or Diderot. What we have, then, is an enormous research program, in which the received—or receivable—categories of academic scholarship must not be trusted.[27]

According to Derrida, there are no strict divisions and no essential difference between literature and other discourses. This is not to say that there is no difference between those discourses at all. While there is no essential difference, there is an institutional difference. It is in virtue of the latter that Derrida can add:

[I]f literature is somehow privileged here in my eyes, it is on the one hand, because it thematizes the event of writing, and on the other hand, because of what, in its political history, links literature to the authorization in principle to "say everything"—which in a unique fashion relates it to what we call truth, fiction, simulacrum, science, philosophy, law, right and democracy.[28]

As an institution different from other institutions, literature functions differently, setting for itself different goals and standards: to reflect on the event of writing, or to contest all possible limits to what can be said. In "thematizing the event of writing," literature addresses itself, revealing that it is both an institution and a counterinstitution (*à la fois institution et contre-institution*), taking place in the space of difference that an institution produces with itself (*placée à l'écart de l'institution, à l'angle que l'institution fait avec elle-même pour s'écarter d'elle-même*).[29] It is this position of literature, as both self-reflexive and self-differing, that allows it to be critical not only with respect to itself but also with respect to other institutions. This institutional affiliation—which has at least as much to do with the expectations that we have of literature (with the way we read it) as with the plain content of a literary work—is what still makes it possible for us to retain some distinction between "philosophy" and "literature."

Derrida's claim that literature can say everything (and we can reasonably take him to imply here that other institutions, philosophy among them, cannot) might be taken to suggest that the literary prerogative is all-encompassing. Thus, its realm would include the realm of philosophy:

everything that is said (including philosophy) can be treated as literature, whereas the reverse is not the case for philosophy. However, Derrida always speaks of literature in terms of works that have a philosophical potential (which would make literature, as he understands it, a part of philosophy as much as philosophy is a part of literature). One might object that it is not certain that all literary works have this potential; however, Derrida's glossing of literary works as those that have the ability to "say everything" makes it necessary that the literary includes the philosophical. As long as a literary work is able to "say everything," it must be able to "convey philosophy" (and hence it can be treated as a philosophical work, or rather as an infinite set of philosophical works—possibly even contradicting one another). That is why Derrida is able to compare Joyce's project of gathering to the Odyssey of the *Phenomenology of Spirit*.[30] In this sense, Derrida is not very far from thinking of great works in Heidegger's terms—as finding themselves at an intersection of what we commonly associate with literature or philosophy: *denkerisch-dichterisch*.

In so characterizing Derrida's understanding of "literature," I have already parted with the idea of literature as a collection of works in different genres in which it would be possible to discern some steady paradigm or formal principle of configuration—for example, the paradigm of a (quasi-) plot in the genre of the novel. Rather, I am interested in a quite limited group of works that succeeded not only in bringing about a schism or paradigm shift but also in "exploding it from within." These are the works Derrida refers to as "[making] the limits of our language tremble," including ones by Stéphane Mallarmé, James Joyce, Paul Celan, Georges Bataille, Antonin Artaud, Maurice Blanchot, Francis Ponge, Edmond Jabès, Franz Kafka, and Samuel Beckett. Even though they belong "institutionally" to the domain of literature, in the sense that they are *à l'écart* these works can all be situated in the difference of the literary institution, where literature "differs from itself"—that is, they are all *denkerisch-dichterisch*.

The texts addressed here not only bear witness to the crisis in the literary institution but also embody a critical experience of literature. It is not enough to say about this kind of literature that it is self-reflexive, for one cannot just introduce a self-reflexive moment into a literary work if what one wants is to give it the force of a genuinely critical experience. The self-reflection staged here is not face-to-face—which would make literature closed in upon itself and indifferent to the outside world—but at an angle, *à l'écart*, which means that in differing from itself, it is also open to what is beyond it.

Derrida says about these texts that "the force of their event depends on the fact that a thinking about their own possibility (both general and singular) is put to work in them in a singular work."[31] In other words, next to its being self-reflexive and paradigm breaking, the force of literature depends on its being encapsulated within a singular achievement. The impact of the literary seems to be intimately related to its singularity. And the singularity in question is no longer the property of a subjective judgment (Kantian singular judgment of taste)[32] but of the moment in which the subject and the work encounter each other (what Heidegger calls "subjectity," and Derrida, following Artaud, the "subjectile"). After attempting to look at literature through the ordering focus of paradigms and formal principles, it seems like a defeat to have to recognize that what is most powerful in literature is that which resists or is marginalized by this approach. We will see, however, that the singular brings with it its own universality—in fact, that all claim to universality of the literary work is founded on the singular.

The singular appears repeatedly in contemporary philosophical reflections on literature. It has been addressed not only by Derrida but also, variously inflected, by Gilles Deleuze, Jean-Luc Nancy, and Alain Badiou, among others. For some, the singular addresses just the unique, "one-time-only" quality of what is represented. Thus in Badiou's eyes, poetry is primarily concerned with capturing in language the singularity of the presence of the sensible: "Fundamentally, a poem addresses not so much a sunset in general as this sunset, not so much the color of the tiles in general as the color of those tiles there. The poem never succeeds here absolutely, but nevertheless this is its goal."[33] The goal of the poem is to recover the singularity of the sensible. The only development that poetry has undergone with respect to this point is, according to Badiou, a change of focus of poetic enunciation. The modernist poem replaced the effort to recover the singularity of the sensible with the meditation on the singularity of the poem itself. Nonetheless, the primary aim of poetry remained the absolutization of the singular moment. In this sense philosophy, in its concern with the truth (the latter understood by Badiou as a relationship between the singular and universal), situates itself in the extension of the poetic concern with singularity. Poetry summons the absolute of the singular, and to this extent philosophy relies on the condition in which the poem finds itself. Philosophy must recognize that in its work of thought it faces "the *successive forms* of this experience of the incandescence of the visible that the poem attempts to capture."[34] Whereas Badiou grants that the movement of a poem toward the singular (and, in consequence, toward its own disappearance and self-consummation) does not have to be essential to poetry in general (nor even to the sort of poetry he prefers), this kind of poetry epitomizes for him the task of philosophy. This task is the "ethical task of thought"—namely, the welcoming of the unpredictable (which philosophy must do differently, in a systematic way).

Derrida's concern with the singular is interesting in a philosopher who throughout his career pursued the idea that everything is iterable,[35] claiming that there is no "first time" and no "one time only." It signals that next to the philosophy of repetition, there is a certain dream of that entity which repeatability cannot capture, that which constantly effaces itself—the absolutely unique and ineffable. At the same time, this repeated insistence that nothing is absolutely unique (or rather that the absolutely unique is absolutely repeatable) makes describing what the singular is a far from easy task. Is it that which resists subsumption into general laws? Is it the idiomatic? The idiosyncratic? We know that for Kant, singularity is a property of the judgments of taste—subjective judgments in which we refer to the feelings (of pleasure or pain) caused by aesthetic objects in an immediate fashion and not by means of concepts. They could gain universality by being expressed conceptually, but then the direct sense of beauty, which relies on the free play of our cognitive powers (which comes to an end with conceptualization), would be lost.

Derrida's notion of singularity, at first sight not directly (and on closer examination not exclusively) linked to the situation of a judgment of taste, addresses itself to kinds of relations that are in some ways analogous to such a judgment. One of them is the singular relationship of the literary work to itself, a self-pronounced judgment of taste so to speak, a singular attempt of a literary work to universalize itself. In Kantian terms, Derrida's question is then, How does the singularity of the literary work universalize itself while continuing to elicit the free play of the faculties—that is, without having to undergo formalization in concepts? How, in other words, can we think systematically something that exists in opposition to the notion of the system? In Derrida's *Signsponge* we read: "What could a science of the *alea* be? . . . We are at the threshold of such a science, which engages itself in a rather singular relationship with the very name of science."[36]

The above discussion of Derrida's notion of the singular is only preliminary. It might look for the moment as if, compared to Kant's singular aesthetic judgments, the singular in Derrida has been shifted from the side of the free play of faculties of the judging subject to the side of the self-reflective activity of the aesthetic object. This is not quite correct. While no longer something primarily on the side of the subject (in Kant, a singular judgment is primarily subjective and is represented as objective only on the basis of the subject's presupposition of speaking universally), the singular in Derrida is not purely on the side of the aesthetic object (conceived as Hegel's singular "this") either. Rather, in accordance with Heidegger's "subjectity" (or what Lacoue-Labarthe and Nancy call "subject-work"[37]), it is an interaction of both—the place where the subject and the object coincide in the work. It is there, in the subjectile, that the singular is to be addressed.

From the above we can already see that the singular is not the same as the particular, which by its nature is always mediated by a concept or presupposes a concept. The singular is not mediated in this way. It is starting from this constatation that Hegel sets upon his project of the *Phenomenology of Spirit*. Yet we know that the Hegelian singular "this" is bound to disappear because it cannot be addressed otherwise than by a universal concept and thereby negated in its singularity.[38]

Derrida's interest in the singular does not betoken an attempt to ignore or refute this conclusion. Rather, it draws our attention to the fact that also in Hegel, this disappearing singular is nevertheless the starting point of the Odyssey of spirit. In other words, even though it is "never given as a fact, an object or existing thing,"[39] the singular has an impact, the potential to become an institution. The question then is not whether, or in what way, we can grasp something in its absolute singularity (we cannot) but in what way a singular event can affect us or generate a series of effects beyond itself. It is for this reason that Derrida insists on singularity never being punctual, "never closed like a point or a fist."[40] In other words, Derrida's search for the singular is expressive of the question of how a highly individual moment (like that of a creative work) can have an impact, or force, that gives rise to a law or an institution. Derrida gives an answer on two related levels: the force that the singular mobilizes is both differential and formalizing.

"Force" is not a term that appears here by chance. The force in Hegel is what lets the phenomenon appear. Hegel's example of such force was electricity producing a bolt of lightning. Even though the singular "this" is bound to disappear, it can to an extent be recovered, Hegel says, when consciousness looks "through the mediating play of *forces* into the true background of things."[41] Kojève explained this in his lectures on Hegel thus: "an entity revealed by force (*Kraft*)—this is the phenomenon (*Erscheinung*)."[42] Derrida expresses Hegel's claim more radically: "[T]o say that force is the origin of the phenomenon is to say nothing. By its very articulation force becomes a phenomenon. Hegel demonstrated convincingly that the explication of a phenomenon by a force is a tautology."[43] In other words, for Derrida to address force, he must address phenomena.

As he himself indicates, Derrida often takes recourse to the term "force": "in the many texts considered 'deconstructive,' and particularly in certain of those I've published myself, recourse to the word 'force' is quite frequent, and in strategic places . . . decisive."[44] It is enough to note some of the titles of Derrida's essays: "Force of Law," "Force of Mourning," "Force and Signification." In these texts, Derrida emphasizes the "differential character of force":

[F]or me, it is always a question of differential force, of difference as difference of force, of force as *différance* (*différance* is a force *différée-différante*), of the relation between force and form, between force and signification, performative force, illocutionary or perlocutionary force, of persuasive and rhetorical force.[45]

Considering that "by its very articulation force becomes a phenomenon," Derrida's use of the notion of "differential force" (which brings together all of the aspects mentioned above) is strategic in that it reopens the whole phenomenological tradition. It refers after all to the grounds of the determinateness of appearance. When Derrida thus speaks about literature in terms of the "force of the literary event,"[46] he is in fact posing the question of what makes the singular literary event appear, come to presence, as a phenomenon. Modifying the Hegelian metaphor of electricity and the bolt of lightning, Gilles Deleuze says that "thunderbolts explode between different intensities."[47] This gloss on Hegel that Deleuze uses to explain his notion of difference is helpful for understanding what the "differential force" of a literary event might mean. The latter is singular in the sense that there is no fully determinate context that would guarantee its "felicity"; there is no structure, no conceptual network, no convention to which it could have recourse to ensure its success. This is not to say that the singular appears in complete isolation. On the contrary, in order to occur as a literary event, it must, to speak with Deleuze, mobilize different contextual "intensities." It must reshuffle the existent configuration of contexts and thereby let the as yet unacknowledged differential force manifest itself.

Derrida's emphasis on the overall "differential character of force" seems to suggest that for him this description applies to the functioning of all of the forces named above, including those associated with speech act theory—namely the performative, illocutionary, and perlocutionary forces. They, too, would be dependent on the productive mobilization of differences in intensity rather than on fitting into the right context alone. There is much to be said for the latter view, not only as far as literature is concerned but also in the case of jokes. (In this sense, Derrida's insistence on iterability, in the sense of both repetition and productive "othering"—"iter" meaning "other"—as a primary condition of the "felicity" of speech acts can be seen as a broadening of Austinian context requirements. Iterability covers both the condition of fitting into the right context [through faithful repetition] and the possibility of exploiting the wrongness of a context, as in the case of jokes.) In his afterword to *Limited Inc*, Derrida states this in terms that are stronger still:

[T]here is never any thing called power or force, but only differences of power and of force.... [O]ne must start ... from difference in order to accede to force and not vice versa.[48]

As Derrida indicates, the force of a singular literary event is not only "differential" but also "formalizing."[49] While the differential force is responsible for bringing about a productive encounter of differences, the formalizing force is responsible for the literary event's proper articulation in a phenomenon. Through the formalizing force, the impact resulting from the encounter of forces is held together through diverse gathering points of focus. Here the other aspect of force is emphasized: while "differential" concerns the genesis of forces, "formalizing" refers to their principle of articulation. A literary event is never one-time-only; it relies for its success on diverse rereadings, wherein each successive reading differs from the last, while the text nevertheless reinstates itself. (Again, the "other" as the root of "iter" in "iteration" has to be kept in mind; every repetition is an "othering," and every "othering" can be seen as a repetition.) This "othering" repetition is a precondition of a self-generalization or even idealization (in the Kantian sense) of the literary work. The promised totality gives us a prospect, an illusion of a completion (never to be fulfilled in practice), thanks to which we can speak as of a never-to-be-achieved unity and so speak meaningfully of a "literary absolute."

Derrida speaks in similar terms about the "force" of the singularity of the *punctum*, when discussing the work of Roland Barthes:

This singularity which is nowhere *in* the field mobilizes everything everywhere; it pluralizes itself.... I said that the *punctum* allows itself to be drawn into metonymy. Actually, it induces it, and this is its *force*, or rather than its force (since it exercises no actual constraint and exists completely in reserve), its *dynamis*, in other words, its power, potentiality.[50]

The same transition from force to potentiality (indicating that at stake is not an independently existing force but only differences of force) can be found in reference to literary works. (Derrida speaks initially of the "force of their event," then of their "event [as] powerful enough," before concluding, "we will have to come back to this word *power*.")[51]

It is not for nothing that the discussion of forces in Hegel's *Phenomenology of Spirit* culminates in the "law of the force" (which for Derrida becomes "the force of the law" and thus the condition of the possibility of the appearance of the law as phenomenon, of the phenomenon of the law). The two levels, the phenomenal and the ideal, interact. Derrida speaks of the "power" of singularity, or of the "force" of the event of literature precisely in terms of literature's formalizing ability. In other words, the literary phenomenon appears to us in virtue of and as its progressive idealization—that is, its infinite effort of self-completion. If this is the case, then the title "Force of Law" is tautological: the force of the law is (derived from) the law (*Gewalt* means both "violence" and "law"). The effect of the law, which is at the same time the condition of its appearance as a phenomenon (the law appears as being "in effect"), is a result of its self-formalizing repetition.

Another way to put it is that knowing that the singular itself is never given as such, Derrida addresses the forces that this singular mobilizes, both their genesis and formal articulation. Since the singular is never given as a fact, object, or existing thing, there is nothing in a work that would be absolutely singular. Literature repeats: no image or word is absolutely original and even the most hermetic text is not monadically closed in on itself (such that we could say of it that it is "one"). On the contrary, as we have seen in the discussion of force, the force a literary work mobilizes must be such that it attracts that which is beyond it (i.e., differences of force) in order to actualize itself. And yet Derrida calls such works "singular," for they are driven by a desire to become a singular achievement. This is to be achieved simultaneously in and through a gesture of making a singular moment appear, in telling a story of a date that is "one and not many." In other words, "singular" indicates the uniqueness of a creative pursuit of which works of literature are an outcome. The dependence of this pursuit on differences of force indicates that the uniqueness in question can never be located simply in the mind of the writer. Rather, it is a function of the exchange of forces (both differential and formalizing). On the one hand there is the creative pursuit of a mind (itself already the outcome of a powerful difference between the conscious and the unconscious), and on the other the infinite potentiality of what can be conceived as creative matter (words, contexts, experience, the materiality of the world, the unpredictable interpretive frameworks of the readers).

Singularity of the work refers then to the uniqueness of the desire, or of its envisaged telos, which expresses itself in a singular signature that is to gather the effects of all those differences of force. The "signature" is therefore not merely a sign conferring an identity; it is what gathers into itself the singular complexity of a text (like an encyclopedic novel, folding into itself other contexts, the future and the past), functioning as a lens for a unique sequence of events. ("This is how one writes, this is how one dreams of writing," says Derrida in *Monolingualism of the Other*: writing comes from a dream that something happens to language; it is like a tattoo on the body of language.) All those "singularities" are given to us as iterable—they depend on their iterability for their occurrence (even the unique desire must be iterable in order to articulate itself)—and hence, it would seem, they cannot be absolute. On the other hand, they can only be called "singular" insofar as their coming to appear cannot be accounted for merely in terms of the established distinction between the particular and the general.

From the perspective of iterability, which does not discriminate between a condition of meaning and a condition of phenomenal appearance (iterability conditions both in one gesture), there is no difference between the singularity of a work and that of an event (a date, real or imaginary) represented within a work. (Consequently, the event of literature, the event in literature, and the event outside of literature all have the same status.) This is what makes singularity in Derrida's thought such an exceptionally broad notion. In the traditional discourse on literature to which philosophers often appeal, as can be seen from Alain Badiou's definition of poetry (cited previously), the meaning of the singular is limited to its Hegelian definition: the unmediated "this," or "now." Literature's aim is to grasp "this particular sunset," even though it can never fully succeed. While Badiou modifies this definition with respect to modernist poets such as Mallarme, he remains to an extent faithful to its traditional version when reading Beckett's work. The latter is still perceived as a searching tool, which arrives at the representation of singular events by way of the elimination of superfluous "noise." In other words, in Badiou's view, it is not Beckett's literary achievement that counts as singular but only its quite independent object: that which this achievement does or does not succeed in uncovering.

As the above discussion shows, the notion of singularity captures well the problems connected with the eroding borderline between literature and philosophy. It is also the point at which the differences between Beckett's and Derrida's views of literature (and the relation of their works to each other) can be brought out most clearly. Beckett stands here for the kind of literature that is powerful and, to speak with Heidegger, *denkerisch* enough to interrogate its own status and thereby to question the status of other discourses—including that of philosophy. As for Derrida, his thought represents the kind of philosophy (if it can still then be called this name) that would attempt to do justice to literature—what Derrida refers to as the science of the *alea*.[52]

Itinerary between Beckett and Derrida

This book's inquiry begins with the question of how the notion of literature functions in Derrida's discourse, starting from the discrepancy between what Derrida says literature is and the notion that he adheres to while selecting the works he comments on (Chapter 1). Derrida's readings of literature follow a certain pattern of interests, and this pattern, motivating the choice of the works in question, can be used to establish a narrower definition of what constitutes, in Derrida's thought, a "literary event." The articulation of this event depends on the work's ability to "(hyper-) totalize" and to establish its own law or, in other words, in terms of the work's "economical" and "juridical" force.

This notion of the singular literary event appears to be in sharp contrast to the functioning of the (absence of a) unique event in the work of arguably the most "eventless" writer ever: Samuel Beckett. A characteristic feature of Beckett's project is that of generating a world in which nothing happens: there are no dates, no events, and no places that would pretend to have character in any way. "[N]o, no dates for pity's sake."[53] Anyone familiar with Beckett's *En attendant Godot* will have noticed the care with which the author avoids having anything in this play that could be qualified as unique. (In Alain Badiou's study of Beckett's work, he describes "la suppression de toute particularité descriptive,"[54] by which he seems to refer to what he elsewhere discussed under the gloss of "this particular sunset"—that is, to the singular.) One of the things that Beckett excludes in this play is dates (one of Derrida's terms for the singular). For example, the date of Vladimir and Estragon's appointment with Godot cannot be placed. Neither the time:

> VLADIMIR. He said Saturday. I think.
> ESTRAGON. You think. . . . But what Saturday? And is it Saturday? Is it not rather Sunday? [Pause.] Or Monday? [Pause.] Or Friday? . . . Or Thursday?[55]

Nor the place:

> ESTRAGON: You're sure it was here?
> VLADIMIR: What?
> ESTRAGON: That we were to wait.[56]
> VLADIMIR: [Looking round.] You recognize the place?

ESTRAGON: I didn't say that.
VLADIMIR: Well?
ESTRAGON: That makes no difference.[57]

Everything that could be qualified as unique (for example, the difference between this evening and the previous one) is dismissed by Estragon's statement, "I am not a historian."[58] Estragon's amnesia makes it impossible to establish any unique points of reference that could contribute to a differentiation of time and/or space. Has the number of leaves on the tree changed? Is the pair of shoes in the second act identical to or different from the pair that Estragon had left there in the first "yesterday"? (Assuming even that he had any shoes, that there was a "yesterday"—details, of course, that he does not remember.)

Derrida's understanding of literature in terms of the singular allows itself to be understood in terms of his discussion of the role of the *punctum* in Barthes' *Camera Lucida* (Chapter 2). While "*punctum*" is a term Barthes employs for photography and not for literature, Derrida's "Deaths of Roland Barthes" is an essay on essay writing, and thus on writing as much as on photography. In fact, much less than images, Derrida discusses there the writing, the "signature," of Roland Barthes. While other figures of singularity used by Derrida arguably stand closer to his discussion of literature—for example, those of a "postcard," "signature," or "date"—Derrida's essay makes for an attractive approach to the issue. This is because the *punctum* as a metaphor of singularity is possessed of an austere visual simplicity (a point or a piercing; one of its persuasive images is the "crack on the pane")—a simplicity that Derrida's metaphors of a postcard or a signature do not have. Moreover, one of the things Derrida shows in this essay is that a "lens" can under certain circumstances be treated as just another metaphor for writing. (The interpretation of a text would then mean answering the question of what happened in front of the lens, which is not necessarily the same as the question, What did the author see?) Additionally, Barthes' dream of a *mathesis singularis* and Derrida's pursuit of the "science of the alea" were developed almost simultaneously (*Camera Lucida* was published in 1980, *Signsponge* went through a long development between 1975 and 1984).[59]

Barthes' project of a "protestation of singularity" is opposed to that of Joyce, who has been the most important literary figure throughout Derrida's philosophical project. Derrida interprets Joyce's program as one of gathering: it is designed to have accounted for everything, to remember everything, and to anticipate everything, including all that we might say on its topic in advance. In contrast, Derrida interprets Barthes—in his *Camera Lucida*—as wanting to preserve the memory of one unique individual, his mother. Derrida reads Barthes' project of *mathesis singularis* as a journey of the singular through its metonymic avatars, which both fails and succeeds in preserving the singular.

The remarkable austerity of Beckett's project makes one wonder whether Marjorie Perloff was not right in her critique of Derrida after all. Perhaps, as she suggests, ordinary language is a key to Beckett that Derrida simply misses in his philosophical vocabulary. While Perloff proposes reading Beckett's *Watt* in terms of disorders of linguistic context, I examine the possibility that the functioning of iterability as a condition of meaning overrides the necessary presence of any "proper" context (Chapter 3).

In Chapter 4 I return to my initial thesis that Derrida's professed inability to comment on Beckett stems from the fact that, given Beckett's refusal to "totalize," the latter's works just do not fulfill the requirements in terms of which Derrida reads literary works. However, I also return to this motif to show how—to an extent and in a very different way, in terms of a different philosophical filiation—Beckett's work can be read as "totalizing."

Having set up this provisional—and fragile—bridge between the work of the two authors, in the second part of this book I stage three points of "transaction" between Beckett and Derrida, where the singular is at stake. This more specific approach allows me to show the slight but meaningful difference of "tone"[60] that separates the two enterprises. The three points will concern (1) the extent to which it is still possible to speak about a human subject in the works of both authors (Chapter 5), (2) the constitution of a law or a source of authority in a literary work (Chapter 6), and (3) the question of to what degree the motives of "negative theology" present in the work of both Beckett and Derrida can be said to function in an analogous way with respect to the purposes they are serving (Chapter 7).

Let me briefly lay out the themes addressed in these chapters. In Chapter 5 I will address the singularity of the human subject. Many authors, in the wake of Emmanuel Lévinas, perceive singularity as something having to do more with the human subject than with any event. Singularity, whether seen as Lévinasian "being singled out," as being called to responsibility by an other, or as what Paul Ricoeur calls "ipseity"—a narrative identity—refers us back to the contested notion of a subject. Habermas thinks himself to have justly condemned Derrida (together with the late Heidegger) for allowing "the disintegration of transcendental subjectivity," but it is not at all certain that "the philosophy of the subject is overcome"[61] in Derrida. It is not for nothing that in his reading of the "*yes phenomenon*"[62] as that which structures and gathers James Joyce's *Ulysses*, Derrida insists on the various senses the "oui" translates. Thus: "what the French translation, co-signed by Joyce, translates by 'oui' is not yes, but once, 'I am' and once 'I will.' "[63] And further: "this yes-laughter reaffirms control of *a subjectivity* that draws everything together as it draws itself together."[64] This link between the iterability of the "yes" and the constitution of subjectivity is quite crucial for Derrida. (It must be kept in mind that the "yes" is "pre-ontological," "pre-performative," and even "pre-transcendental.") I show a similar structure at work in Beckett.

The sixth chapter, which concerns the way in which a literary work establishes for itself a singular law or a source of authority, addresses three possible ways of looking at literature. First, that of so-called New Criticism and structuralist aesthetics, in which the authority of literature, which follows from its autonomy, is limited to the work itself. Second, the diametrically opposed perception of Alain Badiou, according to whom the task of the linguistic work of art is to raise issues that would also be relevant in contexts exceeding the literary work. Finally, I consider the view of Derrida, which oscillates between the two approaches. In other words, Heidegger's famous question, "What are Poets for?" can be answered in a threefold way: (1) the task of literature is to produce autonomous unities that allow all their elements to be gathered around one central unifying theme; (2) literature's task is to reveal to us something that is not properly or essentially literary (say, the historicity of Being); and (3) literature's task is to address that which exceeds the scope of literature, which it does by means of provisional gestures of self-formalizing. This self-formalizing aspect of literature is repeatedly shown by Derrida to exceed the literary context. The third way of answering Heidegger's question permits us to see literature as what Barthes dreamt of: *mathesis singularis,* in the sense of "the science of the singular" but also of "a singular, aleatory science."

Derrida's path of thinking has often been compared to that of negative theology; *différance,* for example, is never explained in positive terms but always in terms of a "neither this nor that" pattern. In negative theology, an account that proceeds via an accumulation of negations is intended as a means to attain a singular (in the sense of "unmediated") insight. Starting from this consideration, I will show that whereas both Beckett and Derrida could be read in this way, the singular that they envisage may yet be different (Chapter 7).

1

The Question of Literature

Fiction and "the Works That Make the Limits of Our Language Tremble"

Could literature as understood by Derrida accommodate a literary event like that of Beckett's work? To ask such a question is to approach literature in a certain way—as a space ready to welcome works-events. Admittedly, this might be deemed inconsistent with Derrida's vision of literature that, rather than aiming at any systematic account of literature, insists on its otherness, lack of essence, and indefiniteness. Indeed, in a recent text, *Demeure*, Derrida says: "the name and the thing called 'literature' remain for me, to this day, endless enigmas . . . nothing to this day remains as new and as incomprehensible to me, at once very near and very alien, as the thing called literature."[1] However, even those cautious words inevitably betray a certain conception of literature. For example, a certain vision of literature can be ascribed to Derrida's choice of the semantically rich word "enigmatic." This recalls the name of a famous World War II encoding machine, containing moreover a "fable" (*ainos*) in its etymological root. (In Derrida's own words, the word "enigma" "indicates . . . the *récit*."[2] Elsewhere, he observes that "*ainigma*, in Greek, is often a relation, a story, the obscure words of a fable."[3] This "obscurity" points in the direction of the encoding machine.) This suggests a vision of literature as an encoding—or a confabulating—machine. At first sight, this representation seems to be coextensive with the vision of literature we can discover in Beckett's texts: a "fable of one fabling with you in the dark."[4] But is it?

In order to be able to answer this question, we need to analyze in depth Derrida's notion of "literature." Much of what concerns the latter is formulated in the negative, which already indicates that nothing can be taken for granted in this understanding of literature. It is concerned neither with beautiful words nor with formal conventions; neither genre nor any other formal criterion can sustain it. Such a negative delimitation of the field of literature in Derrida has already received critical attention. It has been argued that Derrida's "literature" must be distinguished both from the common understanding of the noun (belles-lettres, poetry, etc.) and from the Heideggerian *Dichtung*. It has also been claimed that Derrida's project is quite distinct from that of literary criticism. Furthermore, it has been maintained that literature is, for Derrida, not an issue standing on its own but a part of his wider preoccupation with phenomenology (and in particular with Husserl).[5] Although this negative approach makes us alert to the fact that nothing in this perception of literature can simply be assumed, it is perhaps not impossible to address the issue in positive terms. After all, even Derrida does not limit himself to the rhetoric of negative theology with respect to literature, his discourse on literature therein differing significantly from his discourse on "God." My claim is that, pace Derrida's insistence on the nonessentiality and indefiniteness of literature, it is still possible to conceive of an underlying notion of literature that implicitly accompanies all his interventions concerning the literary. Literature is an institution and as such a construct, an artifact. Its precarious institutional limits are threatened at every moment, but this does not mean that they cannot be named, albeit provisionally, with a term that exceeds the specificity of a genre and thereby attempts to account for any innovation legislating over the literature still to come. (This attempt is thus always reaching out ahead of itself and so is at risk of overstretching its own validity, because the act of naming is at the same time premature and belated.) Speaking most generally, literature is a relatively recent, Western institution founded on a principle of "being able to say everything/anything" (*le concept de littérature est construit sur le principe du "tout dire"*).[6] Next to this provision of the freedom to, in principle, say everything (a provision that links it to modern democracy), literature as understood by Derrida is written rather than oral, and it involves signatures and authorial property. Nonetheless, it has no essence, no binding rules: the institution of literature is instituted every time afresh, every time it welcomes a new literary event. (The welcoming of a given event as "literature" is simultaneously the constitutive, reaffirming event of the institution.)

Derrida calls literature a "fictive institution" and an "institution of fiction," which might lead one to believe that it is mere fictitiousness that makes something literature. This is not the case: literature is not necessarily about "telling stories." In fact, in an interview in *Acts of Literature*, Derrida confessed that it is not any interest in fiction, stories, and even novels that is central to his involvement with literature. He states both that he has "probably never deep down drawn great enjoyment from fiction, from reading novels," and that "telling or inventing stories does not interest [him] particularly."[7] In another text, while referring to such features of literature as "the inscription of a proper name," "a certain autobiography," and "a certain fictional projection," Derrida hastens to add: "not that all fiction and all inscriptions of proper names have had a literary dimension or a relation to the work of art as such."[8] And, finally, in "Before the Law":

> [I]t is not as narrative that we define *Before the Law* as a literary phenomenon, nor is it as fictional, allegorical, mythical, symbolic, parabolic narrative, and so on. There are fictions, allegories, myths, symbols, or parables that are not specifically literary.[9]

Derrida is concerned not with mere fiction but with the principles associated with it in the modern institution of literature: writing, freedom from censorship, and signature. But these principles only seem to help us narrow down our conception of fiction (thereby excluding oral and anonymous fiction). In fact, in Derrida's terms (according to which speech is always mediated [i.e., contaminated] by writing, and a signature does not always need to have the shape of a proper name), there is neither strictly oral nor strictly anonymous fiction. We are left with a very general, indiscriminate definition of fiction; even romances sold in supermarkets correspond to these criteria.

Such a broad definition of literature makes literary practically anything that is accompanied by the above-mentioned set of socio-juridico-political principles. Opposed to this, however, is a much narrower definition of a smaller group of literary texts in which Derrida is interested, consisting of authors such as Artaud, Mallarmé, Genet, Ponge,

Blanchot, Kafka, and Celan. Here, "being able to say everything" remains the binding rule but means something other than a socio-juridico-political principle guaranteeing the author freedom from censorship. This choice to approach literature as a group of texts resembles closely Beckett's observation that "painting as such does not exist, all there is are paintings."[10] A characteristic consistency in the selection of authors above indicates that Derrida is only interested in the broad definition of literature when the stakes are not strictly literary (for example, when addressing political issues or the issues linked to Speech Act Theory). When speaking about literature specifically, Derrida selects his texts according to a much narrower definition. This refers to "texts-events"—that is, the "texts which in their various ways were no longer simply, or no longer only, literary."[11] The idea of "being able to say everything" is a very flexible one. It seems itself to be able to say, or convey, everything: it addresses the political freedom of literature; its fictitiousness; and also, where necessary, what Derrida takes to be the real source of literature's force or power—its ability to "totalize."[12] This is where Derrida locates "the force of their [that is, the works'] event":

> To say everything is no doubt to gather, by translating, all figures into one another, *to totalize* by formalizing, but to say everything is also to break out of [*franchir*] prohibitions. To *affranchise oneself* [*s'affranchir*]—in every field where law can lay down the law.[13]

The force of literature depends on this ability to totalize. Perhaps this is surprising: the desire to totalize certainly seems odd in an author who is known for having criticized the totalizing impulse of speculative thought. Moreover, this expression is not a *hapax* in the above-quoted interview, and it is not accidental at all: "I can analyze it, deconstruct it, criticize it, but it is an experience I love, that I know and recognize,"[14] says Derrida about his desire to "hyper-totalize." Derrida has not forgotten the affiliations of this term, though; he is fully aware that the "motif of *totality* circulates here in a singular way between literature and philosophy" (his emphasis).[15]

This totalizing singular is the first element of Derrida's narrower definition of literature—that literature that is not merely fiction but a set of texts-events that "make our language tremble." Derrida formulates his definition of those texts twice:

> [T]he force of their event depends on the fact that a thinking about their own possibility (both general and singular) is put to work in them in a *singular* work.

[I]n them are brought together the two youthful worries or desires I was talking about a moment ago: to write so as to put into play or to keep the singularity of the date (what does not return, what is not repeated, promised experience of memory as promise, experience of ruin or ashes); and at the same time, through the same gesture, to question, analyze, transform this strange contradiction, this institutionless institution.[16]

Gathering and Law: the Economico-Juridical Character of the Literary Work

As Derrida says, at stake is always a singular work that contains two gestures: the archiving ("to write so as to put into play or to keep the singularity of the date") and the critique ("to question, analyze, transform") of the literary institution. The same is at issue in the first of the above quotations where the two gestures are addressed as "a thinking about their [that is, the works'] own possibility (both general [i.e., critique] and singular [i.e., archiving])." In other words, characteristic of a singular work-event is that it gathers both singular events (that to a degree account for its singular possibility) and a universal reflection on its own possibility. The power of a singular work is thus perceived as economico-juridical in character. Its economic power allows it to condense history, language, the encyclopedia; its juridical power permits a reflection on and critique and transformation of the law.

According to Derrida, it is a property of every singular work that it gathers and condenses—each of which is also always iterable.[17] Think, for example, of the condensation in the "sponge" in Derrida's reading of the name "Ponge," or of Derrida's reading of Joyce's *Ulysses* as "the hypermnesic machine capable of storing in an immense epic work Western memory and virtually all the languages in the world including traces of the future."[18] (This gathering function of literature is also exploited by Chantal Zabus in her book *Le secret: Motif et moteur de la littérature*, with a preface by Derrida, where she interprets a book as a receptacle, a *secrétaire*—a piece of furniture called a secretary.)[19] The event archived in a literary work has two faces. It is defined as "what does not return, what is not repeated"—or, in other words, as "nothing" (for otherwise it would fall prey to the principle of iterability and precisely be repeated)—and, significantly, as an excess of iterability, being repeated in everything else. It is this excess of iterability that allows the work "to gather, by translating, all figures into one another, to totalize by formalizing." The two issues that Derrida isolates in a work-event—archiving and recording (collecting dates and instances), and critique, transformation, and reflection (on the general in the singular)—can also be approached as two desires: the desires to preserve the singular in its singular purity and to address the generality of that preserving gesture. It is my contention that all of Derrida's work on literature addresses those "two youthful worries or desires," the latter being the prism through which the works-events are read. Derrida's claim, in "Before the Law," that the law "is not to be seen or touched but it is to be deciphered"[20] testifies that the two hang together closely. Were Beckett's work to frustrate this desire to decipher, it would be a reason, a structural reason, for Derrida to keep his silence with respect to that work.

Gathering, Sponging, Archiving

Let us first focus on the economic aspect of literature. If Derrida were looking for a gesture of archiving or recording in Beckett's work, it would not be difficult to find. Besides Krapp's well-known taped archives, there are all kinds of devices in Beckett with which one might gather economically time and space: sacks, tins, and other memory containers—including "the skull." But do these archives function in the same way as the Derridean ones? Beckett's archives are rarely like the Derridean "seals" that "hide, so as to keep a reservoir of meaning." The young Beckett did have an admiration for that kind of verbal gathering, as can be seen in his encomium of the "savage economy of hieroglyphics" found in Joyce.[21] Krapp echoes this phase in Beckett's work when he needs a dictionary to decipher the forgotten meaning of the word "viduity," which appears in his archive. He relishes the semantic riches contained in the encyclopedic entry. Krapp's forgetfulness, however, indicates the beginning of the malfunctioning of the verbal archives in Beckett. The forgetfulness of words becomes a powerful motif in Beckett's work, indicating that Beckett distanced himself from Joyce, whom he later explicitly criticized for "believing in words." This is not to say that verbal archives disappear from Beckett altogether: they are just empty (e.g., "What / What is the word" begins the last poem Beckett ever wrote).

Beckett's characters salivate over the archives; some of his characters—Krapp, for instance—are addicted to them because they offer the possibility to relive things, to "be again."[22] Once is never enough. Their desire—to exhaust and ruin the archives by repeated intoxication (described as something of the order of the carnal, animal)—is to "devour" what there is to relive. This is preserved in the archives in "irreproachable freshness, laurel felicity,"[23] or, on the contrary, dead and rotten, until all is gone and there remains nothing to do but "lick chops and basta."[24]

Grant only enough remain to devour all. Moment by glutton moment. Sky earth the whole kit and boodle. Not another crumb of carrion left. Lick chops and basta. No. One moment more. One last. Grace to breathe that void. Know happiness.

Hence, the ultimate goal in Beckett is not to hyper-totalize, not to archive as much as possible—and more—but to exhaust the archives, in order to be able to "breathe that void." The economy of the archives is always frustrated in Beckett. There is no sponge quality here, none of the powerful economic gathering of a sponge "inflated or emptied (expressed)" that Derrida exploits so well.[25] Instead, there are only "some reflections . . . on the fragility of euphoria . . . of . . . sponges. . . ."[26] Archives and recording have an ambiguous status in Beckett. On the one hand, there is the power archiving of Hamm, Moran, and the young Krapp. Here the archives in Beckett never have the positive value that they have in Derrida. In fact, Beckett is an unappeasable judge of the desire to archive; in *What Where*, the words of a voice that announce the replaying of a tape—"I switch on"—echo the words of an executioner switching on the electric current. On the other hand, there are weak, minimal memories: for example, that single moment of value that Krapp cherishes—the memory of the thigh of a woman he loved frescoed by scratches from gooseberries—and also those "frescoes on the skull" that diminish slowly to the size of three "pins" in *Worstward Ho*.

Some issues in Derrida's unrelenting pursuit of what in various guises can function as a reservoir of meaning communicate rather awkwardly with Beckett's work. Is an idiom a semantic treasure box, as Derrida seems to suggest? Or is it merely, as it is for Beckett, a demonstration of power, an unnecessary tour de force, the "euphoria of a sponge"? In

Monolingualism of the Other, Derrida states that the reason one writes is "the dream that something happens to language."[27] The event happening to language is the production of an idiom that resists translatability—an incision, a mark on language. The particular attention that is given to language in literature in the act of carving a personal idiom inside it is, again, not an essential and absolute property of literature but an element that has until now played a role in its institution, and one with which Derrida chooses to go along.[28] The personal idiom (or *shibboleth*) that leaves a mark on language and that, through it, leaves a mark on those of us who read it—this last element being what Derrida describes as the circumcision of a word or the resurrection of language—has for a long time now been associated by us with literary writing. Derrida represents this idiom as a tattoo, an inscription on language constituting a secret reservoir of meaning.[29] Whereas obviously Derrida is not unaware of the aspect of mastery involved in tattooing (Deleuze observes that a tattoo is a mark of territoriality),[30] he emphasizes the semantic enrichment that comes with it. In Beckett, the production of scars that constitutes a tattoo primarily emphasizes a relation of power, even though it is connected to language in a way very similar to Derrida's. It is meant to make one's victim speak, and in this it is no different from the thumps Molloy applies to his mother's head to make her react, or from Bam's saying "you will be given the works until you confess."[31] The status of the tattoo as a device for semantic enrichment is therewith rendered problematic. (Whereas we tend to laugh at Molloy's treatment of his mother, it is different from the inscription "do you love me cunt" that the character of *How It Is* carves, with the help of a can opener, on the body of his victim.)

For Beckett, gathering—even in the form proposed by Derrida—remains a figure of power, and he deliberately renounces this form of writing—that is, the form of writing that would have an "economic power."[32] This is perhaps the reason why "it would not be possible . . . to extract a few 'significant' [and this means semantically rich, 'powerful,'—A. S.] lines from a Beckett text," and why Derrida goes on to call them "decomposed." If there is a discernible element of critique in Beckett texts, it is directed precisely against this economic power, which Beckett so admired in Joyce in his youth. Beckett's literature is not merely about tramps but is itself the tramp (the nomad, Deleuze would say) of literature. It accuses all approaches to literature, even the most delicate, the most balanced approach, driven by the best of intentions. Consider the example of Molloy, who expresses this protest by throwing away the social worker's gift.[33] The fact is, nobody can handle Molloy and the kind of literature he represents.

Is it fair to oppose Derrida's approach to literature as a territorial drift to Beckett's as the wandering of the expelled? After all, even the expelled have a territory—as Deleuze has shown—but it is a closed territory, a "black hole": "[t]his is what happens under conditions of precocious or extremely sudden deterritorialization, and when . . . paths are blocked."[34] And Deleuze goes on to quote the characteristic of a black hole:

> A star that has collapsed so far that its radius has fallen below the critical point becomes what is called a black hole (an occluded star). This expression means that nothing sent in the direction of such an object will ever come back.[35]

The property of a black hole so defined is that it gives us nothing (to be perceived, touched, etc.). And this is precisely the ambition of Beckett's oeuvre: "all I say cancels out, I'll have said nothing."[36] The fact that this ambition is impossible to fulfill does not change the nature of the project. (On the other hand, Derrida also demonstrates that the quasi-totalizing operation he is tempted to perform is never possible in an absolute sense; that it is rather aporetic. In other words, all he seeks to totalize remains ultimately singular, non-totalizable. This again shows a difference of objective, even if the net result remains to an extent structurally parallel.)

Having established this difference between Derrida and Beckett—a difference in the kind of territory created by their work—two steps are possible. Since we have just discussed the archive aspect (i.e., the economical aspect) of Derrida's notion of literature, we might move on to the juridical aspect, which will lead us to the problems of an oeuvre reflecting on its own event. Or, since we have just addressed the work of Beckett as a "black hole," we might follow up this figure that for Deleuze stands for subjectivity. (I will return to this issue in Chapter 3.) These two follow-ups have much in common and, as we will see, become intertwined.

A Shift in Derrida's Work

For each of these steps, a detour is necessary. In order to move from the economical effects associated by Derrida with literature to consideration of both the effects of law and the problems of the speaking subject (testimony), we must take into account a shift in emphasis in his work. I will later address this shift as a move away from anonymity. It is a shift from the issues of writing as contrasted with speech and of the effects of language, to the discussion of literature as the representation of an event, to issues of testimony, responsibility, and signature. To put this another way, Derrida's interest moves from the *repetition* of an event to the repetition of an *event*.

In early Derrida, where literature is "writing" and an effect of language, literature seems to be more autonomous in the sense that both the speaking subject and the represented event are of secondary importance; literature is directed toward itself, toward its own representing capacities. In that period, Derrida questions Heidegger's perception of art as world disclosure, suggesting instead that the only thing art discloses to us is the ambiguity of the hymen.[37] The event represented by literature is, as in Mallarmé's *Mimique*, a nonexistent event, internal to the act of representation, which means that the real concern is with the event of representation. In this context, Derrida is concerned with showing representation standing apart from and precluding the presence of the represented, in accordance with his larger project of dismantling the myth of living speech and of the metaphysics of presence (by alerting us to the all-pervading work of *différance*, spatial and temporal deferral). Literature enhances the effects of language, especially the economy of language that allows for a dissemination of meaning, turning every text into an endless structure of referral. This is especially the case with the early texts on Rousseau, Mallarmé, and Artaud (*Of Grammatology, Dissemination*, and "The Theatre of Cruelty," respectively). The relationship between speech and writing is central to those texts. If we take into account Derrida's general predilection for the figure of death, in this period—roughly spanning the sixties and seventies—we can clearly see that death (as synonymous with writing) always takes over from life. (The "live" voice is shown to be pervaded by death.)[38] This emphasis is partially responsible for the interpretations of Derrida's work exemplified by Habermas: as an extension of the work of later Heidegger, discarding subjective responsibility in favor of the anonymous occurrence of language.

In the later texts by Derrida, the issues of speech and writing decrease in importance. Literature is no longer perceived as merely anonymous writing (hieroglyphics, or Heidegger's *die Sprache spricht*); the emphasis is now on the idiom as a private sedimentation of language—that is, as a signature. As a consequence, we see survival/"hauntology" instead of death (death is now seen as conducive to life); private testimony instead of the play of signifiers; and the exploration of the relationship between the author and his signature rather than of that between speech and writing. The interest in the singular receives much more emphasis in the texts published in and after the eighties. The later work by Derrida, with its interest in the authorial signature and responsibility, is more likely to accommodate Beckett's work than was his earlier interest in the economy of language, which Beckett so explicitly rejected.

Although it must be underlined that the change is only one in emphasis, this shift from literature as an economy of language to literature as a testimony is basically a move away from anonymity: one can economize anonymously, but one cannot testify anonymously. This movement away from anonymity has implications for the perception of language in literature. Here there is an analogous change: from the sense of being submerged in a language that dictates its laws to us (where grammar constitutes the framework of our experience and where, to quote Heidegger, "even the structure of the thing as thus envisaged is a projection of the framework of the sentence"[39]) to the affirmation that it is possible to produce one's own individual incision in language. Derrida modifies Heidegger's approach to language where *die Sprache spricht* (where, that is, one does not speak but one "is spoken") in that he compares language to "the mother." While all the "situatedness" already takes place within and starting from language,[40] this does not preclude our developing a personal, responsible inflection of this language—that is, a private signature.

It has often been noticed that Beckett's work emphasizes this Heideggerian "being said" by language: the "novel" *How It Is* is staged in the form of a quotation, and the late prose work *Worstward Ho* urges: "be said on." Beckett perceives language as sclerotic, demented, and eventually dead—like Molloy's mother in the *Trilogy*—and his characters say, "I am in my [dead] mother's room" as if they mocked being in language, or being in what Heidegger called the "house of Being." To what extent this work also involves the grafting of the private, or what Derrida calls "a testimonial message on the epidermis of fiction,"[41] remains to be explored.

(I address the sense of the impossibility of achieving this as explored in Beckett's *The Unnamable* in Chapter 5.)

The search for Beckett's private signature brings us to the question of the position of the speaking subject in his work, to the constitution of that subject, and thereby to the occurrence of self-reflection. The latter is not a phenomenon or a mental operation reserved for philosophy. In the gesture of literary self-reflection (the *mise en abyme*) are grounded both the self-constituting law of a literary work and the reflexive relation between the author and the work (where the latter is conceived as the author's testimony). This gesture organizes a literary work with respect to itself; it constitutes the work's "law" on the basis of the iteration of its various elements. Furthermore, it provides a link between the subject/author and his work without representing this work as the straightforwardly intentional product of the author (i.e., without giving in to an intentional fallacy).

The understanding of the work's self-reflection as that which generates the work's singular "law" brings me back to Derrida's notion of literature. Until now I have addressed only half of what determines Derrida's interest in the literary works he comments on: their ability to archive in a powerful way, to hyper-totalize. As I argued before, the other half consists in what we might call literature's relation to its law. This relation is primarily that of critique; it involves analysis, and formalizing laws and their transformation. Let us now focus on this latter aspect.

The Law of "Before the Law": Derrida's Reading of Kafka

At stake here is the relation of a work to its own law (this being more than merely the form of a work) and to the institution of literature in general. This is a gesture with a double function, by which the work of literature both sets up its law and subverts and transforms the literary institution (such that the affirmation of the singular law of the work is at the same time the subversion of the general law of literature). But can this gesture be formalized? Speaking about law requires formal observations, for even though there can be an infinitely delayed or deferred law, there cannot be a totally formless law. Hence, we need something of an order of structure to account for a law's generality, and it is for this reason that Derrida speaks about literary "formalizing" ("totalizing by formalizing"[42]). Yet since "the law" of a literary text, even though not entirely new, has each time a different configuration, we cannot make any general observations about the law of literature. (We can speak about signatures, titles, copyright, the fact of being written rather than oral—yet although these things accompany a text's being literature, they do not make something literature in the specific sense we are addressing here. Whatever may be said about them, these elements, as relevant as they are, are only so in virtue of the singular relation they hold to a given work.) Since each text is singular and moreover produces its (singular) law in a singular way, we cannot seek any regularity in the way a singular text produces its law. The minimal observation we can make is that in order for the law to apply to the text's event, there must be a movement of communication between the text and its law that reflects on the relationship between this law and the literary institution in general. The only permanent factor here is that there is a relation of the text to its law (by which a text affirms itself, makes itself iterable) and thereby a critical relation to the literary institution (isn't this what the critic is looking for in a work, each time anew?).

What does this communication proper to "a form of literature which bore a question *about* literature"[43] consist in? Derrida calls it a "turning back on the literary institution": "[t]hese texts operate a sort of turning back, they are themselves a sort of turning back on the literary institution." The return performed in those texts cannot be complete, says Derrida; the texts cannot be only "reflexive, specular or speculative" or "suspend reference to something else."[44] A purely self-referential text would not only malfunction as an archive (i.e., fail in its hyper-totalizing function); it would, to the extent that it approximated to a pure singularity, run the risk of annulling itself. However, even though a literary text cannot be only "reflexive, specular or speculative," it must also be such. The latter is for Derrida a prerequisite, a minimal condition; it is only in this way that the texts he is reading can effectuate "the thinking about their own possibility" that, according to Derrida, gives their event the necessary force ("the force of their event"[45]). It is my contention that Derrida exploits the motif of the specular reflection—in various guises (including, for example, the refraction of sound)—in all of his readings of literature that address the latter's critical and constitutive function. This is most prominently the case in *The*

Double Session, Dissemination, Signsponge, Psyche, and "Before the Law." For example, in *Dissemination* we read:

> Imagine Plato's cave.... Imagine that mirrors would not be in the world but that things "present," on the contrary, would be in them. Imagine that mirrors (shadows, reflections, "phantasms," etc.) would no longer be *comprehended* within the structure of ontology and the myth of the cave—which also situates the screen and the mirror—but would rather envelop it in its entirety.[46]

This fragment, speculative in itself (the injunction "imagine..." is already speculative), demonstrates the extent to which Derrida is willing to exploit the figure of a mirror image. If shadows, reflections, and phantoms are all "mirrors" that envelop every conceivable relation between being and thought "in its entirety," then this game of mirrors is not just a philosophical reflection, because it enfolds both philosophy and literature.

In saying this, I am not disregarding Rodolphe Gasché's argument in *The Tain of the Mirror,* which represents Derrida's work as a critique of reflexivity. I fully recognize the "nonreflexive" character of deconstruction to the extent that reflection is conceived as a tool of the logos, which achieves its ultimate fulfillment in the unifying function of the absolute or speculative reflection.[47] On the contrary, I am rather following the conclusion of Gasché's argument: namely, that Derrida's thought brings reflection to a crisis precisely because it "takes reflection's exigencies seriously" (239). By reinscribing the reflective gesture into what exceeds it (i.e., into "doubling," as Gasché calls it, adding that it could also be addressed as "iterability" [225]), Derrida makes it impossible to think of the "hyper-totality" thus achieved as a rationally conceivable unity "without engaging in a conceptual monstrosity" (237). The latter condition is not to be neglected because the philosophical telos of the mirror's play is "the actualization of all that is reasonable" (238). However, this telos of the mirror's play is a distinctively philosophical telos. It is possible that the status of literature with respect to the claims made by Gasché in *The Tain of the Mirror* might be a little different. This at least is what Derrida seems to suggest in an interview given after the publication of that book, in which Derrida expresses his doubts as to whether general textual effects permit us to address that which is specifically literary and, consequently, as to whether it makes sense to treat literature in terms of infrastructures, suggesting that rather than starting with textual effects to address literature, we should perhaps start with literature to address general textual effects:

I wonder whether literature is simply an example, one effect or region among others of some general textuality. And I wonder if you can simply apply the classic question to it: what, on the basis of this general textuality, makes the specificity of literature, literariness? I ask this question for two reasons. First of all, it is quite possible that literary writing in the modern period is more than one example among others, rather a privileged guiding thread for access to the general structure of textuality, to what Gasché calls the infrastructure.[48]

If literature is to be a seen as a "privileged guiding thread for access to the general structure of textuality," it is perhaps because literature is not limited, in the way that philosophy is, by the telos of "actualisation of the unity of all that is reasonable." The literary gesture of "hyper-totalizing" is not affected by the threat of producing a "conceptual monstrosity" in the way that philosophical discourse clearly is.

As is well known, Derrida's entire project grew out of his examination of the difference between hearing and seeing (speech and writing). The figure of "hearing-oneself-speak" is misleadingly suggestive of a moment of "pure presence," and it required the vigilance of Derrida's reading (combined with Husserl's meditation on temporality) to discern in "hearing-oneself-speak" an endless deferral (that Derrida calls an auto-affective "pure speculation") instead. The deferral involved is more obvious with respect to seeing, which requires the mediation of a mirror. (In Derrida's words, "what can look at oneself is not one.") In Hegel, the subject and the world, or thought and being, are conceived as two mirrors facing each other. This mediation, even as it carries the Hegelian promise of pure speculation leading to absolute totality, undermines its own effect. It offers not only the promise of identity by self-recognition but also the threat of dispersal and abyssal decay (*s'abîmer*) through the effect of an infinite regress of mirror reflections, the *mise en abyme*.[49] When we take into account that the figure of a mirror reflection stands as much for a unifying movement as for an infinite structure of deferral (and provided we do not require that it produce a "unity" of "what is reasonable"), it becomes possible to interpret the entire splitting movement of difference as mirror-based. If we approach the principle of iterability starting from Derrida's words that "what can look at itself is not one," the latter suggests that perhaps the reason that in Derrida nothing is one (the "originary doubling") is because everything iterable has always already "looked at itself." Thus construed, iterability is in itself a kind of self-reflection. Also, if it is the case that "what can look at itself is not one," then the oneness can only be attained by the suppression of what divides it. If we want to render justice to what is thus suppressed, mirroring, reflection, and speculation can no longer be seen as absolute, unifying, and constitutive of identity; on the contrary— they are an ever-deferring principle. The mirror only confirms identity by dividing it: "the reflection, the image, the double, splits what it doubles."[50] Because it intensifies the effects of language—that is, intensifies the effect of a deferral of presence (language becoming a representation of a representation, a citation of a citation)—literature enhances this threat of abyssal decay. While reason mobilizes reflexivity and speculation to attain unity, literature, unlike philosophy, thrives as well on the side that must remain hidden in rational speculation, beyond the conceptual stability of the mirror surface—the fading side of infinite regress and decay of identity.

But this effect of the deferral of presence visible in literature is not only responsible for revealing the inherent naiveté of conceptual thinking. The structure of an infinite regress (of the origin, of presence, of validation) set in motion by the gesture of the *mise en abyme* described earlier also produces something in a positive sense. According to Derrida, specific to the literary institution is a "revealing power," located in "what literature does with language" and shared by literature with law ("literature shares a certain power and a certain destiny with 'jurisdiction'"[51]). This revealing power or "force" is constitutive of (literary) phenomena. (In the Introduction I discussed Derrida's frequent switching from the differential and formalizing "force" to "power." The motivation for this "inconsistency" was to emphasize, while not losing the link to Hegel's way of thinking about phenomena, that at stake is not an independently existing force but only differences of force.) It is precisely the repetition inherent to the infinite regress described earlier that lets this formalizing power—the law of literature—articulate itself. "This abyss [of representation, the representation of representation, etc.] is not an accident.... An entire theory of the structural necessity of the abyss will be gradually constituted in our reading," states Derrida in "... That Dangerous Supplement...."[52]

A part of the abyssal structure of literature is that its mirror leaves undecidable whether what it reflects is real or present—or merely a quasi-event: literature "produc[es] events whose 'reality' or duration is never assured."[53] And just as well; the figure of two mirrors facing each other (*abyme* and *contre-abyme*) serves as much to produce identities as to shatter them. The conceptual proximity of "*mise en abyme*" and "*s'abîmer*" helps Derrida emphasize the imperfection of the mirror image that immediately dissolves whatever stability it produces. While philosophy must feign here a certain "evasion of insight,"[54] even if only to prevent dissolution of the purity of conceptual meaning, literature depends on this imperfection.

Derrida's reading of Kafka's "Before the Law" is exemplary here for a number of reasons. More explicitly than in any other reading, it addresses the issues that interest us here: the relation between literature and law, and the abyssal structure of the law. It is also a reading that shows that a text's "thinking about its own possibility" is effected through various mirror effects. These effects include, among others, the putting *en abyme* of things that are usually considered external to any work of literature: the author, the critic, the reader, the experience of reading, and another work, functioning as a *contre-abyme*. (Thus, Derrida's reading of Kafka relies on a figure of two mirrors facing each other.) The text in question tells a story of the condition of its own possibility by reinscribing in itself what might be considered its margins. This shows that the *mise en abyme* is not only a gesture of infinite deferral but also a totalizing gesture, since everything can be pulled *en abyme*. This is no less a totalizing than the Hegelian equivalent but in a different way, since—as opposed to the Hegelian reading—this totalizing does not overcome differences, does not sublate anything.

Derrida reads Kafka's story about a man waiting at the gate of the law and a guardian who denies him entrance as (among other things) a story of the functioning of the story, a literary text about literature. This is a self-reflexive structure in itself. But, more importantly, at the center of this self-reflective story is a gate—a door that symbolizes the text itself, the condition of possibility of our entering the text. It is my conviction that this entrance turns out in fact to be a mirror, for how otherwise could we make sense of Derrida's subsequent insistence that this text, Kafka's "Before the Law," produces its law by reflecting itself in the *contre-abyme* of its twin version contained in Kafka's *Trial*? The equivalence of the entrance and the mirror is the founding invention of this text, and even though not verbalized by Derrida (who played with the same thought in *Dissemination*), it certainly did not pass unnoticed by him. Rather, it functions as the tacitly assumed center of his interpretation. It is this equivalence that makes the door, like death, singular and universal at the same time (a universal mirror producing different but singular reflections-interpretations in those who approach it). The parable represents the literary work as a "text before [which] we the readers appear as before the law," a text that "makes the law" (214/132) and that is protected by "guardians (author, publisher, critics, academics, archivists, librarians, lawyers, and so on)." The supposition that the guardian and the man from the country are in fact one and the same person is based on the assumed equivalence of the entrance and the mirror. And that makes the law function as a mirror (in a more general sense, we might compare it to the motif of the refraction of voice in Heidegger's *Sein und Zeit,* where the voice of conscience that Dasein hears is in fact its own voice: "In conscience Dasein calls itself"[55]).

A text has the power "to make the law," Derrida tells us, "on condition that the text itself can appear before the law of another . . . text" (214/132). In order to make the law, the text must also appear before the law; in order to function as a mirror it must face a mirror. In this sense, the whole structure of "Before the Law" presupposes the existence of its mirror reflection in *The Trial.* It presents those of us who come before it with an infinite series of entrances because it sees itself refracted back from another text. The figure of the *mise en abyme* accounts for the way in which the law of this text functions: it represents the vanishing origin of the law as well as its structure of repetition. On each doorstep, the whole situation (two men on both sides of the doorstep and the doorstep—the gate of the law that is at the same time the text and the mirror) repeats itself. In the end, it is not the content of the law that is at stake (the man in the story does not gain access to it) but its structure: the structure of repetition in the abyss that produces endless deferral ("endless *différance* till death" [211]). ("From hall to hall there is one doorkeeper after another, each more powerful than the last. The third doorkeeper is already so terrible that even I cannot bear to look at him" [183].) It is this structure that accounts for Derrida's claim that "the origin of literature at the same time as the origin of the law" is "not an event in the ordinary sense of the word" but a "quasi-event" that is "the simulacrum of narration and not only . . . the narration of an imaginary history" (199).

Precisely this structure of a mirror *vis à vis* another mirror, organizing

Kafka's "Before the Law" (together with its *contre-abyme*, *The Trial*), makes it a work that, as Derrida would put it, "contains [a] thinking about its own possibility." A mirror is a receptacle that can—fictively and provisionally—hold anything. It reflects the other mirror and, in doing so, reflects itself again. In reflecting the other mirror (*contre-abyme*), it is a container of reflection—a reflection that is then reflected again as content (second level) and yet again as a container (third level) and so on, endlessly, producing the effect of the inclusion of the container within itself. Furthermore, since the reflecting surface of the origin itself interferes, the reflection of the origin is endlessly deferred: the origin is a mirror that is already doubled, facing itself and in virtue of this its presence (representation) is endlessly deferred. This brings the margins of the image closer to their origin. This gesture of *mise en abyme* not only allows Derrida to problematize the oppositions among set/member, center/margin, and origin/copy but also, as we will see, in virtue of the power of the text to include its own margins, issues of signature, authorship, and testimony.

I have bestowed this much attention on the issues surrounding the *mise en abyme* not only because they allowed me to account for the way in which the law makes its appearance in Derrida's perception of literature, but also because of their relevance to the work of Beckett. Even though the motif of the *mise en abyme* seldom explicitly appears in Beckett, it structures a certain aspect of Beckett's work: the fact that he as an author keeps projecting himself into his work, making this gesture of self-projection a part of his literary experiment. This interest in the function of the author provides an excellent occasion for the discussion of the manner in which Derrida approaches the issue of law in literature. Even though it is difficult to determine with precision the routes of intellectual influence, it nevertheless seems certain that Beckett's interest in the function of the author (an interest that has a lot in common with Blanchot's interest) prepares the way for this part of Derrida's reflection on literature.

The One Who Signs

We have now said that according to Derrida, the privileged access of literature to the law consists in literature's being able to set up and challenge its own "constitutional law"[56] (in Derrida's project, literature has no essence but does have a constitution, which it itself produces and challenges). Now, the primary concern of constitutional law is the distribution of sovereign power. But what is the sovereign power of literature? Who is in charge? This question brings us closer to understanding Derrida's concern with such juridical aspects of literature as copyright, signature, and testimony, which all have in common their relation to a certain *I*. Derrida makes this explicit in *Demeure*, his recent work on Blanchot: what he calls "a passion of literature" consists in "the slippage between the three I's"—that is, between "these three instances (author, narrator, character)."[57] Without suggesting that those three instances are the same (quite the contrary), Derrida speaks about what he calls an "identity of compassion" as the way in which sovereign power (and responsibility) is distributed in the literary institution. The "constitutional law" of literature places the sovereign power in the spectral bond (or what Derrida calls "the haunting") between author, narrator, and character—the bond that produces an infinite regress of responsibility, a *mise en abyme*.

It is characteristic of Beckett that throughout his work he is preoccupied with the voice that is telling stories, the hand that is writing them, the site of making fictive personages, and the authority that stages and directs situations. Beckett practices this self-reflexive gesture while being aware that it is impossible for an author simply to retain his presence in his work, to remain in control of a signed oeuvre. As a result, we find in his works the unmistakable portrait of an author losing himself in his work, an author watching his own decomposition (*s'abîmer*). This self-reflexive gesture, which is everything but mimetic, can be made only on the condition of drawing implicitly on the resources of the *mise en abyme*.[58] (The same consideration applies to the work's witnessing or bringing about its own decomposition—the disintegration of its singular law. This characteristically Beckettian gesture is also the consequence of a mirror effect. I have already quoted Derrida's "what can look at itself is not one," thereby implying that there is a schizoid effect in a mirror reflection, distorting the equivalence of one-to-one into one-to-two. Rather than producing identities, a mirror decomposes them.)

Beckett's Characters and Deleuze's Law of the Nomad

Before we go on with the discussion of the *mise en abyme* in Beckett, we need to address a caveat: there is a more evident and straightforward way in which the law manifests itself in this author's work. To the extent that the *mise en abyme* in Beckett assumes primarily the sense of decomposition (and not, as in Kafka, of a hierarchic structure of infinite regress), the law makes here its appearance as something that is wasting away and disintegrating. This gives way to what Deleuze called the "fundamental indiscipline" of the nomad[59] (the *nomos* is hence closer to anarchy than to a constitution). Deleuze's discussion of *nomos versus polis* in *A Thousand Plateaus* offers a view of the law that at times strikingly resembles the perception of the law we find in Beckett. (The nomadic "law" (*nomos*) of Molloy finds itself in tension with the chesslike law of its counterpart, the *polis*, in *Endgame*.) We cannot fail to notice in Beckett a "fundamental indiscipline" that obstructs the law of the *polis* (i.e., the law "proper") and in contrast to which the nomadic represents "stupidity, deformity, madness."[60] Nor can we remain indifferent to the debilitating impact the appearance of the nomad has on the law of the *polis* (and vice versa, the nomad being equally baffled by the latter):

And suddenly I remembered my name, Molloy. My name is Molloy, I cried, all of a sudden, now I remember. Nothing compelled me to give this information, but I gave it, hoping to please I suppose. . . . Is it your mother's name? said the sergeant, it must have been a sergeant. Molloy, I cried, my name is Molloy. Is that your mother's name? said the sergeant. What? I said. Your name is Molloy, said the sergeant. Yes, I said, now I remember. And your mother? said the sergeant. I didn't follow. Is your mother's name Molloy too? said the sergeant. I thought it over. Your mother, said the sergeant, is your mother's—Let me think! I cried.[61]

The inefficiency of this exchange paralyzes the law (of the *polis*), including the archives, whose function is to support it. For what is to be entered into the archives if Molloy can only with difficulty recollect his name and if he, when asked for his papers, can produce only the bits of newspaper that serve him as toilet paper? Molloy's name (as Henry Sussmann quite rightly observed in one of his lectures) suggests that he mollifies, softens, weakens the law (*loi* in French), and he says as much himself: "[T]o apply the letter of the law to a creature like me is not an easy matter. It can be done but reason is against it."[62] In Beckett's later work, especially in the so-called *Second Trilogy*, the nomadic character of the Beckettian experiment is worked out even further. Even as the law retains its ambulant character with "on" as a main principle, it is no longer, as in *Molloy*, merely debilitating and disorienting (which is what the nomadic war machine must appear when perceived from outside—from the point of view of the *polis*) but develops into a problem-oriented strategy.[63] (This is especially the case in *Worstward Ho*, the supreme exercise in "unsaying": "The void. How try say? How try fail?"[64])

The tension between *nomos* and *polis* described by Deleuze prompts us in the direction of interpreting the law in Beckett as the *nomos*. It not only seems a better, more encompassing figure (and intuitively more persuasive to anyone acquainted with Beckettian tramps) than that of the *mise en abyme*, but also seems in conflict with any self-reflexive structure. This "law" (*nomos*) is not interested in itself; it does not watch itself and does not want to see itself represented. Unlike the law of the state, it has neither representatives nor subjects.[65] In this sense, this "law" is not a constitutional law and hence fails to account for the institutional aspect of literature. This makes it inadequate to the purpose of Derrida, even leaving aside the question of whether literature is, or is not, unlike any other institution.[66] Derrida insists that literature "is an institution which consists in transgressing and transforming, thus in producing its own constitutional law," and that this cannot take place without a gesture of self-reflection. (That which produces its own constitutional law is a *polis*—the nomads having no constitution.) If it is the case that a work of literature cannot be critical either of itself or of the literary institution without the latter gesture, the figure of the *mise en abyme* returns to us with a force of necessity.

The *Mise en Abyme* as Failure and Decomposition ("*S'abîmer*")

There can hardly be any doubt that the idea of the *mise en abyme* of the authorial voice organizes the majority of Beckett's work. In later chapters I will explore this in more depth, discussing the narrator of *How It Is* and the character named Bam in *What Where*. Also, works like *The Unnamable* or *Company* focus on solitary characters who tell themselves stories "for company"—who, in other words, speak to an alter ego, created by the mirror. (It cannot be emphasized enough that the aspect of companionship in Beckett is both schizophrenic and mirror-born: the companion is a ghost, a product of a mind divided by a mirror.) In those works, the speaking voice preserves and perpetuates itself in and through its stories while experiencing the dispersal of its (sovereign) power in the *abyme* of a work. *The Unnamable* formulates explicitly what is here at stake: Is it possible for me, the author, to become incarnate in my creation, to make my voice descend into my work and not to lose it (my voice, my self) in the bargain? "Me, utter me, in the same foul breath as my creatures?"[67]

That a mirror reflection in Beckett does not constitute identity but shatters it can be seen in *That Time*, a strongly autobiographical play, in which during a visit to an art gallery, the narrator sees his face reflected in the glass surface that protects a work of art, a portrait added on the surface of a portrait.

[T]here before your eyes when they opened a vast oil black with age and dirt someone famous . . . behind the glass where gradually as you peered trying to make out gradually of all things a face appeared had you swivel on the slab to see who it was there at your elbow . . . never the same after that . . . not believing it could be you.[68]

In this experience, a (schizophrenic) mirror reflection divides identity instead of confirming it—the "me" is next to me: "at my elbow." This crucial experience (the narrator was "never the same after that") of seeing a reflection of oneself embedded in a work of art prepares and announces Beckett's experiments with putting himself, the voice of the author, *en abyme* in his own work. (In this case, *mise en abyme* through its kinship to *s'abîmer* means also "ruin," "decomposition," "putrefaction.") This development in Beckett comes as a consequence of seeing oneself as somebody else, thereby putting that other *en abyme* (but also *s'abîmer*) in somebody else's work and seeing that work as an abyss. (Thus the work is shown to contain its margins—its audience—within itself.)

Similarly, in the *Calmative*, it is not only the narrator who "never wished for anything . . . except for the mirrors to shatter" and who is "too frightened to listen to myself rot [*pourrir*]."[69] Those are also confessions of the author who anxiously witnesses the decomposition of his sovereign "I" in his work. This image prepares the interchange of *abyme* and *s'abîmer* (based on the similarity of the homonyms *abyme* and *abîme*) explored by Derrida in *Signsponge*.[70] (Since *s'abîmer* means "to decay," *mise en abyme* means both "ruin" and "self-representation" at the same time.)

But the *abyme* of the work hosts more than the specter of the author. Next to containing within themselves the spectral reflection of the author,

Beckett's texts can be read as attempting to put *en abyme* their own event as a shadow of the event to which the text testifies. In fact, for Beckett, the speaking "I" is a special case of such an event: see, for example, the "black, hard, solid rubber ball" given to the dog in *Krapp's Last Tape*. This ball, symbolizing the event of the death of Krapp's mother, reappears in *The Unnamable*, where the narrator describes himself as such a ball, also given to a dog ("Sirius in the Great Dog").

I am a big talking ball. . . . I always knew I was round, solid and round. . . . I am round and hard. . . . All the rest I renounce, including this ridiculous black which I thought for a moment worthier than grey to enfold me.[71]

Beckett's texts also reflect on the successfulness of this attempt to put *en abyme* their own event, for in Beckett's work, the event of an oeuvre is at the same time an event of intrinsic failure. One particular reflection of a text on its own being bound to fail can be found in the hedgehog fragment of *Company*.[72] This pet animal of Jena romanticism[73] is a figure that traditionally brings philosophy and literature together—through the motif of the fragment. It was chosen not merely to represent the new literary genre but also as a subversive way of writing beyond genres such that philosophy and literature would coexist. "A fragment, like a small work of art, has to be entirely isolated from the surrounding world and be complete in itself like a hedgehog." (It was, moreover, as a fragment that it was envisaged so that the Kantian Idea of the Good might finally be presented.) In the Fragment 206, Schlegel's hedgehog symbolizes a detached totality of the fragmentary writing,[74] its struggle for completion, the "literary absolute." The episode in Beckett's *Company* in which a hedgehog makes its appearance recounts an event out of the "listener's" childhood in which, driven perhaps as much by an altruistic impulse as by the need for distraction, he went to some trouble to keep and protect a hedgehog. In this episode, the listener-child places the animal in an old hatbox and leaves it there with some provisions, only to find its body decomposed to a formless mush on the second visit: "You have never forgotten what you found then. . . . The mush. The stench." (In the French version: "Tu n'as jamais oublié ce que tu trouvais alors. Cette bouille. Cette infection.")[75] The episode, which appears to be a veridical memory from Beckett's own life (as is another episode described in *Company*, that of the diving lesson), functions in the text as a childhood memory that returns to the listener by virtue of its being "unforgettable." However, the equivocal status of this and similar episodes appearing in Beckett's work—making it often impossible to establish whether what is at stake is an ironic bringing-up of a weak sentimentality, an allegory, or the representation of a "real" experience—should not prevent us from interpreting them.[76] In Derrida's words: literature is about "events whose 'reality' or duration is never assured."[77]

Read in the tradition of the transcendental poetry of Jena romanticism, the hedgehog episode in Beckett becomes an example of literary self-reflection, a writing that reflects on the conditions of its own possibility. It looks just like the fragment that Schlegel envisaged: an independent island of writing that can be read in detachment from the rest. At no other place in the text is the hedgehog episode alluded to; in fact, one might wonder why it stands there at all, since there does not seem to be any internal exigency that would make the inclusion of this episode necessary, or even clearly motivated, for the sake of the whole. What makes this particular fragment special is not only that it is "like a hedgehog," an embodiment of a Romantic fragment, but also that it contains a hedgehog in itself *en abyme*. The hedgehog in *Company* stands not only for the status of the episode in which it appears, suggesting that we have to do with a poetic fragment, but also for what, at least in Derrida's view, is essential to poetic writing, namely an event that provokes writing. Paul Celan calls it "the unrepeatable . . . / something that can go, ungreeting,"[78] the "Zuspruch der Stunde."[79] In Derrida's words, written in response to Celan, the event is that which "calls or assigns the poem, provokes it, convokes, apostrophizes and addresses it, it and the poet whom the hour claims."[80]

In this case, the event arrives in the shape of the hedgehog crossing the path of the protagonist. And since the episode is written in the second person, the hedgehog can be seen as crossing our path (the mirror is turned toward the reader) and thereby appealing to our capacity to do "good" by keeping and saving it. The hedgehog episode captures the arrival of the event (*l'occurrence*) as that which "crosses our way" (*croise ton chemin*)[81] and, in doing it, at the same time reflects on this act of capturing. The attempt to keep and save the event that crosses our path (which is invariably done by containing it somehow, and moreover containing it in something that is "old hat" [-box]) results in failure ("mush," "stench" [in the French version, *bouille*, "infection"]).

What is at the core of the so-described failure? Is it just that in attempting to capture an event by naming it we risk the loss of the original force of the event (as the English word "mush," a synonym for "weak sentimentality," would suggest)? The "death" of the hedgehog would reflect then the inevitable loss of the individual by subsuming it under a concept. In the decision to "keep" and "contain" the hedgehog, the animal's fate would be sealed. It is impossible to represent an event because any attempt to "keep" the event inevitably entails the loss of its original force and singularity, a failure due to the insufficiency of language (namely that there are no "proper" concepts to designate singular events).

Another possibility is that the fate of the hedgehog is sealed by the fact that it is subsumed under the wrong concept rather than just by its being subsumed under a concept at all, since of the two containers available for housing the hedgehog, one is intended for keeping inanimate objects (hats); and the other, for rabbits. Whereas the rabbit cage is left open so that the animal can "come and go at will," the same is not true of the old hatbox inside, so that the freedom given to the hedgehog is merely apparent. A hatbox has the round shape so favored by Beckett in his prose; its space allows the animal captured inside to move only in circles, an isolated movement of pure self-reflection. In this the hatbox has the form to which the Romantic fragment aspired and seems suited to capture the absolute singularity of the event. But the purity cannot sustain itself without compromising itself, without entering into relation with difference. It should not need mentioning that for Beckett there are only wrong concepts. They are wrong if they are pure, precisely capturing the event, because then, in the resultant isolation, the hedgehog dies. They are wrong if they are impure, contaminated with other meanings, because then they cannot capture the hedgehog. This is the reason for Beckett's words that "there is nothing with which to express" and for his desire for "unsaying." We are structurally obliged to use hats and rabbits to refer to hedgehogs. The use of the expressions *bouille* and "infection" in the French version seems to complement the latter interpretation. It suggests that independent of the verbal dexterity of the writer who tries to preserve the "pure" quality of the event in words, the "contamination" and thereby the loss of the singular in the impurity of language, which is tainted by all kinds of intercontextual interventions, is inevitable.

The question that arises now is whether the intrinsic failure of the effort to contain the event is a reason to give up the attempt itself. Such a possibility is voiced in the text: The character experiences a "great uneasiness" at the "suspicion that all was perhaps not as it should be. That rather than do as you did you had perhaps better let good alone and the hedgehog pursue its way." To "let . . . the hedgehog pursue its way" without trying to keep it is equivalent here to not responding to an event—or, in the words of Celan quoted above, of allowing "the unrepeatable . . . to go, ungreeting." On the one side we have the possibility of renouncing the temptation to keep the event; on the other side, the possibility of giving in to it, which entails, in Beckett's words, that we will "fail again. Fail better."

That the resolution to "keep" the event is here presented as the consequence of an ethical consideration, one that would be opposed to "letting good alone," concurs with Beckett's overall view that there is something like the "obligation to express" and thus that for a writer, the decision to write is an ethical decision. In the hedgehog episode, this "ethical decision" is already in itself flawed, certainly in the Kantian sense. It is taken for all the wrong reasons—*pour tuer le temps d'une lenteur mortelle*—and perhaps also in view of a reward in the shape of *la petite flamme allumée par cette bonne action, un petit chaud au cœur*. Insofar as the hedgehog fragment might be interpreted as an aesthetic idea symbolically presenting the morally good, in Beckett the link between the two is always shown to be flawed: "you had perhaps better left good alone and the hedgehog pursue its way."[82] While this exemplifies the essential failure of writing, it does not relieve one of the "obligation to express."

In this chapter, I have suggested that Derrida's event of a singular literary work appears to be economico-juridical in character. The work economizes on the space it takes while attempting to gather an infinite multiplicity. It does so by appealing to all networks of significations (existing ones and those only as yet to come), thereby presupposing the possibility of an infinite expansion of meanings. By allowing the gathered items to appear as echoing each other, the literary work permits them to arrange themselves into series of iterations. These series form the law of the literary work in the sense that they determine its force. (The force of the law stems from the necessary possibility of its being repeated or cosigned.) Derrida reads Kafka's parable as staging the working of (among other things) the law that determines the question of the "literariness" of a text. Consequently, the law before which the countryman comes consists in a series of iterations: "from hall to hall" and "guardian after guardian."[83] The law itself, concludes Derrida, is "nothing other than that which dictates the delay."[84] It is through such self-reflective series of iterations (and as one of them) that the author's signature inserts itself into the work. From then on, the signature is both, and undecidably, a "receptacle" assuming responsibility for the (hyper-)totality of textual effects produced by the work, as well as just one of the infinity of the gatherable singular items. It attempts to embrace the textual event of the work as a whole but is at the same time itself embraced, put *en abyme,* by the latter.

2

A Singular Odyssey

The Work as a Singular Event

In the previous chapter, I examined Derrida's notion of literature to find out whether it is universal enough to be applicable to Beckett's work. Whereas "literature" in Derrida's thought names an institution that is continually redefined by works-events and hence could, in principle, account for any work, Derrida's discourse consistently privileges certain texts in accordance with a much narrower definition of literature. On that narrower definition, the singular works-events that make up "literature" have two gestures in common. One of them aims at saying an infinite number of things within the finite space of a text. This gesture, on Derrida's own account, reflects his desire to say "everything": to gather dates and significations, to hyper-totalize. The other one consists in the reflection of the work on its own law and thereby on the nature of law and on universality in general. Having taken those two gestures as a starting point for a possible dialogue between Derrida and Beckett, I argued that whereas Beckett's work lends itself to a reading alongside the latter gesture (reflection on the law), it is particularly recalcitrant to—and critical of—the gesture of hyper-totalizing. This recalcitrance, which might explain why Beckett does not belong to the canon of works discussed by Derrida, marks a point of difference, of dissent perhaps, which has larger implications for the discussion of the function, or "essence," of literature.

The consensus that there is no such thing as an essence of literature does not put an end to the discussion of what it is that we expect from literature or what its relation, contribution, or relevance to philosophy might be. It has often been said that even if literariness is not an intrinsic property of texts, our reading of certain texts can be specifically literary. But Derrida claims that literariness is not something that resides in our intentional attitude alone. Certain texts do lend themselves better to certain readings. "The literary character of the text is inscribed on the side of the intentional object, in its noematic structure, one could say and not only on the subjective side on the noetic act."[1] The literary character of at least some of the texts or a possibility of reading them as "literature" must hence also, at least in part, be inscribed in those texts. In a recent interview, for example, Derrida explicitly opposed the "mixing up" of literature and philosophy, thereby "reducing the one to the other." Whereas he does not renounce the idea that literature, too, can be "argumentative," he says that it is so "in another way, with different procedures."[2] This confirms Gasché's observation that rather than "leveling the difference between literature and philosophy" (as Habermas has argued), "since *The Origin of Geometry*, Derrida has been working in light of the difference between the literary and the philosophical text."[3] Philosophy and literature become what they are in their respective difference. For example, philosophy contains elements of literature that are not full-blown but appear only *in nuce*. Narrativity can be seen as such an element; while traditionally understood as the core of the literary, it is not always absent from philosophical discourse. Derrida has asserted that the expression "as if" in Kant's formulation of the categorical imperative functions as an element of narrativity and fiction at the source of the law. Gasché, commenting on this issue, emphasizes that "with the 'as if,' narrativity and fiction are said to be only *almost*, or more precisely, *virtually* present in the pure and in principle unrepresentable law."[4] This is so because philosophy attempts to suppress in itself the features of the literary, and it is precisely in virtue of this resistance to other kinds of writing that philosophy becomes what it is, Gasché argues.

If philosophy and literature become what they are in their respective difference, then the same holds for literature: it contains elements of philosophical discourse but suppresses them and, in so doing, creates its own identity. The work of literature would resist being read as a philosophical text by privileging the singular and opposing it to the overt ambition of universality characteristic of philosophy. "The man from the country had difficulty in grasping that an entrance was singular or unique when it should have been universal, as in truth it was. He had difficulty with literature,"[5] Derrida observes, commenting on Kafka's story. In other words, the man from the country attempted to read literature as philosophy when he should have known better—when he should have known that the passage through the singular was inevitable because "there is no literature without . . . an absolutely singular performance."[6] Derrida immediately adds that the entrance that presented such an obstacle to the man from the country was not only singular but, "in truth," also universal in the sense in which Heidegger wrote about death, which has the feature of being "always mine" (*Jemeinigkeit*), such that it is absolutely individual and universal at the same time. So again, literature does not exorcise the universal from itself but negotiates an intersection of the singular and the universal within itself as a singular work.

The definition of literature as a set of singular works that simultaneously gather and formalize[7] makes double use of the term "singular": the singular is not only the work but also what it gathers—that is, the singular dates-events that the work gathers and that make the work possible. Therefore the singular becomes a central notion for addressing the literature, which we can define as the gathering (and formalizing) of the singular, in the singular. In this chapter, I will pursue this discussion of Derrida's understanding of literature by examining the notion that is central to it: the singular event.

Even though the singular is an old issue, it has been pointed out that as a third notion, next to the particular and the universal, the singular appears only with the arrival of Hegel's speculative thought and that only there the notion of the singular acquires a greater depth.[8] As Jean-François Marquet argues, Hegel's thought is a philosophy of the singular par excellence: it is in the singular (*das Einzelne*) that the other moments of the Absolute (the universal and the particular) come to completion.[9] A reading of Hegel's *Encyclopaedia* §§ 163–65 shows that, at the conceptual level, singularity ("*Einzelheit*," rendered here as "individuality") seems to include the less complex moments of universality and particularity. "Individuality [is] the reflection-into-self of the specific characters of universality and particularity; which negative self-unity has complete and original determinateness, without any loss to its self-identity or universality."[10] What is of interest in this definition is that the singular moment of the concept is self-reflective (*die Reflexion in sich*) and that it is both concrete (specific) and general. Similarly in his *Ästhetik*, Hegel describes the singular both as self-knowing and as the center where the universal and the particular coincide. Derrida's thought is very faithful to this Hegelian motif. The idea of this intersection of the particular and the universal, the empirical and the transcendental, is characteristic of Derrida's thinking of the singular.

In his book *Guillaume d'Ockham: Le singulier*,[11] Pierre Alféri discusses the origin of the notion. There are two types of singularity in the thought of William of Ockham, Alféri argues: one that has a numerical unity (the ontological singular, the one that is "extra *animam*," beyond mind), and one that has a unity of signification. (The latter is the sign for the singular thing that allows the singular thing, through the mediation of the mind, to enter into a series.) The latter is said to have a transcendental pertinence because without it, it would be impossible to organize the objects of perception into a series. In other words, the whole division into the universal and the particular is dependent on the transcendental concept of the sign. For Ockham, these two types of singularity are irreducibly different, and the major difference is that the "ontological" singular is "before" all particularity. While Derrida seems to align Ockham's ontological singularity with the utopia of the absolute singularity, Ockham's privileging of the other sense of the singular (the sense of the unity of signification) as a transcendental condition of thought seems to be very close to Derrida's philosophical project.

Thinking about a literary work in terms of a singular event is not a Derridean idiosyncrasy but is common to all recent philosophical attempts to understand the phenomenon of literature from within the French postwar philosophical tradition. Authors such as Gilles Deleuze, Maurice Blanchot, Jean-Luc Nancy, Philippe Lacoue-Labarthe, and Alain Badiou share the interest in the singular. It is in and through the singular event that they try to capture literature's relevance for life and for thought. The discussion of this issue is complicated by the fact that the above authors differ (and, moreover, often inexplicitly so) in the meaning they give to the terms "event" and "singularity." Hence, we need to ask: What is an event? (This question is pertinent not only in relation to literature but also in a broader sense: Derrida's whole project is dependent for its coherence on a certain articulation of the notion of the event.) We are familiar with Deleuze's exemplary answer to this question: the event is "la prise de la Bastille." Badiou's examples of events are comparable: May 1968, the Chinese Cultural Revolution, and the Solidarity movement in Poland.[12] Derrida seems to voice the same intuition when he defines a founding event as "a revolutionary instant that belongs to no historical, temporal continuum."[13] However, whereas in Deleuze's discourse an event is something beyond the regime of signs (an event is "becoming in itself" [*un devenir en lui-même*]), for Derrida, no event can be thought "in itself" but must express itself in a self-imposed "code" of doubling. While Deleuze does not conceive of the event as having a numerical unity—"an event is a million of droplets"—his notion of the event is nonetheless closer to Ockham's ontological singularity in that as "becoming in itself," it does not necessarily require the mediation of the mind, and could just as well take place "extra animam." In Derrida's thought, as shown earlier, the logic of iterability does not discriminate between events and their signs, which means that an event does not have any distinctly ontological quality (according to which "being" would be opposed to meaning or sense): "an event . . . marks." This is why it is so easy to use the words "event" and "date" interchangeably: "date" means both that which is given—the datum (the event, that which happens)—and the numerical sign for it that marks the event on the calendar. If doubling (iterability) is taken to mean representation, then Derrida's event is always at the same time its own re-presentation (as in Ponge's phrase, "By the word *by* commences then this text."[14])

The "*Mathesis Singularis*" of Roland Barthes

Although Derrida addresses the singular in many of his texts, he does it in perhaps the most visually appealing form in his "Deaths of Roland Barthes," an essay responding to Roland Barthes' *Camera Lucida*. Derrida's essay is perhaps not an obvious choice for the discussion of the singularity in (and of) literature, but it has the advantage of being an antecedent to his later, more widely discussed attempts to rethink the relationship between the singular and the universal. (*Shibboleth* appeared only five years later, in 1986.) Even more importantly, Barthes' project of a "protestation of singularity," while significantly differing from Beckett's (which aims at the effacement of singularity), is no less significantly opposed to the literary project of Joyce that we have seen at work in Derrida's views on literature as gathering. Joyce's program is designed to have accounted for everything, to remember everything, and to anticipate everything—including all that we might say on its topic—in advance. In contrast, Barthes, with his *Camera Lucida* (in Derrida's interpretation), wants to preserve the memory of one unique individual—his mother.

Barthes' essay—a "protestation of singularity" born out of a "desperate resistance to any reductive system"—addresses a number of points that return in Derrida's project. Notably, Barthes considers the tension between the effects of iteration and the singular (understood as that which should transcend iteration).[15] Already the first sentence of Derrida's response, "How does one reconcile this plural?" makes his purpose clear. How does one reconcile the grammatical oddity of "the deaths" with the individual human being to whom they are attributed?

In the early stages of Derrida's exposition, Barthes' name functions in the text as a singular signature, gathering a "terrifying and endless series"[16] of deaths. Among those deaths are real ones, like Barthes' own and that of his mother. There are also those momentary, symbolic deaths produced by the click of a camera, which freezes, or "deadens," the photographed object. Finally, there are those deaths by naming—the dialectical effects of negation, of which Blanchot speaks in *La part du Feu,* when, in the wake of Hegel, he compares the act in which Adam gave a name to every creature to an "immense hecatomb."[17]

There is another sense in which the singular appears, or rather disappears, in Barthes' essay. This essay, Derrida argues, is governed by the remarkable absence of a photograph of Barthes' deceased mother—the absence of the photograph mimicking the absence of the mother. This absence stands for the ineffable singular, for that which is without a double. The utopia of absolute singularity comes to light in the discussion of this missing image—the so-called Winter Garden Photograph. This image (addressed in capitals, as in a proper name) is the only one that does not accompany the text that nevertheless speaks about it—perhaps, as Derrida suggests, only about it. It seems to be the invisible focal point around which the whole essay is gathered. When Barthes speaks about this absent photograph, one is reminded of the strategy proper to negative theology, the *via negativa*. It cannot be "read," "reflected," "interiorized," "contemplated"; it is "undialectical," "unnamable," "invisible," "outside of meaning," and can only appear by "assuming a mask" (passim). What is the power of resistance of this photograph that makes it so singular, so different from all the others? According to Barthes, the impossible right or power of this image to resist iterability is drawn from the "originality of suffering."

I might say, like the Proustian Narrator at his grandmother's death: "I did not insist only upon suffering, but upon respecting the originality of my suffering"; for this originality was the reflection of what was absolutely irreducible in her, and thereby lost forever.[18]

When Derrida says that "love . . . protests against . . . [the] metonymy" of the *punctum*, he addresses Barthes' intention to single out his mother's death, to grant it the status of a singularity that precludes any external relation, of an event that does not have anything in common with any other event. The picture of the mother must not be shown in order to preserve the absolute singularity of the event.

Derrida, who sets out to show that it is impossible to think the singular without thinking about it as repeatable, is aware of a potential criticism of this enterprise: the repeatable is no longer the absolutely unique; iterability destroys the singular. "The deaths of Roland Barthes: because of the rather improper brutality of this plural, one might think perhaps that I resisted the unique," says Derrida. And he answers: "[P]erhaps, but how do we speak otherwise without taking the risk? Without pluralizing the unique or generalizing that which is held most irreplaceable in it, his own death?" In other words, it is only by employing the resources of iterability that we can speak of the singular. Moreover, Derrida insists that there is nothing disrespectful in this; according to him, the metonymy that allows us to speak about what is otherwise ineffable is as much a way of "speaking" as of "keeping silent."[19]

Paradoxically, it is also the iterability that permits Derrida, albeit in a ghostly fashion, to address that non-iterated absolute singular that transcends our conscious experience ("that which does not return, which is not repeated, the experience of ruin and ashes"). Derrida is in fact saying here that if even absence is subject to metonymic expansion, everything can be talked about (is effable). He puts it defensively—"how do we speak otherwise?"—but then he also says, "this way we can speak." This again is consistent with Derrida's hyper-totalizing desire "to say everything: what happens and what fails to happen." In this sense, Derrida does not weaken the singular by depriving it of its uniqueness; on the contrary, he reinforces it by allowing it to serialize, to pluralize itself, by the power of what Barthes calls "metonymic expansion."

In Beckett's *Krapp's Last Tape,* the death of the mother appears without appearing in a manner almost identical to that seen in Barthes. The event itself is not named. With the narrator sitting with the mother's window in view, all we hear is that "mother lay a-dying" as he was "throwing a ball for a little white dog as chance would have it," and that then "the blind went down, one of those dirty brown roller affairs." This is all that is said.

> I sat on for a few moments with the ball in my hand and the dog yelping and pawing at me. . . . In the end I held it out to him and he took it in his mouth, gently, gently. A small, old, black, hard, solid rubber ball. . . . I shall feel it, in my hand, until my dying day. . . . I might have kept it. . . . But I gave it to the dog.[20]

Perhaps, Krapp muses, he should have kept that "small, old, black, hard, solid rubber ball" as a token of his mother's death. But he gave it away, consciously or not, permitting the figurative substitution of that singular moment of the transition from life to death by any other moment: "Moments. Her moments, my moments. [Pause] The dog's moments."[21] Yet it is the same movement of iterability that both causes the loss of the ultimate singularity of the moment and allows for memory to keep it: Krapp would not remember his mother's death if there were no original division, reproduction, repetition, in the event itself, which made it possible to substitute the event with something else. It is ultimately through the detour of the "ball" Krapp has given away that he remembers: "I shall feel it, in my hand, until my dying day."

As mentioned earlier (see the discussion of the *mise en abyme* of personal signature in Beckett in the last section of Chapter 1), the "black, hard, solid rubber ball" reappears elsewhere in Beckett's work. In *Krapp's Last Tape,* the ball stands for the moment that divides life from death; in *The Unnamable,* for the point of transition between the author and his work (I return to the latter transition in Chapter 4). I bring up this resonance here to show that in Beckett and Barthes alike, the absolutely singular serializes itself, producing a "terrifying, endless series," a singular serialization that can be seen as constitutive of memory, of subjectivity, and of Beckett's singular signature.

In his recent film adaptation of *Krapp's Last Tape* (for the "Beckett on Film" project), Atom Egoyan explores and deepens Beckett's idea of ruining the archives, of archiving ruin and silence. Egoyan's realization of the play follows the script in almost every detail, with one significant exception that emphasizes the context of elision or erasure. We know that in Beckett's text, at the spot where Krapp remembers the death of his mother, the script has Krapp elide the information that his mother died. We are able to guess it, knowing that Krapp reflects on the time when his "mother lay a-dying," and from the custom of lowering the blinds in the house of the dead. Under Egoyan's direction, we merely hear the sound of the tape recorder being switched on and off without seeing Krapp perform this action. This leaves open whether it is the sound of Krapp acting now or whether it is a replayed trace of an earlier erasure, one in a series of them, that we hear as a piece of archiving by silence.

Without expansion (metonymic or other), the radical consequence of treating the singular as absolutely unique (i.e., in the way we intuitively tend to construe it, as that which happened "one time only") is its self-effacement. The singular as unique, "alone," without valence, "is" not. It can only be thought as an absolutely "unsubstitutable" absence, insists Derrida. Not only does it have to be "unredeemable" and nondialectical, since otherwise it would be easily turned into presence, but every way of thinking it otherwise must be prevented. (It is in order not to turn the absent singular into a presence that both Derrida and Barthes insist that singularity precludes mourning, for mourning sublates death.)[22] We cannot even say that it so much as dissimulates itself, appearing in the guise of something else, because the "guise" would function as its double. It is that which has always already effaced itself. Nothing can be said about the singular, not even that it leaves an empty space in its wake, for that already allows substitution. The failure of Barthes' undertaking of protecting at any price the singularity of his mother's death is thereby made clear. Derrida plays with the near-homophony of the expressions "the law of the name" and "the law of the number" (*nom/nombre*) to show that a name, intended to single out an individual, always already gathers a series, a number, a multiplicity. In the place that Barthes wanted to keep empty and thereby singular, "substitution repeats itself . . . , retaining of the irreplaceable only a past desire."[23]

The guiding thread of Barthes' undertaking in *Camera Lucida* is his dream of *mathesis singularis,* or the "impossible science of the unique being"[24]—the impossible generalization of the singular, so to speak. What becomes apparent very soon is that there is nothing singular about the medium on which Barthes focuses to initiate this science. Photography resists attempts to conceive the nature of its object as "unique," as being "without a double." A doubling, a repetition (the referent and its representation), is inherent in this medium. In this sense, singularity in Barthes cannot be opposed to duality: the *punctum* of the camera's click does not pretend to be "one"; it is precisely that which causes doubling. But the singularity of the *punctum* gathers more than its own doubling alone. It is not the case that the doubling forms a purely self-reflective circle that does not point to anything outside of itself. Barthes shows how what we see in a photograph divides itself, lending itself to metonymy, which points ultimately beyond the photographic image and beyond that which is represented in the image: to other places, moments, photographs. Similarly, the singularity of the *punctum* oscillates between a detail of a photograph and the act of reading that the photograph evokes; again, the *punctum* is a "lightning-like"[25] negotiation between these two points of view. In this sense, Barthes must see the singular as a relation. Easily detectable in photography is the rapport between the photographic image and its referent (even though Barthes, unlike Derrida, insists on the "existential," distinctive singularity of the photographed event: "What the Photograph reproduces to infinity has occurred only once: the Photograph mechanically repeats what could never be repeated existentially"). Some rapport is also brought about between (the significant fragment of) an image and the viewer who is "touched" or "animated"[26] by it. Eventually, all these doublings become aspects of the larger movement of the singular, which multiplies relations and thereby forms series (since images refer, by resemblance, meaning, or even pure coincidence, to other images). This is what Barthes calls the "metonymic expansion" of the *punctum*. If we take into account this larger movement, photography's mimicking of reality (again, both by preserving and negating it) becomes just one more aspect of this movement. Both the potential iterability of the experience of the *punctum* and the trajectory in which the *punctum*, moving like an arrow, produces a series are cases of this self-pluralizing expansion of the singular.[27] All these examples are those of an inherent doubling and serialization at stake. In other words, the singular displays here the structure of a relation originating in the "uncompromising and punctual decision, which takes place in the almost no time of a [camera's] click." This "almost no time" signals that, while the relation is forged with the velocity of an electrical discharge or a "shot," nonetheless it does have a temporal nature. Although it has practically no duration—like a flashover, or like the momentary "explosion" of the "active reading" that makes a "star on the pane of the ... photograph"[28]—it does not suspend time altogether. (This is to say that, like the temporal "now," the moment in which the photographic image is captured is always already fissured.)

It is only apparently that a *punctum* is a point, Derrida tells us. In his words, it is "a point that is not a point," for were we not told by Barthes that the *punctum* is a point that punctures? ("[T]his element ... [that] rises from the scene, shoots out of it like an arrow, and pierces me.") If it does do this, it must be in movement that has a direction, and this movement must be something like a line. It only looks like a point from a very special position—when we are "in the line of fire," face-to-face with the oncoming arrow. Indeed, if we look in this one-dimensional way, it may even seem like there is nothing to be seen. But in fact the *punctum* has a "whence" and a "thither," even if the reversibility of its direction makes them interchangeable; as Derrida makes clear, "the *punctum* points to me at the instant and place where I point to it."[29]

Iterability of the Singular

Derrida's patient reading of Barthes merely emphasizes what the latter has said himself: the *punctum* is both singular and plural. This brings Barthes' study of the "metonymic power of expansion" of the *punctum* very close to Derrida's investigation of the iterability of the singular. In both cases, the repetition at stake is not an identical repetition; it involves change. Derrida says of the singularity of the *punctum* that it "mobilizes everything everywhere. It pluralizes itself."[30] But there is more to it. The *punctum* not only produces a multiplicity (in Derrida's terms, it mobilizes a differential force) but also organizes it (this is its formalizing force). Derrida emphasizes that Barthes is saying that the *punctum* is the "inner Law." It is here that Derrida elaborates the interplay of what appeared in Barthes as a pair of absolute opposites: the *punctum* and the *studium*—the first being the "uncoded beyond," and the second the "always coded."[31] "I would like to show that the concepts which seemed the most squarely opposed, or opposable, were put in play by [Barthes], the one for the other, in a metonymic composition."[32] *Punctum* and *studium* are in fact metonymically substituted. In virtue of this substitution, the *punctum* (that appeared to be the "uncoded beyond") functions paradoxically as the law itself and thereby as the code that organizes the *studium*. It is with good reason that Derrida emphasizes[33] that "luminosity" refers both to the *camera lucida* (*la chambre claire*, the apparatus anterior to photography—in other words, that which captures and codes all) and to the central *punctum* of the whole essay, the mother's face. This makes the mother, the *punctum* of the whole essay,[34] metonymically replace the gathering camera. In virtue of this substitution, Derrida is able to destabilize Barthes' notion of the *punctum*. The *punctum* is no longer simply beyond the law; it produces the law.

The poignant singularity does not refute the generality, it does not prevent it from having the force of Law but . . . signs it.[35]

Derrida's addressing the *punctum* as the supplement and the "ghost" (i.e., a doubling) and his suggestion in the text that he substitutes his own signature for that of Barthes make it clear that, to a large extent, he identifies his own project with this particular reading of the *punctum*.

One thing becomes clear from the above discussion: the poles of the singularity and the law must coexist. Singularity is a conjunction of both the "irreplaceable" and the very law that gathers the substitutions of that "irreplaceable." The latter can reveal itself in no other way than through the process of substitution. The *studium* and the *punctum* are not simply opposites of each other, just as the other and the same (or the singular and the universal) are not; a necessary interaction is taking place here, even if only in the form of haunting. The absent *punctum* pluralizes itself, finding its way to reveal itself through the multiplicity it gathers. Iterability—as the ability to expand, to pluralize itself—is indeed the *punctum*'s force, the way in which the *punctum* operates. An "irreplaceable event" like the one of Barthes' book can only be produced by the metonymic expansion of the *punctum*.[36]

Even though Barthes' project, in its attempt to account for something unique and irreplaceable, seemed totally opposed to that of Joyce (who exploited the equivocity and substitutability of language in order "to say everything"), Derrida's reading of Barthes shows the respective projects to be very similar. Granted, Barthes did not produce an encyclopedic novel like Joyce did but a highly personal essay. Yet what the one wanted to resist and the other embraced—the series-forming principle, iterability, as a condition of the possibility of writing and experience—is at the core of both projects.

The power of the singular event, Derrida says, resides in its ability to formalize.

> What is fascinating is an event of a singularity powerful enough to formalize the questions and the theoretical laws concerning it.... [T]hat a singular mark should also be repeatable, iterable, as mark. It then begins to differ from itself sufficiently to become exemplary and thus involve a certain generality. This economy of exemplary iterability is of itself formalizing.[37]

In other words, the self-generalization of a singular event, its law-producing force, is a consequence of its iterability—an iterability that at the same time conceives the event of its own representation. (Note the smooth passage from "event" to "mark" that is for Derrida characteristic.) The misleadingly simple definition of an event that Derrida gives in *Sauf le nom*, where it is defined as "what comes, what there is and which is always singular,"[38] might make us think that the event is something that happens only once, at random, unexpectedly. We should not fail to notice, however, that the word "singular" is preceded by "always," for this is quite essential to Derrida's definition of singularity. An "always singular" event houses this contract and hence has some universal properties—a grid of predictability. Thus, paradoxically, no chance event is fully unexpected.

Derrida's understanding of an event, as opposed, for example, to that of Jean-Luc Nancy, is indissociably connected to a mark; whereas for Nancy an event is merely "empty time" ("temps vide")[39] and is not presentable, a Derridean event "marks." Derrida always links the event to the figure of writing: it is "what can happen to me through writing,"[40] "poetic writing is an event that marks."[41] It is this marklike quality of an event that allows Derrida to make a passage from the singular to the universal. When Derrida speaks about his interest in famous works of philosophy and literature as the interest in "what happened one time only, while dividing itself already," he addresses iterability as the property of a mark: "the ideal iterability ... forms the structure of all marks." Derrida's argument is that a singular event-mark is always iterable—that is, it can be repeated across contexts and still retain (a part of) its meaning. Because repetitions across contexts are not identical repetitions, the repeated mark begins to differ from itself, becoming one of its many repetitions. Each of the latter can be taken as an example of the totality of the iterations of the mark. But to be exemplary is to be both one of many and one standing for many—and to stand for many is to be in possession of something that is common to many (i.e., it is equivalent to having acquired a certain generality). It is in this way that the singular acquires its claim to universality. This genesis of the universality from the singular by way of substitution makes clear the importance of interpretation in Derrida's project. Interpretation, relying on the general assumption that something stands for something else, is needed for both gestures associated by Derrida with literature. In the case of the juridical, the generality of the law can only arise due to the exemplarity of the singular, which differs from itself and thereby stands for many. Likewise, the economical gesture in literature would not be possible without interpretation. The economy of means of expression can only be achieved by entrusting one item with the function of replacing, standing for, and thereby gathering in itself a multiplicity of other items.

The Odyssey of the Iterable Singular

I mentioned before that the serialization of the singular through the "metonymic expansion" in Barthes is not unlike the gathering gesture of Joyce's *Ulysses*. This is confirmed on further examination: Derrida speaks about the singular moments in Barthes not only in terms of a series but also in terms of an itinerary; the "orienting tombs" of the deaths Barthes discusses draw a circular route, an odyssey from himself to himself. Beckett too can be said to have written such an odyssey. At a certain point in his writing career, the robust style of the "talking black ball," which was still easily induced to laughter and bouncing off to new topics, evolved into the austere consistency of the "monster of the solitudes." Thus, we can understand the being that lends its voice ("I quote") to the story of *How It Is*.[42] That "creature in the mud" tells us a story of a journey between places, a permanent, almost immobile, tortuous odyssey to the rhythm of minor displacements in the series of creatures numbered from 1 to 1,000,000. That the million creatures conceal in fact a (dispersed) unity of one point of enunciation is disclosed at the end of the "novel": "only me yes alone yes with my voice yes in the mud yes . . . never crawled . . . never suffered . . . never abandoned."[43] He (she? it?) is, just like the Derridean universal singular, one of many (as any particular link in the self-created chain) and one standing for many (the signature that gathers this odyssey and assumes responsibility for its "justice"). In this sense, *How It Is* looks almost as if it was designed for a structuralist reading (the French version was published in 1961, when structuralism was at the heyday of its influence). We can discern in it the two gestures through which structuralism proceeds. The first is a combinatory description of the multiplicity of discrete beings, subject to preexistent laws of contrast or position. This static abstraction of distinct entities named Pim, Krim, Bom, Bem, would remain "opaque"—that is, would not produce sense without the second gesture, in which a singular entity, an "empty square," is isolated within the structure in order to set it into motion as a sense-producing machine.[44] (This, of course, was the main question posed by structuralism: How is sense produced?) In this case, the couple of victim and tormentor plays the role. The couple sets the machine in motion in the literal sense, too: the result of its interaction is "a pursuit without hope and a flight without fear."[45]

The odyssey (the circular movement of the million creatures in the mud) of *How It Is* proceeds through violence. The million having differentiated themselves into victims and tormentors, in every couple the tormentor inflicts wounds on his other ("the unbutcherable other") with a tin opener. The necessity of this repetitive motif for the meaning of the novel as a whole becomes clear only when the phrase "tin opener" suddenly appears in the form of the phrase "I opener."[46] The wound inflicted by the narrator (and any like him in the series) on his temporal other that extorts "a sigh" from the latter is an "eye-opener" but also an "I opener"—something that produces a fissure in the "I." (It seems as if at stake here is something analogous to what Deleuze discovers in Proust. Deleuze opposes the traditional reading of Proust as a meditation on involuntary memory; for him, Proust's novel is a machine for the production of resonances of which involuntary memory is only one type. In Beckett's *How It Is*, literally this time, we witness a representation, as well as the working of a machine to produce "sighs." Some of those sighs are memories.) Even more so, it is a gesture through which the "I" opens and discloses itself, both to itself and to the outside world, by telling (or writing, or carving—with a can opener on its "other") its story. The "I" presents itself to us thereby as the early Romantic embodiment of the subject-work, where the progress of writing and the becoming of the subject of writing are one and the same project, narrated by carving on the temporal incarnations of the "I."

In what way is this singular odyssey different from the undertaking of Joyce's *Ulysses*? (After all, we know that Beckett has chosen not to follow the path of his master Joyce.) In what way are the twin couples of victim and tormentor similar to or different from the twin yeses that Derrida has elevated to the status of the founding program of the *Ulysses* machine? (The two yeses are the hyper-totalizing yes of hypermnesis, which has always already accounted for everything, and the affirmative yes of resigned lucidity, which acknowledges the unforeseeable and the failure of the first yes's totalizing project.) To start with, we might observe that the twin yeses are constitutive of subjectivity in the same way that the victim and tormentor couple is in Beckett. However, Joyce's project is more pretentious; for the twin yeses, the subjectivity is just one of many effects. The machine as a whole is designed primarily to collect, by affirming, everything indiscriminately. That indiscriminate greed of Joyce's machine is what makes it (and Joyce was not unaware of this, as Derrida shows) "*in sum* poor literature, vulgar in that it never leaves its luck to the incalculable simplicity of a poem, grimacing from overcultivated and hyperscholastic technology."[47] Beckett's literary project, at least up to a certain moment, is simpler: all it wants to account for are the quasi-transcendental conditions of the point where the "I" produces an oeuvre. The singular in Beckett, to the extent that we can speak about it (i.e., in the sense of Beckett's singular signature), is always situated in this context. If there is an element of gathering in Beckett, it will always be with respect to the subject-production—the overlapping of successive "I"s. Compared to Joyce's project, this gathering, if we can call it that at all, looks strikingly austere. It is not for nothing that Beckett's work has been compared to that of Wittgenstein. By describing Joyce's project as one of an "overcultivated and hyperscholastic technology," Derrida himself has assumed the idiom of the "ordinary language" philosophy that criticizes Western metaphysics as a product of such an "overcultivation." Perhaps we should look more closely at the singular gesture in the context of Derrida's encounter with that branch of philosophy.

3

Beckett, Derrida, and the Ordinary

In her *Wittgenstein's Ladder: Poetic Language and the Strangeness of the Ordinary*, literary critic Marjorie Perloff pleads for an alternative approach to literature to counteract what she sees as the overwhelmingly "continental" reception of a number of literary works—including those of Beckett. (It should be noted that Derrida never accepted the designation "continental philosopher."[1]) *Wittgenstein's Ladder* has been received as a turn away from so-called "theory"—the word that for Perloff is almost synonymous with Derrida—toward the "anti-theory" that she associates with a Wittgensteinian mode of investigation. The main claim of the book is that Wittgenstein anticipates current trends in literary practice and that therefore reading certain literary works through and with Wittgenstein might be productive. Perloff, known as a "militant critic," makes no secret of her conviction that Wittgenstein has more to offer than Derrida on the problem of literary language. It is not my intention here simply to contest this claim. There is no doubt that Wittgenstein provides us with remarkable insights in almost any domain. Stanley Cavell, in his repeated attempts to show the inseparability of the aesthetic practice of "The Investigations" from its argument, has shown that Wittgenstein's work must offer us, however implicitly, some reflection on (its own) literariness.

Nonetheless, Perloff's exposition might be thought somewhat question-begging when it comes to the question of the relative merits of the ordinary language and "continental" approaches to literature. Especially since more and more critics are coming to recognize that there are

> very strong affinities between deconstructive thought and the thought of later Wittgenstein.... Belatedly, analytic philosophers are coming to realize that deconstruction has common ground with "analytic" philosophy both in presuppositions and in strategies.[2]

For example, it has been argued that Quine's polemic with the distinction between analytic and synthetic can be read as an example of deconstruction, comparable to Derrida's deconstruction of the distinction between expression and signification in Husserl.[3] Also, Cavell notes that the form of the critique of skepticism within the Anglo-Saxon philosophical tradition bears strong affinities to Derrida's deconstruction.[4]

In spite of the apparent obscurity of his formulations, Derrida's arguments might turn out not to be incompatible with the conception of the world offered to us by ordinary language philosophy (the world of language games and family resemblances).[5] Admittedly, formulations in which he evokes the "mystical" and confesses his "taste for the secret" might suggest otherwise. But provided that we adopt a broad understanding of Wittgenstein's heritage—an understanding that discourages our thinking about grammar and criteria as provided by a framework of rules—a certain congeniality between the different approaches to philosophy is surely not out of the question. The main remaining difference is that whereas Wittgenstein's vocabulary has freed itself from the discouragingly huge legacy of the philosophical and literary canon, Derrida's vocabulary embraces this legacy. Derrida does not just play with the unnecessary excesses of the metaphysical tradition. Rather, his approach reflects the observation that the sedimentations of our culture are, through our language, always implicitly presupposed in our thought, and that therefore using everyday language meaningfully means obeying the same principles as those that gave rise to Western metaphysical thinking. Whereas those principles can be seen as sheltering a certain urge toward essentialism, it does not entail that they are bound to give in to it. A similar thought can be found in Cavell, who insists that what he calls "living our skepticism" is an indelible part of the ordinary. (To Cavell, skepticism is the final and the most consistent expression of our urge to metaphysics.) If this is the case, then the distinction between the ordinary and the metaphysical might turn out to be less sound and less rigid than it appears to be. The language in which the metaphysical treatises of the past were composed was, after all, the language of everyday use (at least for the most part). Cavell observes that whereas Wittgenstein sees metaphysics as a consequence of ordinary language, Derrida sees ordinary language as an effect of writing.

(Here Cavell tries to stay close to Derrida's grammatology. Whether or not Cavell realizes it, the "general writing," used by Derrida to distinguish this particular effect from the common meaning of writing as putting signs on paper is an extension of what he, elsewhere, endorses under the name of "impishness," or the "perversity" of our language.[6] By this he means its endless [and often chaotic] referentiality; that its "cells" or particles [so not simply words, and not always clearly detachable morphological units, but sometimes even less-determined fragments] carry residual meanings with them that tend to disturb the meaning of what is said. For Derrida, the system of speech, consciousness, meaning, presence, truth, would be only an effect of this referential structure. [Derrida himself emphasizes that the term "writing" is used here "provisionally and strategically."]) If this diagnosis is correct, rather than posit a stable dual opposition between the ordinary and the metaphysical, we would have to characterize a continuous process in which writing sediments into the ordinary, from which in turn human beings are tempted to distill the metaphysical. While this is not what Cavell thinks (he seems to identify at least certain aspects of Derrida's work with the metaphysical), such a reading would at least explain why Cavell finds "Derrida [to be] every bit as opposed . . . to the metaphysical voice as Austin and Wittgenstein are."[7] In view of the possibility that Derrida's notions of iterability and the singular event could be read as an attempt to formalize most generally how a language game functions, I have placed "general writing" at the beginning of a process of which the metaphysical is the endpoint. Derrida's work could then be seen as pursuing the question of how a language game grows and changes over time (although again this project does not fall under the scope of the present research).

One chapter of Perloff's book is devoted to Beckett's novel *Watt*. This witty and intelligent book describes a tramp on the move, making his way to the house of the mysterious Mr. Knott, where he becomes an employee. In a hopeless attempt to come to understand his master's household,

Watt works his way up the hierarchy of servants before finally being turned out of the house—ending up as a tramp on the road once more. Despite Perloff's statements to the contrary, this is a quest novel with the object of the quest seemingly as important as it is undetermined. Thus, the novel can be read as a staging of the pursuit of truth, self, God, beauty, the good, nothingness, meaning, and so on. Details abound that would corroborate any of these interpretations and at the same time corroborate none of them in particular. The bemusement that we feel in trying to make sense of this undetermined quest—perhaps best described by Wittgenstein when he said that perhaps the door is "unlocked," but we are pushing instead of pulling it[8]—makes the mental exercises we perform in trying to make sense of *Watt* different from any straightforward interpretation.

Watt is a novel about the crisis of language. One cannot but think that Perloff is unfair to Beckett criticism when she says that this reading of Beckett has been neglected. In fact, such an interpretation of *Watt* is widely acknowledged. That Perloff does not see this may have something to do with the fact that almost all of the works on Beckett that she quotes are quite dated—from the sixties and seventies. Perloff reads *Watt* as supporting her claim that literature is a Wittgensteinian experiment—that its function is to "interrogate the 'bumps' we get from running up against the limits of language." Anticipating the argument to come, one might ask how this differs from Derrida's interrogating the works that "make the limits of our language tremble."

In stating her case against the "various deconstructionists,"[9] Perloff's treatment of Beckett focuses on the idea of a "context deficiency." (As we shall see, this reading seems to be motivated more by the debate around Derrida's *Limited Inc* and speech-act theory than by any reading of Wittgenstein himself.) According to her interpretation, the crisis of language to which *Watt* bears witness is caused by not knowing how to assign the right context to words that are, precisely, "cut-out" from their contexts. What does it mean, she asks, that Watt, the protagonist of Beckett's novel, is supposed to feed the remains of the meal to the dog if there is no dog on the premises?[10] Perloff takes this to illustrate the idea that the meaning of our words is context dependent. (She takes for granted that "context dependent" in its narrow sense is what Wittgenstein means when he says, "the meaning of a word is its use in language.")[11] This context dependence arises because words don't carry their definitions with them. As Wittgenstein famously pointed out, the word "cow" isn't always attached to a picture of a cow—and even if it were, this wouldn't explain its meaning.

However true, this is not helpful in letting us see where Derrida's shortcomings lie. For although Derrida questions the idea that context alone determines the meaning of our words, this does not entail that he adheres to the Platonistic view that words must carry their definitions with them to be meaningful. Nowhere does he suggest this. Moreover, Derrida pushes his argument precisely to the opposite extreme: he argues that our words can be meaningful even when entering a context that is totally new or that is flawed. This is precisely what happens in *Watt*: a whole multiplicity of more or less viable hypotheses are proferred concerning the nonexistent dog. The absence of Mr. Knott's dog does perturb our ability to make sense of his desire that it should be fed, but it doesn't make his request meaningless. *Perloff's* "Wittgenstein" would perhaps say that these explanatory hypotheses, together with the dog, litter an otherwise well-functioning language and should be removed from it. But then, is *Watt* not a well-functioning book?

Perloff reads *Watt* as an interrogation of language issuing from Beckett's acknowledged objective to penetrate behind the veil of words, and ending in the realization that this is impossible. She interprets this desire as equivalent to the search for a steady, ideal meaning of words or an ideal referent (leaving aside the fact that Beckett does not exclude the possibility that behind words there is merely "nothingness"). "Words, Beckett suggests, function only in large sequences, and, even then, everything depends on how they are used."[12] Perloff presents us with a clear opposition between the meaninglessness of single words "cut-out" (123) from any contexts and their meaningfulness in contexts (where these contexts determine their meanings). (The term "cut-out" stems from the vocabulary of the resistance in World War II and is central to Perloff's interpretation of Beckett. It refers to a certain manner of encoding wherein utterances were taken out of the contexts of their production to convey messages that thereby remained unreadable to outsiders.) Again, seeming more to take issue with Derrida's engagements with J. L. Austin and John Searle than pursuing Wittgenstein's way of thinking, Perloff insists that words function only in their proper context: "only in large sequences."[13] Derrida, on the contrary, argues that words can be meaningful with a diminished attachment to any particular context, even in the absence of the intentions of the one who produces the words. Iterability accounts for the words' remaining meaningful—though not immune to change—across contexts. In Beckett's novel, despite the elusiveness of the intentions of the unfathomable Mr. Knott and without any indication of what the "right" conventions might be, there are still many ways in which Knott's instructions could be made intelligible. Watt's speculations are related to us and are summarized with an (apparent) mathematical precision.[14]

In the end, Perloff does not convincingly show that her argument for a Wittgensteinian approach to literature would be preferable to the "continental" approach. The only charge that she formulates against Derrida is that his own discourse seems to be "exempt from aporias of undecidability" and "abounds in authoritarian statements."[15] Perloff mistakenly associates Derrida with the normative theoretical discourse that she blames for sustaining the opposition between "ordinary" and "literary" discourse, and for advocating the separation of the practices of theory and literature—but this is not an accurate reflection of Derrida's project. Moreover, most of the credos on which she relies to justify her approach are ones that Derrida's project could only be seen as corroborating. Among them are her conviction that literature and philosophy are inseparable; her belief in the need to undermine "Grand Theories"; her aspiration that any critical project should take place "in the trenches" (presumably to be contrasted with the "authoritarian statements" of Derrida's metatheoretical discourse); her understanding of literature as a discourse relying on passwords (hence its being an encoded discourse); and, finally, her idea that our "running against the boundaries of language" has an ethical dimension to it, suggesting that the resistance performed by (literary) language has an ethical urgency.

If we leave Perloff's insistence on "context deficiency" aside, the remaining differences between the "analytical" and the "continental" approaches seem to be, first, the emphasis, in Wittgenstein, on the "instinctive" or "natural" understanding of words—on what Cavell calls the "ordinary" or the "everyday" (*Watt*, Perloff tells us, is "a book about the problematic of language use in the ordinary transmission of information"). A consequence of this emphasis is a more specific, second difference, coming to light in Perloff's interpretation of literary works: a disregarding of the (literary and philosophical) canon (as the realm exceeding the ordinary), offset by the introduction of real-life situations (war and resistance, for example). Perloff's renouncing of the figurative application of language demands that she take an important passage in *Watt* about the loss of the hammers in the piano literally and not as symbolizing—for example, as the loss of language and thus as illustrating a step made by Beckett on his way to silence. More generally, attempts to renounce the figurative understanding of literature (if this is even possible) and to disregard the canon of the writings that make up our tradition limit the scope of possible interpretations of literary texts. This again does not seem to support Perloff's claims of the superiority of the approach that she advocates.

Furthermore, the ethical claim that Perloff makes on behalf of the language of resistance remains perfectly intelligible and legitimate inside the framework of Derrida's thought. Thus, at the end of *Watt*, the main character receives a "free pass" to a "language that *resists*, . . . that is not . . . '*contiguous* to anything else.'"[16] (Strangely, Perloff associates Watt here with Beckett himself, in a reading that is symbolic, not literal.) This image of Watt's language of resistance as a language of high uncertainty—that is, without any essentialist guarantees—is compatible with Derrida's thought. (While Wittgenstein himself would likely resist the claim that ordinary language is generally unpredictable and uncertain—at least to anyone practically attuned to the ways and lives of others—the attunement Wittgenstein appeals to [while distinct from interpretation] does not free us from all of the moments of uncertainty that characterize ordinary language use. That is, even granted our practical attunements to the language use of others, moments of uncertainty still arise. These moments call for interpretation.) The free pass thus becomes a *licentia poetica*, which is the prerogative of literature. Whereas Wittgenstein's disinterest in the literary canon is almost proverbial, it is by no means certain that the shaping of the meaning of words through their use in what Wittgenstein calls "language-games" is very different from the shaping of the meaning of the words through the progressive, infinite sedimentation of the meanings given to them in different contexts that Derrida describes. The fact that in this book I often rely on the vocabulary associated with "continental" philosophy does not therefore mean that the validity of the claims I make should necessarily be limited to that strain of philosophy. Furthermore, in view of the often distinct interests pursued in those two strains of philosophy (the "analytical" strain tends to care more for the nature of the use of language we encounter in literature, while Derrida attempts to account for what it is that makes something a literary work or literary institution), I see the two traditions as complementing rather than contradicting each other.

Derrida and Austin: On the "Non-Serious Uses of Language"

Until now I have been discussing Derrida's notion of literature by starting from the notion of singularity and making a passage to iterability (the necessary serialization of the singular moment). Now I would like to take iterability as a starting point—as that which leads to the production of the singular. In "Signature, Event, Context" (considered by many to be the shortest and most effective way to approach this issue), Derrida shows "literature" to be dependent on the general possibility of language to be iterated across contexts.[17] This possibility of language is more explicit (because pushed to its extremity) in literary uses of language (and what Austin called the "non-serious uses") than in some other uses of language. Consequently, Derrida argues that we might want to investigate the literary use of language in order to gain insight into iterability. Again we are facing the coexistence of singularity and iterability: On the one hand, literature—or the "literary use of language"—is important to us because it teaches us about iterability. On the other hand, it is also paradoxically the place par excellence where the singular appears. We have two apparently competing definitions of literature: one focused on the singular event of a literary work, the other emphasizing the iterability of the literary use of language. Again it must be concluded that these two aspects—iterability and singularity—do not exclude but rather reinforce each other.

The argument about the status of literary language in speech-act theory, of which Derrida's *Limited Inc* offers an account,[18] was perhaps the most aggravated of the recent philosophical disputes that touched on the problem of literature. It is important for our discussion because the question of the literary thereby made its entrance into and a subsequent substantial contribution to a discussion that had previously considered the literary as more or less irrelevant to its field. It is even possible that Derrida's critical interest in the status of speech-act theory in general started with literature. (The first longer discussion of the issue was directly provoked by J. L. Austin's exclusion, in *How to Do Things with Words,* of the fictive and other "non-serious" uses of language from his theory.)[19] In his endeavor to account for the conditions of successful ("felicitous") speech acts as the combination of sets of intentions and conventions that would together form the context of any given utterance, Austin noted that there are cases his theory does not cover—those cases where we still do something with words but without satisfying the conditions Austin stipulated for "ordinary" speech acts. Austin qualified these as the "non-serious" uses of language and limited his investigation to the "serious" ones.

Anyone as interested in literature as Derrida is could see at least two problems with this exclusion. The first is possibly of minor importance and addresses our intuitions about literature. Assuming that what Austin presented was a general theory of speech acts—that is, a theory that pretends not to lose any of its validity by excluding the literary use of language—at stake is a value judgment about what we can learn from the literary uses of language. What Austin's exclusion asserts is that the cases of "non-serious" uses of language are not of essential importance to our knowing how language functions. More important is the second problem (which again becomes pertinent if one assumes that Austin's work is to be read as a general theory of speech acts): the theory assumes that a distinction between serious and "non-serious" uses of language is fundamental to language. But should this apparently arbitrary distinction not be primordial, the whole theory is undermined.

A possible conclusion, and this indeed seems to be Derrida's conclusion, is that the theory itself is somehow at fault. Since it is in the treatment of context (the conventions and intentions accompanying the utterance) that Austin cannot account for the literary use of language, it is likely that this is the weak point of the theory. Austin excluded the "non-serious" uses of language on the grounds that they either openly violate any context or are simply indifferent to it. By contrast, Derrida stipulates that the possibility of the "non-serious" precedes the serious or that the two are equiprimordial (and thus that in any case, the "non-serious" is not derivative with respect to the serious).

As a result, context no longer appears to us as the sole universal criterion for a communicative action's being successful. (Derrida does not deny that intentions and conventions play a role in communication but only that they are capable of determining communication in the absolute sense. And since they cannot explain the "non-serious" uses of language, he postulates to give more attention to those uses, insisting that they have something precisely essential to teach us about the nature of linguistic phenomena, something that is missing from Austin's theory.) Derrida argues that the "force" of iterability overrides the importance of the context: "a written sign carries with it a force that breaks with its context."[20] To get into the right context is no longer a sufficient condition of meaning (where "meaningful" is understood as a speech act's being "felicitous"). We can clarify it in terms of validity: both for Austin and for Derrida, at stake is what makes a speech act a valid one. Whereas in Austin the power of confirming validity is delegated to the context (if the context is right, the given speech act becomes a valid—i.e., felicitous—example of itself), in Derrida the singular produces its own validity by being iterable. By being iterable across contexts (but independent of any particular context), the singular speech act becomes exemplary—that is, it becomes a valid example of its possible iterations, which is equivalent to its being a valid example of itself. Any speech act, serious or non-serious, confers its validity on itself in virtue of its ability to be iterated across different contexts. Whereas for Austin the context provides the rule for the validity of the speech act, for Derrida the singular itself (its iterability) produces its own rule.

This is not to say that the singular is absolutely independent of context. It does seem, while moving from one context to another, to transmit with it traces of its previous contextual attachments. Yet it never belongs to any context absolutely, in virtue of its original difference. Whereas Austin presents successful utterances as fitting perfectly into the predestined "slots" of appropriate contexts, Derrida argues that they fit much less perfectly, always only provisionally, and that this is sufficient. A corollary is that there is no hierarchy (from serious to "non-serious," or otherwise) of contexts. Any context, not necessarily a "serious" one, will do. Contrary to what was maintained by the speech-act theorists, what the literary use of language teaches us better than any other use is that words can be meaningful even without any immediately discernible contextual attachment. It is possible for a text to be meaningful even in the absence of what might be taken to belong to its context: both the intentions of the one who produces it and the specified set of conventions required by the given situation.

Words can also be meaningful in literature with a lesser attachment to any narrowly understood "ordinary meaning" than speech-act theory (as Perloff interprets it) would have it. (From within the "analytic" tradition, Donald Davidson gives a clear and coherent account of such a possibility.)[21] In an earlier paper, Derrida describes the paradoxical (in)stability of the sign in the following way:

[T]he identity of the mark is also its difference and its differential relation, varying each time according to context, to the network of other marks. The ideal iterability that forms the structure of all marks is that which undoubtedly allows them to be released from any context, to be freed from all determined bonds to its origin, its meaning, or its referent, to emigrate in order to play elsewhere, in whole or in part, another role. I say "in whole or in part" because by means of this essential insignificance the ideality or ideal identity of each mark (which is only a differential function without an ontological basis) can continue to divide itself and to give rise to the proliferation of other ideal identities.[22]

The mark, in its movement across contexts, moves "in whole or in part." When a freshly coined metaphor sends us back to its antecedents in a (narrowly understood) "ordinary meaning," often what we are referred to, or what we are able to recover, is also "a whole or a part." It is this condition of the mark that makes possible the detours of (literary) language. If one part is hidden from us (for example, the "ordinary meaning"), this does not necessarily prevent us from grasping a meaning. Another part, within an immense filiation of the sign, can stand in its place.

According to Derrida, "iterability," which he defines as the "necessary possibility that any meaningful item of language will remain meaningful through its repetition across contexts," is an even more fundamental condition for the meaningfulness of language. First of all, this means that language is possible only if signs can move freely without becoming meaningless across contexts (even if their meanings change somewhat in that movement). Second, it means that iterability is a condition of the possibility of meaning (and, since iterability confers the interpretive component without which we would not be able to experience something *as* something, it is also the condition of all experience). In case we might have been tempted to think that the law of iterability does not necessarily exclude the possibility of exceptional, singular cases that would not obey it, Derrida helps us out of this illusion. In his own words, "the iterability of an element divides its own identity *a priori*"; what "seems to have occurred only once ... is in itself divided and multiplied in advance by its structure of repeatability."²³ Yet this would not necessarily have to entail that, as the result of an identical repetition, "everything is the same." Iteration (the word is derived from *iter*, i.e., "other") brings alterity, change.

One might expect that once Derrida had demonstrated the workings of iterability—of which a corollary is that nothing can be absolutely singular—the notion of singularity would be rendered superfluous. Yet even in a text that insists on the logic of iterability as much as *Limited Inc* does, the singular remains, even though the use of this term might here be thought incidental (cf., for example, the "singular" "chain" of argumentative "points" [44]). In particular, Derrida's texts dealing with literature abound in singular others, decisions, texts, and events. This is consistent with Derrida's understanding of literature as the place where the dependence of meaning on the stability of context is questioned, where we regularly witness singular uses of language in which the attachment to the usual context is weakened or even severed altogether.

At an earlier stage, I suggested that in the case of literature, iterability and singularity are correlates of each other. I hope to have made clear since then that the gathering force of the singular resides precisely in its iterability. What the singular gathers are the products of its iterability—its iterations—of which it is always one. The hyper-totalizing force resides in the singular, which treats everything else as its own iterations. In a sense, the singular gathers nothing else but itself. It is important to note that the status of the gathering singular is equal to that of any of its iterations: each of them can gather equally well, and none of them can gather absolutely. If, following Derrida, we call that which effectively gathers the multiplicity of a text "a signature," each element of a text can function as such. Recall, for instance, that when reading the texts of Ponge, Derrida finds Ponge's signatures everywhere ("sponge" and "pine" are examples).²⁴

Literature is here in focus because, unlike in the cases of the "serious" uses of language studied by Austin (the "I do" of a marriage ceremony, for example), each work of literature must produce its own singular claim to validity. It is not sufficient for a work of literature to place itself in the right context. Neither the author's intentions nor the fulfilment of any linguistic conventions says anything about the "felicitousness" of a literary work. According to Derrida, the criterion here would rather be the singular work's gathering potential—its "force"—that at the same time involves the production of a law.

The gathering signature is the exemplification of the singular par excellence; when Derrida speaks in *Shibboleth* of the gathering potential of dates ("Several singular events can concentrate in the same date"), we must keep in mind that he also says, "the date is always a type of a signature."[25] In gathering, by a *mise en abyme,* the signature produces and questions its own law. In the encompassing structure of this figure, the gathering shibboleth puts the entire work into its own *mise en abyme,* just as much as it inserts itself in that work. This double self-absorption of work and figure is the reason why Derrida, as I argued in the previous chapter, considers the figure of the *mise en abyme* a case of (flawed, because provisional) self-reflection, an instance of the self-undermining law. And this is where he locates the possibility of critique. Therefore, gathering and the law—the economical and the juridical—turn out to be two sides of the same coin. The production of archives (the gathering of the singular) is coextensive with the production of the law. Iterability is coextensive with self-reflection (albeit always partial, always flawed, where *mise en abyme* becomes *mise en abîme*). Where the mirror is, is representation: iterability is self-representation (not in the mimetic sense that presupposes the original and the copy, but at another level, "before" this distinction and hence "before" mimesis). The iterable singular is always already, in its original difference, a *mise-* and *contre-abyme.* It contains its own iterations and is one of them.

The oscillation between singularity and iterability, which we were witnessing in "The Deaths of Roland Barthes," results in something that we might call the "stretching" of a point into a line, or the stretching of the unique into a rule. In this text, recalling the *studium/punctum* opposition in the texts of Roland Barthes, the *punctum* is read as a singularity. At first, the *punctum* seems to indicate a unique "detail," a single point in a larger configuration—temporal (a "punctual decision . . . in a [camera's] click") or spatial (the "referential"). But very soon the "point of singularity" is represented as the "becoming a line" of a series. The word "punctual" renders this ambiguity quite well: it refers to the properties of a point but also denotes a regular occurrence. The point produces a line that can be contracted back to it. Barthes' life, too, can be contracted back to such a single point—and stretched again into a "terrifying and endless series" of "solemn moments, orienting tombs."[26]

Beckett's Singular Language Game

I have retraced Derrida's discussion with Austin at considerable length as a response to Perloff's one-sided treatment of the "continental-analytic" debate, but also to show that the serialization of the singular as described by Derrida is not just a motif at work in literature (or in Barthes' project of *mathesis singularis*). Rather, throughout the descriptions of the singular that serializes itself, Derrida presents the iterability (or "citationality") that rules this serialization as a general condition of meaning. Iterability underlies (and hence is prior to, and must be presupposed by) Austin's theory of successful performatives. I hope also to have made clear that the fictive, the "non-serious," and thereby the literary gains in Derrida are in a sense (if only a sense) privileged in the process of the constitution of meaning, as opposed to Austin's theory of language wherein those cases are put aside as less relevant. It is namely in those uses of language that we can see iterability overriding in importance the Austinian criteria for an utterance's being successful (i.e., the intentions of the speaker and the generally accepted set of conventions).

In his article "What Did Derrida Want of Austin?" later reworked into the second chapter of *A Pitch of Philosophy*, Stanley Cavell confesses his disappointment with Derrida's treatment of ordinary language philosophy in both *Of Grammatology* and "Signature, Event, Context."[27] Coming from a former student of Austin, and one of the few sympathetic readers of Derrida on the side of "ordinary language philosophy," Cavell's critique must be taken with the seriousness it deserves. At the same time, it is worth keeping in mind that since, as Cavell puts it, Wittgenstein sees metaphysics as a consequence of ordinary language, and Derrida sees ordinary language as a product of writing, Cavell does not see a common denominator under which those projects could be brought. The point of Cavell's critique is not merely that Derrida fails to acknowledge sufficiently the originality of ordinary language philosophy. As Cavell sees it, the stakes between Derrida and Austin are ethical.[28] Even if both Austin and Derrida start from similar premises, namely that there is no ground or founding principle that would guarantee the meanings in our languages and thereby release us from skepticism, the next steps that they take are very different. Whereas Austin privileges voice with respect to writing, Derrida privileges writing with respect to voice. In doing so, Austin attempts to lessen the distance between the utterance and the one who utters it, "tethering" the one who speaks to his words and to his responsibility: "*our word is our bond.*"[29] This implies that Austin's notion of intentionality must be reexamined. Cavell emphasizes the ethical consequences of this gesture of "tethering," urging that we are responsible for our words irrespective of whether we pronounced them intentionally or not. Cavell reminds us that "our word is our bond" is Austin's answer to the words uttered by Euripides' Hippolytus: "my lips swore but my heart did not."[30] "[T]he price of having once spoken . . . is to have spoken forever, to have entered the arena of the inexcusable."[31]

Cavell seems thereby to imply that Derrida's interpretation of Austin is a misreading in that it overemphasizes the requirement of intention that must accompany a speech act in order to confer the validity ("felicity") of the act. Given the absence of any intention from Hippolytus' utterance, it could be argued that no context determined the meaning of these words, thereby providing an excuse or extenuating circumstance should these words need to be retracted. However, Cavell interprets Austin as being against such a reaching down to the depths of the (unfathomable for the world) speaker's intentions in order to establish his or her responsibility. Such an interpretive "excess of profundity" is, in Cavell's eyes, proper to the metaphysical voice, as opposed to the ordinary voice. Derrida, in his critique of the privilege of the voice against writing, would fail to recognize that Austin and Wittgenstein "distinguish between the metaphysical and the ordinary voice."[32] "Our word is our bond" is an expression of the ordinary voice.

Cavell also seems to imply that in not acknowledging the distinction between the metaphysical and the ordinary—and as a result, rejecting (in Cavell's words, "suffocating") the voice, thereby increasing the distance between the written word and its author—Derrida is unable to offer an answer to the situation of having spoken unintentionally, in which Hippolytus finds himself. (It is this situation, and not literature, that for Cavell exemplifies what Austin refers to in the expression "non-serious uses of language.") Derrida is, in other words, unable to account for Hippolytus' sense of responsibility, which overrides his lack of intention. It is, in Cavell's words, Derrida's "flight from the ordinary," "contribut[ing] to th[e] suffocation of the ordinary,"[33] that limits "my . . . presentness to the world and others in it," hence leaving a way open for not acknowledging those others and my responsibility to them. I doubt strongly whether Derrida's critique of the metaphysical privilege of speech can be seen to entail this kind of dissipation of responsibility when it comes to actions. Cavell is right, to the extent that Derrida's thought presents us with no ethical solutions. Neither does literature—at least not literature as conceived by Derrida. But then again, neither does Austin, in his "Plea for Excuses," as Cavell acknowledges.[34] In recognizing the importance of the (ordinary) voice as the expression of the assumption of responsibility, Cavell credits Austin with providing us with an ethical impulse. But if no present mental intention is needed to sustain that voice, then it is not significantly different from Derrida's speaking of responsibility in terms of writing.

This discussion of Cavell and Derrida does suggest something about Cavell's view of literature—and, by extension, about ordinary language criticism's view as well. To treat literature as offering us representations of moral problems to be shared and responded to—in other words, as inviting us to exercise and sharpen our moral judgment, our ability to discern—is to read it in a manner that is either Platonic (didactic) or Aristotelian (therapeutic). While this does justice to one of the aspects of literature, in limiting itself to this aspect only, it limits our notion of what literature is, inevitably making literature subservient to ethics. It also induces us to part with the idea that a literary work can "produce its own truth"[35] (as Alain Badiou puts it) or that it is capable of pursuing its own singular universality as a work of art (as Derrida might put it).

A related aspect of Cavell's critique is that Derrida misunderstood Austin in reading the latter as opposing ordinary to literary language. The opposition Austin has in mind, Cavell says, is between the ordinary and the metaphysical, not between the ordinary and the literary. Cavell is here faithful to Wittgenstein, who—even though acknowledging that literature ("poetry") is a different game from the game of giving information[36]—insists that as a game, literature is a case of ordinary language. In his own readings of literature, Cavell often presents it as the realm of the "natural," which provides us with a possibility of "tuition." Whether Derrida's views can be reconciled with this interpretation depends on how we understand the word "ordinary." But to presuppose, as Cavell does here, that it would be possible for us to know the indisputable essence of Austin's argument (i.e., the opposition between the ordinary and the metaphysical, and not between the serious and the non-serious) and thereby exclude

Derrida's alternative reading is to ignore that not only Derrida but also Wittgenstein and Austin himself argued against essentialism of meaning. (To say, with Wittgenstein, that not all understanding involves an interpretation [cf. *Philosophical Investigations,* § 201] does not mean that our understanding is always beyond dispute. Consequently, even if the meanings of Austin's words are not in the first instance interpreted, they nonetheless remain apt for interpretation and reinterpretation.) One might wonder whether language—for example, that used by Joyce in *Finnegans Wake*—could still be called ordinary or "natural" without stretching the explanatory detour that this would necessitate to monstrous proportions. It would be easier to believe that it could were the critics to come up with an ordinary-language-interpretation of that language and of the ordinary, "natural" tuition that it offers.

> Hark!
> Tolv two elf kater ten (it can't be) sax.
> Hork!
> Pedwar pemp foify tray (it must be) twelve.
> And low stole o'er the stillness the heartbeats of sleep.[37]

What would it mean for those words to be brought "back . . . [to] the language-game, which is its original home"?[38] And what would remain of Joyce's experiment once we succeeded in doing it?

Transporting Wittgenstein's words from their original context of the essential/ordinary distinction to Derrida's abnormal/ordinary distinction, we might ask: Does the fact that some of the above words might never find a (legitimate) way to their "original home" mean that they have no right to be used? "The concept of the 'ordinary,' thus of 'ordinary language' is clearly marked by this exclusion" (of the "*abnormal, parasitic,*" etc.).[39] Derrida's defense of the abnormal and parasitic is not equivalent to the defense of the metaphysical—on the contrary, on Derrida's reading, it is Austin's "ordinary" that is complicit with the metaphysical.

Obviously, for a philosopher who is primarily interested in the "ordinary," or "natural" in the narrow sense, literature must belong to this sphere to be relevant at all. In other words, a privilege will be granted to the reading that requires the shortest possible interpretative detour. This interpretative detour shortened to a minimum will simulate the preservation of a "literality" of meaning in exactly the same way as in Derrida's reading of Husserl, for whom "the voice simulates the conservation of presence" (and we know that "presence" stands for "ideality of meaning," hence for what must be interpreted as an essentialist gesture).[40] In other words, the shortening of the interpretative detour favored by ordinary language philosophy partakes in the same metaphysical structure as the one Derrida discerns in Husserl.

The role of literature in this framework is to serve as a reservoir of exemplary utterances and situations—exemplary for either the failure or the success of ordinary language. Cavell's readings of literature tend to emphasize the "literal," "natural," or "ordinary" meanings of language, and certain works by Beckett lend themselves perfectly to such purposes. One of Cavell's first attempts in this direction was a reading of Beckett's *Endgame*, published in *Must We Mean What We Say?* In this essay, Cavell presents Beckett's language to us as "imitat[ing] . . . the qualities of ordinary conversation among people whose world is shared." Cavell, emphasizing the "*hidden literality*"[41] of Beckett's language, was among the first to observe Beckett's ability to exploit the banal, the everyday. This literalizing and banalizing of language in Beckett serves on Cavell's reading a quietist purpose: the ultimate objective is to cease to mean.

True, Cavell is an unorthodox and open-minded reader of Wittgenstein. Thus, according to Cavell, Wittgenstein's criteria do not function as rules. Rather, our mutual understanding is governed by what Cavell calls our "attunement to forms of life." Throughout our lives, we are continually "initiated" into different forms of life that, precisely, cannot be formulated as rules. Yet he does make a distinction between the "legitimate" and non-legitimate projections we can make in our language,[42] as well as between the "natural" and "unnatural" ones (the latter ones being the origin of metaphors). A child learning the word "pumpkin," for example, might acquire some irrelevant associations when learning the word (due to the word's superficial similarity to "Mr. Popkin" or "pumps"). Cavell grants that some of those irrelevant associations will never get totally discarded—even though we might presume that the child will later discover them to be illegitimate. If I understand him correctly, Cavell seems to acknowledge here that what will count as "legitimate" is something that is "sorted out," selected from the illegitimate.

As I have shown in my discussion of "Signature, Event, Context" above, Derrida defends what was here called "the illegitimate" and "the unnatural" (or the "abnormal, parasitic") because they show us the working of iterability as a primordial condition of meaning. Already for this reason alone, his literary examples must be different from those used by ordinary language philosophy. (Note that Wittgenstein speaks of "family resemblance" and not of "legitimate family resemblance"; this is not very different from the "machine of filiation—legitimate or illegitimate, . . . ready to domesticate, circumcise, circumvent everything"[43] that Derrida finds in Joyce.) The link between Molly's name and perfume in Derrida's reading of *Ulysses* will inevitably be seen as specious, as will the link between perfume and performative ("perfumative"). These "unnatural," farfetched links are forged by Derrida in full awareness that they are such. Heidegger was perhaps the first to introduce to philosophical discourse supposed filiations of words under the cover of pseudo-etymology. Derrida does the same, albeit in a much more overt fashion, to show that language can and does function independently of the legislation of the ordinary.[44]

It seems that for ordinary language criticism, the illegitimacy, or "non-seriousness," of language is primarily the product of a misplacement of context (Perloff's reading of context disorders in *Watt*).[45] Literature does no more than exemplify (and explore the strangeness of) ordinary language; for "our word" to be "our bond," our meaning has to be an everyday meaning. There is consequently no reason to question what literature is, because all it does is provide us with examples of statements and situations that we might just as well encounter in real life. As a subspecies of ordinary language, literature is not worth any philosophical investigation of its status as a separate institution. The radicality of Derrida's step is to examine the literary institution as testifying to the general illegitimacy of our language. His choice of Joyce as an exemplary author confirms this.

Cavell argues that a "non-primitive" language (i.e., a language that possesses general concepts) arises given projections that must be legitimate (the validity of projections is "deeply controlled"). For Derrida, they might just as often be illegitimate, since the distinction is for him quite artificial. If we read Beckett's work as an experiment with ordinary language, the fact that it followed upon Joyce's linguistic bastardy might be taken as confirming the view that the "unlaw" comes before the law; and the illegitimate, before the principle of legitimacy can even be contemplated. (At the very least, the second cannot claim any ontological or axiological primacy with respect to the first.)

However, putting all those differences aside, we might also ask whether there is not a similarity or "family resemblance" among (1) what Wittgenstein, Austin, and Cavell call a "language-game," (2) what Derrida calls the working of iterability, and (3) what in Beckett might be called "the banal." All three cases are to an extent about an utterance that falls—whether happily or otherwise—into the "predestined grooves" of its own repetition. (The following limerick is reported by a critic to have been one of Beckett's favorites: "There was a young man who said, 'Damn! / I suddenly see what I am, / A creature that moves / In predestined grooves, / In fact not a bus but a tram.' ")[46] Is there a difference between the singular event that must serialize itself and produce its own law (Derrida) and the exploiting of the commonplace that is a product of an endless and already legitimate repetition (Beckett)? To be interested in the singular event means to explore the possibility of the derailment of an utterance that nonetheless, in an unpredictable and unaccountable fashion, becomes a success.[47] Would we say that a language game does not allow for such a derailment and therefore has a non-eventful character? One would be tempted to think so, since the events that will be seen as relevant in the context of a given game can only be those that are seen (even if only *après coup*) as conforming to its rules. On the other hand, it only makes sense to speak of a literary work in terms of an event (i.e., to an extent, a "revolutionary instant") if it can be seen as an illegitimate projection, one that sets up its own, singular "game." A work becomes an event if it changes things in an unpredictable way. We do need what Cavell calls "attunement" for this, and we do need "legitimacy"—but not in any preexisting manner.[48]

While it is possible to see some shared ground between the various ways of thinking about the repeatability of words (in Wittgenstein, Austin, Cavell, Derrida, and Beckett), this does not eliminate the contrast between Beckett and Derrida. It is possible to read Beckett as an ordinary-language writer and in this way to account for Derrida's inability to comment on him. Beckett has been repeatedly seen as an author who exploits the commonplace and the banal (the plays *Happy Days* and *All That Fall* can even be said to consist of that)—and the banal does not gather. What we call banal has been used up so exhaustively that all it conveys is its own emptiness.

But, having acknowledged this feature of Beckett's language, we might still want to ask, What, then, is its "tuition"? Would not looking for such "tuition" make us inevitably regress to a reading of Beckett that had him forcing us to confront the absurdity of our existence? If Beckett was indeed an ordinary-language writer in the sense Cavell attributes to this expression, his work has been seriously neglected (its "tuition" is not at all clear), and its proper appraisal is only yet to come.

On the other hand, Beckett's work does have the features of ordinary language, and it did arrive as an event—as many thinkers were prepared to acknowledge. Perhaps we can speak of the singularity of the commonplace? If so, this would be because the ordinariness of that work is not its main purpose but its material. This is why its ordinariness is so striking. Taking phrases out of that work as if it were just another case of ordinary language in use will not say much about the reasons for its success. It still says nothing about why the ordinariness of certain phrases strikes us so much in Beckett when in real life or in a bad novel we would not pay attention to them. It will still not, then, tell us what kind of game is being played. In the next chapter, Deleuze will be shown to provide us with the hint of an answer: the game played is an exhausting one.

4

Beckett's "Exhausted" Archives

The Advantage of Being Poor

One of the assumptions accompanying my argument from the start has been that Beckett's work, at least to a degree, resists interpretation in terms of the gesture of gathering (gathering figures, meanings, dates, events, etc.) that is intrinsic to Derrida's thought about literature. This is, after all, the core of what repeatedly strikes Beckett's audience: the propensity of his discourse to say less rather than more, to "unsaying" rather than to "saying everything." From the gradual impoverishment of the language of his early works to the sterile landscapes and interiors later on, Beckett's gesture was the renunciation of gathering. Perhaps the most consistent feature of this discourse is that it poses or stages its own fundamental questions—questions fundamental to the writing process—and at the same time empties them of any answer, committing them to the impersonal, anything-whatever generality of a cliché. "Who?" "When?" "What?" "Where?" "How to proceed?" "What is the word?"—Beckett's work is punctuated with questions, from *Waiting for Godot* through the *Unnamable*, the titular *How It Is* and *What Where*, until the very last poem Beckett wrote, "What Is the Word."

Little can be gathered in a discourse that has set out to empty itself of "those demented particulars."[1] Beckett's is such a discourse. The dismissal of "demented particulars"—and of "the beastly circumstantial"—

by one of *Murphy*'s characters is considered by Beckett scholars to be "one of Beckett's most important statements."[2] However, it is often interpreted *a rebours*, as expressing Beckett's (as opposed to the quoted character's) fascination with the particular. On this reading, Beckett dismisses the general instead of the particular. The reason for this inversion is the statement of the young Beckett that:

[W]hat I want is the straws, flotsam, etc., names, dates, births and deaths, because that is all I can know.... Rationalism is the last form of animism. Whereas the pure incoherence of times and men and places is at least amusing.[3]

However, the qualification "at least amusing" says it all: Beckett's attitude to the particular was in fact as ambivalent as it was to the seductions of rationalism. As early as *Murphy*, written in the same time period as "The German Diaries," the protagonist contemplates "conquer(ing) his prejudice against the anonymous."[4] With Murphy's body and soul exhausted and dissipated in ashes, the novel ends, ominously, with the repeated summons "All out" (158). The conjunction of this "most extreme dissolution"[5] and the above series of questions left unanswered—the typical landmarks of Beckett's landscape of thought—give it its characteristic barrenness, which stands in contrast to Derrida's perception of literature as hyper-totalizing.

It is well known that Beckett made the major decision to write in French (a language that for him was a second language) so as to be no longer haunted by the sedimentations of his own mother tongue. Ludovic Janvier recounts Beckett's words explaining the advantage of renouncing the privileges of writing in English: "C'était ma chance d'être plus pauvre."[6]

The impoverished language of Beckett is precisely something of which Derrida might be apprehensive because he associates it with a reductive attitude to history. It is ahistorical because it has bracketed its historical sedimentations. In his introduction to Husserl's *Origin of Geometry*, Derrida finds himself having to defend Husserl against precisely this charge: "Husserl does not make univocity, as could be feared, the value for *a language impoverished and thus removed out of history's reach*."[7] Rather, in his pursuit of univocity (a univocity that is never absolute and that always shares in equivocity), Husserl sees in it a condition of all historicity. The absolute univocity (which Derrida shows to be "absurd") would "sterilize and paralyze history in the indigence of infinite iteration."[8] Yet it is the latter that seems to be precisely what Beckett aimed at. This is not to say that Beckett's ahistorical language has washed its hands of history out of indifference or contempt, or that he aimed at a reduction of history in the pursuit of some abstract, generalized totality. Beckett's project of "giving up" cannot be seen as a choice between univocity and equivocity: both of them would be too "saturated" with contents.

On the other hand, I showed in Chapter 2 that Derrida understands literature as an institution in which the juridical and the totalizing gesture are unthinkable without each other. If we are to adhere to this, then demonstrating that it is possible to read the cases of *mise en abyme* in Beckett as a work's reflection on its own law indicates that archiving must be part of this work as well.

In this chapter, I am going to explore the possibility that Beckett came up with an alternative for gathering. This will be glossed in terms of Gilles Deleuze's "exhausting," an alternative that, despite the formal resemblance of its result to gathering, has features that account for those aspects of Beckett's work that would escape any archiving gesture.

"The Nearly Total Affinity": Derrida on Deleuze and Beckett

"The Exhausted" is not the title of a text by Beckett—although it sounds like one ("The Expelled," in particular). Instead, it is the title of a remarkable reading of Beckett by Gilles Deleuze, which does justice to the intuition that Beckett's work is primarily a gesture of renunciation. Does Deleuze's description of Beckett's work as "exhausted" constitute a challenge to Derrida's understanding of literature as gathering or economy? In the latter thought, literature functions as a container (*le secrétaire*, again) that, even though it is finite itself, has an infinite potential for gathering. It seems at first sight that exhausting is, somewhat like the emptying of the *secrétaire*, opposed to gathering, and hence that Deleuze's essay can be read as containing a silent critique of Derrida.

Janvier opposes Beckett's *désir de se rapprocher du presque rien*, to the *exhibitionnisme inévitable* of, among others, the celebrated author of Derrida's example of the literary, James Joyce. Leaving aside the question of whether the almost Franciscan tone of Janvier's moral approbation of the spirit of renunciation in Beckett's work does justice to the meaning of that work, it is difficult to disagree that the overwhelming spirit of destitution (of language, but equally of mind, memory, body, and world) in Beckett's work remains in sharp contrast to the wealth (of all the above) that we would associate with a gesture of gathering. The characters in Beckett own little, remember little, know little, and are able to do little. They are, in all respects, "exhausted." This indicates that the gesture of "lessening" does not concern only how much is said. It is not only the words that falter: all life in Beckett is impoverished, impaired, and disabled. The merit of Deleuze's reading of Beckett lies in his having shown, through the closely related notions of exhaustion and exhaustivity, how two characteristic aspects of Beckett's work are interconnected. The rhetorical enterprise of unsaying reveals itself to be coextensive with and parasitic on the physiological exhaustion of Beckett's characters.

Whereas Derrida likes to identify his project with Joyce's hypertotalizing enterprise (he devotes a chapter of *Deux mots pour Joyce* to give a reading of his own philosophical itinerary in terms of an ongoing response to—or dialogue with—Joyce),[9] Deleuze prefers to draw on the work of Beckett. In addition to having quoted Beckett in many of his works (especially in *A Thousand Plateaus*, co-authored with Felix Guattari, but also in *Dialogues II*, *Essays Critical and Clinical*, and *What Is Philosophy?*), Deleuze wrote two texts on Beckett. One of these—"The Exhausted" (1993)—was among the last texts published before his suicide in 1995.[10] His response to Beckett had been, as he himself stated, "immediate and instinctive"; furthermore, he recalled that "few authors had ever made him laugh more than Kafka and Beckett."[11] (Interestingly enough, Deleuze emphasized that his appreciation of Beckett did not require "literary" training [formation]— unlike, for example, the work of Robbe-Grillet.) Commentators on Deleuze did not fail to note this; in his book on Deleuze, Alain Badiou singles out two literary characters as "Deleuze's heroes of thought": Melville's Bartleby, the scrivener (who says, "I would prefer not to") and the protagonist of Beckett's *The Unnamable*.[12] (Indeed, Deleuze himself brings Bartleby together with Beckett—speaking of "Bartleby's Beckettian formula"—in a text that I will discuss further below.)

Given these identifications, Derrida's assertion that he feels himself close to Deleuze raises similar doubts as to his self-proclaimed affinity with Beckett. Derrida mourned the former in similar words to those he used when speaking about the latter—"closeness..., nearly total affinity.... The one... to whom I have always judged myself the closest"[13]—but despite these postmortem assurances, he had never actually entered a philosophical dialogue with Deleuze. The abandoning of dialogue on the side of someone like Derrida (who makes a point of his interest in the "blind spots," the places in other authors' discourses where they renounce explication, where dialogue is therefore least likely) is in itself something that asks for special attention.

Beckett's Exhausting Project

Deleuze's "The Exhausted" is a short yet complex text (addressing Beckett's entire oeuvre), which has until now received little critical attention.[14] While evoking Spinoza in its opening sentences, it relies at least to the same extent on Deleuze's analysis and development of the work of Bergson in his own work on the cinema. (This is particularly relevant since, in focusing on images rather than texts, Deleuze's reading does not dwell on the exclusively literary aspects of Beckett's work.) Perhaps the philosophical filiation to which Deleuze appeals (a lineage that stems from Spinoza and Bergson) will prove to be more fruitful than the framework of Derrida's discourse for the discussion of Beckett. There are three ways to complete the title of Deluze's essay: it addresses the exhausted person, exhausted possibilities (e.g., the totality of possibilities for action), and the "exhausted quality" of Beckett's prose (i.e., that it appears to us as "exhausted").

Deleuze attributes the exhausted quality of Beckett's work to a consciously realized program. This program of exhausting, Deleuze suggests, is Beckett's way of overcoming the subject-object dualism. Deleuze shows the project of accounting for the world (through the enumeration of all its possibilities, possible objects, and facts) and the physiological and spiritual fatigue of the subject that accompanies the realization of this project to be two sides of the same coin. This program is subservient to the larger pursuit of the point where a state of total, comprehensive exhaustion is attained (i.e., the program is realized) and "the exhausted person" is released from his or her efforts.

A possible objection to such a reading of Beckett's work could be that both Beckett's credo—"I can't go on, I'll go on"—and his commitment to writing until the end of his life show that he never disregarded the "obligation to express."[15] Thus, in spite of his relentless pursuit of the point of total silence where the accumulation of words can cease, he must have been aware of the impossibility of giving up archiving altogether. Nevertheless, we might still wonder whether the expressing of which Beckett speaks should be construed as a gesture that involves archiving. Even construed as a positive content, this "obligation to express" could not possibly fill the vacuum gaping in

> the expression that there is nothing to express, nothing with which to express, nothing from which to express, no power to express, no desire to express together with the obligation to express.[16]

In fact, the pertinence of Beckett's pursuit of silence is in no way diminished by his following the imperative to go on. On the contrary, the unresolved question of the reasons of this "logically impossible"[17] pursuit against all odds acquires with it an additional urgency that is even reinforced by the contradictory interpretations to which this work gives rise. It gives the audience the sensation that "nothing happens" (or, at least, very little), but it might also be argued that everything happens (or, at least, everything of importance): that this work addresses the "event."[18] How else can we explain this work's tendency to say less and less, its suspending, bringing into doubt, or even explicitly canceling what it has said (cf. the disempowering rhetoric of the "Irish bull" in Beckett so astutely analyzed by Christopher Ricks)[19] and at the same time its remaining "affirmative"?[20] These questions are closely linked to the question I pose in this chapter regarding the reasons why speaking of Beckett's work in terms of "hyper-totalizing" is so problematic.

The Possible

Deleuze defines the exhaustion of the possible in its opposition to the realization of the possible. Whereas to realize means to make decisions or choices that ultimately limit the possible, to exhaust the possible means to consume it entirely, without limitation, to drain it systematically of all its aspects. In realizing the possible, steps are taken that would exclude some of the possible consecutive steps ("I put on shoes to go out, and slippers when I stay in"[21]). In exhausting the possible, no step is better than any other, and none of the steps has any consequences ("shoes, one stays in; slippers, one goes out"). Exhaustion has as its condition that, while being fully aware of the multiplicity of choices that exists, one renounces deciding between them because to be exhaustive means to exclude nothing until one has run out of options. Thus, exhausting requires at the same time an unceasing activity of differentiation and a total indifference to this project of differentiation. The formal structure of exhausting is that of an "inclusive disjunction." Deleuze refers us here to the "art of the combinatory," which allows us to rearrange sequences of sets of items. The permutations of the possible produced in this way indicate all the possible arrangements of all possible objects. The possible is thus opposed to realization, which operates by "exclusive disjunction"—that is, which takes each choice to be consequential with respect to the one following it and hence privileges certain arrangements or certain objects to the exclusion of others (realization is thus merely derivative with respect to exhausting).

While at first sight it is primarily Beckett's early work that abounds in permutations—of stones (Molloy), cookies (Murphy), items of clothing and furniture (Watt)—on a closer examination, the principle of permutation reveals itself as a constant factor in Beckett's work. (See, for example, the arrangement of the protagonists in the late theater play *What Where*.) It is perhaps Murphy who takes the first steps in the "art of the combinatory." Pondering the possible sequential arrangements of the five sorts of biscuits that make up his meal, he only slowly discovers the richness that inclusive disjunction has to offer. This satisfaction comes with the proviso that he must respect "the essence of the assortment," which entails that he conquer "his prejudice against the anonymous" and that he learn "not to prefer any one to any other."

He took the biscuits carefully out of the packet and laid them face upward on the grass, in order as he felt of edibility. They were the same as always, a Ginger, an Osborne, a Digestive, a Petit Beurre and one anonymous. He always ate the first-named last, because he liked it the best, and the anonymous first, because he thought it very likely the least palatable. The order in which he ate the remaining three was indifferent to him and varied irregularly from day to day. On his knees now before the five it struck him for the first time that these prepossessions reduced to a paltry six the number of ways in which he could make this meal. But this was to violate the very essence of assortment.... Even if he conquered his prejudice against the anonymous, still there would be only twenty-four ways in which the biscuits could be eaten. But were he to take the final step and overcome this infatuation with the ginger, then the assortment would spring to life before him, dancing the radiant measure of its total permutability, edible in a hundred and twenty ways!

Overcome by these perspectives Murphy fell forward on his face in the grass, beside those biscuits of which it could be said as truly as of the stars, that one differed from another, but of which he could not partake in their fullness until he had learnt not to prefer any one to any other.[22]

These biscuits exemplify the universe ("the stars"), which Murphy, like God, can only "partake of" in virtue of a certain indifference. This thought brings us to the topic of Beckett's Spinozism.

"Relentless Spinozism"

Exhausting the possible is not equivalent to merely stating the possible in an exhaustive way; the latter is just one of the prerequisite steps on the way to exhaustion.[23] The reverse, correlated side of the project of exhausting the possible is the exhausting of the self that performs the exhausting. Exhausting the possible is thus coextensive with exhausting oneself. This is, according to Deleuze, what is at stake in Beckett's work; Beckett, in a gesture of "relentless Spinozism,"[24] exhausts the possible. It is not accidental that Spinoza is evoked in a text on exhaustion; to Deleuze, he is a thinker whose "tuning into life" went together with a certain fundamental "fatigue."[25] Spinoza is one of the series of the exhausted selves that keeps reappearing in Deleuze's work. Another example is Nietzsche's "spiritually conscientious one," the man who, in order to know "everything" about the leech's mind, lets leeches drink his blood (thereby "increas[ing] his knowledge with his own blood"[26]). The exhaustion of this man is a condition of his exhaustive knowledge of the leech's brain. "Beckett's great contribution to logic," Deleuze says, "is to have shown that exhaustion (exhaustivity) does not occur without a certain physiological exhaustion, somewhat as Nietzsche showed that the scientific ideal is not attained without a kind of vital degeneration."[27]

The scope of this chapter does not permit an explication of the range of Deleuze's network of notions, which can be shown to pertain to literature—for example, "becoming" ("becoming-animal"), "minority," "deterritorialization," and "flight." Nor is that the purpose of this chapter.

Deleuze's approach to literature is to a large extent indifferent to whatever might be termed its literary qualities (writing, text, context, etc.). His reflections on literary works (as opposed to those of Derrida) are almost always motivated by an interest in an anonymous process ("movement," "flight," "flow," "life," "becoming") that does not have any specifically literary properties. In this respect, despite his occasional denials, Derrida is much more committed to a certain idea of the distinctiveness of literature, which can be seen in his sustained interest in the notions of oeuvre, signature, and writing.[28] Whereas Derrida's "grammatology" attempts to extrapolate the relevance of the notions traditionally associated with writing to other domains of life, Deleuze's project goes in the reverse direction: to show the manifestation of "life" in literature. It is neither as writing nor as signature but as life, "becoming," that literature intervenes in life. Spinoza's influence on Deleuze cannot be overstated here; the relation of the writer (or the reader) to the work, the writer's "relentless Spinozism," follows the pattern of the relation of God (*Natura naturans*), who exhausts himself in becoming "everything that he understands"[29] (*Natura naturata*). In this sense, "exhausting" is another word for, or a variation of, God's "becoming" (his becoming the totality of the possible). In its project of exhausting, the self dissipates itself in its possibilities, but it also becomes the possibilities that it exhausts. "The aim of writing is to carry life to the state of a non-personal power."[30] This becoming ("carrying life to the state of non-personal power") is the reason for the writer's exhaustion; "he is only too weak for the life which runs in him or for the affects which pass in him. To write has no other function: to be a flux, which combines with other fluxes—all the minority-becomings of the world."[31]

In what does the "relentless Spinozism" that Deleuze attributes to Beckett consist? In one of his 1980–1981 lectures, Deleuze explains that Spinoza's system as a whole is founded on the radical deconstruction of the category of the possible.

> It is a system in which everything that is, is real. Never has such a negation of the category of possibility been carried so far. Essences are not possibilities. There is nothing possible, everything is real. In other words essences don't define possibilities of existence, essences are themselves existences.[32]

These essences differ from actualized existences only in their degree of "luminous intensity." Similarly, in *Spinoza et le problème d'expression*, Deleuze insists that possible existence is not the same as what we usually mean by possibility. On the contrary, every possible existence, as partaking of God's potentiality (*potentia*), is real rather than "merely" possible. (As Spinoza has it, everything that exists in God's intellect is real.) Deleuze remarks, "C'est précisément parce que l'essence est puissance que l'existence possible (dans l'essence) est autre chose qu'une 'possibilité.' "[33] The reality of the possible is a cornerstone of Deleuze's thinking about the inclusive disjunction. Rather than realize just a selection of the possible, all possibles must be accounted for.

It might seem a little strange that in "The Exhausted," Deleuze, who as we have seen credits Spinoza with the deconstruction of the possible, invokes Spinoza precisely in order to speak about the possible and about the distinction between the possible and realizing the possible. But as can be seen from the previous quote, in Deleuze's reading of Spinoza, "a possible existence" is something other than a mere "possibility." The former, as partaking of God's potentiality, is real, while the latter is not. By the time of Deleuze's reading of Beckett, the possible has fully occupied the place of the real. The statement "there is nothing possible, everything is real" (i.e., there is no "possible" in the sense of "beyond the real") has become "everything that is possible is real" (i.e., the possible is the real). A reversal of the hierarchy has taken place: the real in the colloquial sense is just a derivative of the possible (i.e., the "properly" real); it is not more, but less than the possible. As previously shown, exhausting the possible requires that all personal preferences be suspended in a certain indifference. (This is also a Spinozistic motif: in Spinoza's words, all things are subject to "a certain indifferent will of God.")[34] Since to exhaust the possible is much more than to exhaust the selection of the possible that we are used to calling the real, the former causes exhaustion whereas the latter only leads to tiredness. This is why Deleuze says that exhaustion is "much more"[35] than tiredness (in both a psychosomatic and an ontological sense).

"The Exhausted Person"

Deleuze starts his essay by making us consider what it means to be an "exhausted person." He does not mention it, but "the exhausted person" in Beckett has a predecessor in Murphy, perhaps the most prominent of Beckett's if not visibly exhausted then at least indolent characters (perhaps their indolence is symptomatic of their exhaustion). These are all descendants of Dante's friend Belaqua and have in common that, as Murphy's girlfriend Celia puts it, they do "nothing that she could discern." (Belaqua, who is described repenting in Purgatory, is Beckett's favorite *Divine Comedy* character and appears in name in his work.) Murphy is pressured by Celia to seek paid employment. Since "there was no possibility of his finding in himself any reason for work taking one form rather than another" (the divine indifference of inclusive disjunction again), he is exhausted in advance by the inexhaustible possibilities of choice and decides to entrust his fate to the stars. The consulted Hindu swami, next to a few doubtful prescriptions, pronounces a verdict of which one part is later ominously repeated in the novel: "avoid exhaustion by speech."[36] Throughout the story, Celia keeps reminding Murphy of these words, at first literally (25), but later in a manner that is generalized to "avoid exhaustion" (80). Yet exhaustion is precisely what Murphy wants to achieve when he gives in to his compulsion of rocking in his rocking chair until in a state of "torpor" (61) and being "improved out of all knowledge" (62).

Exhausting the possible is a task for the exhausted person: Why does the name of God appear so insistently in the opening pages of Deleuze's text? Or, to put it otherwise, who (whose self) is exhausted? God, defined as "the sum total of all possibility," is the name of the place where the exhausted self and the to-be-exhausted *possibilia* coincide. In a passage refuting the idea that God might not create everything he understands (i.e., that some things that are possible might not be real), Spinoza says, "my opponents seem to deny God's omnipotence. For they are forced to confess that God understands infinitely many creatable things, which nevertheless he will never be able to create. For otherwise, if he created everything he understood [NS: to be creatable][37] he would *exhaust his omnipotence* and render himself imperfect."[38] Deleuze's reading of Spinoza draws the ultimate consequence of this passage: since God does create everything he understands to be creatable (again, the possible is the real), he thereby exhausts himself. From the very beginning in his reading of Beckett, Deleuze opposes the exhausted demiurge—"the originary or the sum total of all the possibility"[39]—who does not exclude anything, to the tired person, who acts on choices and preferences and thereby proceeds through exclusion. Acting on preferences may sometimes be tiresome, but only indifference (i.e., not excluding anything) is exhausting. In a paradoxical way, Deleuze brings here Nietzsche's "death of God" and Spinoza's pantheism together: God is not tired, and he is also not exactly dead; he is exhausted. He exhausts himself in the possibilities that unfold from his nature: *Natura naturans* exhausting itself in *Natura naturata*.[40]

To assume the place at the limit of all the possible series—which is what the exhausted person attempts to do—is equivalent to taking the place of God. One sets out to do this by first transcending a series and, in particular, by transcending the reverberation of selves—one of the most consistent motifs in Beckett and one that has a special status, because it reflects on the position of the author of a work. Traditionally, God's creation has been compared to that of the author: Leibniz wrote that God is the "author of things,"[41] and Foucault's "death of the author" is in this sense only an extension of the "death of god." (Derrida alludes to this historically somewhat obsolete, Romantic perception of the author as endowed with supernatural powers when he speaks of Joyce in terms of a demiurge: "demiurgue sadique.")[42] After demonstrating how the exhausted person dissipates itself in the inclusive disjunctions of all possibilia, Deleuze states: "[m]any authors are too polite, and are content to announce the total work and the death of the self"[43] (i.e., without showing, as Beckett does, the actual decomposition of the self). Thus, Deleuze confirms the implicit substitutability of "God" and "author." If the possible, the sum total of which is God-author, is being exhausted, then God-author, whose nature is to be exhaustive, is the subject and the object of this exhaustion: exhausted and exhaustive. God, author, and self merge into one here, in absolute consistency with Beckett's work. After all, do we not learn of one of the series of Beckett's alternative selves, Murphy, that he "loved himself with intellectual love?"[44]

The Three Stadia of Exhaustion

Let us retrace the progress of exhaustion in Beckett as described by Deleuze. It proceeds in three steps. In the first step, the *possibilia* (things, objects) are named, designated, in order to prepare them for exhaustion. This is the stage of nomination, the language of words ("language I"). "How could (an object) enter into a combinatorial if one does not have its name?" Deleuze asks. The search for the name recurs throughout Beckett's work, which poses such questions as "How try say?"[45] and the titular "What is the word?" Watt's perplexity with respect to what happened during the visit of the Galls also shows the importance of this search for the name: "if he could say, . . . Yes, . . . that is what happened then . . . then the scene would end, and trouble him no more."[46] Deleuze chooses another example: that of Molloy's puzzlement with the object of which he knows neither the name nor the purpose (the knife holder). Just as in the aforementioned case, when the name of the thing or the event in question remains unknown, it cannot enter into a combinatorial, which prevents it from being "exhausted."[47] "Language I" is "atomic, disjunctive, cut and chopped"; it is "a language in which enumeration replaces propositions and combinatorial relations replace syntactic relations."[48] This language exhausts the possible with words, but it does not exhaust the words themselves.

This is why, in order to be able to continue the task of exhaustion, "another metalanguage" is needed, one that will exhaust the words. In the second step ("language II"), the words are no longer seen as atoms but as parts of "blendable flows" of voices, where the voices are defined as "waves or flows that direct and distribute the linguistic corpuscules."[49] In order to exhaust the words themselves, the voices must be dried up. To achieve this, the voices must be traced back to their owners, among whom are Murphy, Watt, Mercier, and "Mahood and Co." Each of them controls his own "possible world," which remains to be extinguished.

The third step, after having attributed the voices to their owners, consists in extinguishing all the identified flows by getting beyond them. It is this third step that is the most problematic, since it's not obvious how one might reach a position external to the voices that is not itself a voice. "The aporia lies in the inexhaustible series of all these exhausted beings."[50] The search for the limit of the series can only bring a result if one acknowledges that the limit "can be anywhere in the flow." "Language III" pursues the immanent limit that can be found "between two terms, between two voices or the variations of a single voice."[51]

These three steps of exhaustion correspond, according to Deleuze, to the progressive transition in Beckett's work from the novel (the language of words) through the radio pieces (the language of voices) to the television plays (the language of images that transcends the other two). Seen in this way, Beckett's work becomes a project that from the outset was predestined to culminate in the television plays:

[N]o doubt this language (of images) is born in the novels and the novellas, and passes through the theatre, but it is in television that it accomplishes its own mission, distinct from the first two.[52]

Even though Deleuze provides in his essay an account of Beckett's work in general, it is on Beckett's television plays that he ultimately focuses. In fact, Deleuze's essay was written as a prefatorial contribution to the release of an edition of Beckett's television plays.[53] However, it would be too facile to say that the reasons for privileging the television plays in Beckett's artistic itinerary are here purely circumstantial; rather, the text functions as an extension of Deleuze's earlier cinematic reflection on Bergson, which involved a short but crucial encounter with Beckett.

It should be kept in mind that Deleuze's preoccupation with Beckett prior to his writing "The Exhausted" was marked by his interest in film and television. In his book on cinema (*Cinema 1*), which preceded the publication of *L'Épuisé* by nine years, Deleuze refers to what he elsewhere calls *le plus grand film irlandais*: Beckett's early *Film*.[54] Those who have read *Cinema 1* know that Deleuze's discussion of the three varieties of movement-image (perception-, action-, and affection-image)[55] is constantly set against the background of "a-centered," "free" images in general. There is an important difference between the images of the three mentioned varieties and "free" images; the former are "filtered" by a subject, defined as an interval between perception and action. The idea of consciousness as an interval between perception and action comes from Bergson's meditation on the nature of consciousness:

Throughout the whole extent of the animal kingdom . . . consciousness seems proportionate to the living being's power of choice. It lights up the zone of potentialities that surrounds the act. It fills the interval between what is done and what might be done.[56]

The subject exists as such an interval of consciousness that selects and organizes ("centers") the images that it encounters. Opposed to the images that are "filtered" by the subject are "free" or "a-centered" images. These images interact without any order of preference because there is no center that would organize them in any way.

Just as in Deleuze's later essay on Beckett, in *Cinema 1*, Beckett's *Film* appears as an example of (a kind of) exhausting. The discussion of this example functions as an important digression in *Cinema 1* following a path contrary to the direction of the rest of the book—not toward perception-, affection-, and movement-images but toward an undoing of those. Deleuze shows that Beckett's triple "extinguishing" of the three varieties of the (centered) movement-image allows him to look back on the otherwise unthinkable "mother movement-image."[57] Thus, the discussion of Beckett's *Film* aims

> to rediscover the matrix of the movement-image as it is in itself, in its acentred purity, in its primary régime of variation, in its heat and its light while it is still untroubled by any center of indetermination.

Again Beckett is thus depicted as someone who aims at a kind of exhaustion—this time at a purification of the image, reverting to its unalloyed state before the subject.

If we accept Deleuze's claim in *Cinema 1* that what defines subjectivity in the first place is subtraction, then exhausting is a movement away from the subject. (According to Deleuze, the subjective subtracts whatever is of no interest to it; subtraction, just like exclusive disjunction in "The Exhausted," is an inevitable consequence of making choices.) We have seen that, to the extent that it is "indifferent," exhausting is the opposite of subtracting: it does not choose but exhausts the possible, including the exhaustion of the subjectivity itself. (This shows that some of the similarities between Deleuze's reading of Beckett and the reading offered by Badiou are only superficial. For Badiou, Beckett's work is an almost Husserlian exercise in reduction, the goal of which is to arrive at the empty subject. Deleuze's exhausted subject, dissipating itself in all of the possibilities toward which it is indifferent, is something entirely different.) The analysis of the example from *Cinema 1* only confirms what was coming to light throughout our reading of "The Exhausted"—namely that exhaustion is a de-subjectivization. "Free images" can only be "free" on the condition of the disappearance of the subject.

However, at the same time, since the subject exhausts itself in the images, exhaustion is the supreme moment of subjectivity. If the situation of the writer is indeed comparable to that of God, as Deleuze suggests, then writing has little to do with putting signs on paper. Instead, writing is pantheism: "God, who is the sum total of the possible merges with Nothing, of which each thing is a modification."[58] It is only in this way that we can interpret Deleuze's claim that "literature" is "life." Deleuze's reading presents Beckett's work as a transition from things through voices to the subjective interval, which—in virtue of having exhausted the possible—is allowed to cease or die. This culminates in a final step, in which the subject is extinguished as a kind of supreme moment of subjectivity.

There are two domains in which this state of immanent transcendence can be achieved: image and space. Making an image "captures all the possible" but only "in order to make it explode," so that there is "no more possibility." The image then "announces the end of the possible." The other way to transcend the totality of the possible is to "depotentialize space" (i.e., to exhaust the possibilities offered by a given space). Whereas making an image makes use of visual or aural resources (a ritornello or a refrain) to transcend the possible, transcending the possible in space relies on motor resources (as, for example, in the movement of a rocking chair). The movement of the rocking chair in Beckett's *Film*, which symbolizes the auto-affection of the thinking subject, is taken by Deleuze to depotentialize, to exhaust this autoaffection. (Deleuze's insight is confirmed when we remember that the state of exhaustion is what Murphy hopes to attain by rocking in his rocking chair until in a state of "torpor" and being "improved out of all knowledge.")[59] This dual way of transcending the possible finds its parallel in Deleuze's discussion of the face and of space as "two kinds of signs of the affection-image."[60] If the face can be taken to symbolize subjectivity,[61] then to extinguish the face is to extinguish the subject. And, indeed, Deleuze says of Beckett that he "consumes and extinguishes the face."[62]

At first sight, the objective of the whole enterprise of exhausting—its purpose—is to be released from the exigency to create. The self (author, God) is after all only allowed to cease to exist at the end of the possible, after the possible has been exhausted. But there is another side to it—namely the image, which appears when the project of exhausting comes to an end. The image is more than a mere by-product of the whole enterprise. Exhausting the possible opens the way for the "pure image," which Deleuze calls "the indefinite."[63] The exhausted self is released from the exigency to create by creating, as when it exhausts itself in the pure image.

Exhausting versus Gathering: Deleuze and Derrida

It seems at this stage that exhausting, even though it belongs to a conceptual field apparently opposed to gathering ("to exhaust" means "to use up, to empty, to impoverish"), aims, just like Derrida's gesture, at being exhaustive, at accounting for "everything plus n." But even if we decide to call exhausting just another way of accounting for a hyper-totality, we have to remember that it occurs in virtue of its opposite: giving up. This brings us back to the tension that exists between exhausting and gathering. Perhaps the tension between the discourses of Beckett and Derrida that can be evoked by the terms "gathering," "archiving," "hyper-totalizing," and "economy" on the one hand, and "poverty," "exhaustion," and "less-ness" (which is also the title of a text by Beckett) on the other, is not just an issue between these authors; perhaps it indicates a point of dissent between Beckett and Joyce (the hyper-totalizing author par excellence) and a corresponding difference between the Joyce-reader Derrida and the Beckett-reader Deleuze. We might see it as the difference between seeing literature as an institution set on gathering (Derrida) and seeing literary works as "becomings" (Deleuze), which involve a nomadic flight from memory or history[64]—and from institutions.

We might formulate this difference in the following way: even though Derrida and Deleuze share the concern (common to all thinkers interested in literature since Sartre) to demonstrate that the function of literature is more than granting us a short-lived escape from reality, they differ in the way that they deal with this concern. Although Derrida fully recognizes the subversive role of literature, through reading this role in terms of archive, economy, and law, he attempts to demonstrate the relevance of literature to these established institutions (and vice versa—the applicability of the notion "institution" to literature). For Deleuze (who is in this respect perhaps more radical), literature is a flight from these institutions in search of viable alternatives to the forces that the institutions represent. It needs emphasizing that this "flight" is not equivalent to the flight from life but to a voyage of discovery, a search for alternatives.[65] It is these alternatives, where viable, that Deleuze addresses when he says that "literature" is "life." All of the terms that Deleuze uses in this context ("becoming,"[66] "flight," "life," "intervention") emphasize the noninstitutional character of literature. To say that literature is an "institution" is to treat it as a significant practice, hence to acknowledge that one approaches literature in terms of signification and, more generally, mediation. Deleuze's thought is fundamentally opposed to this view.

Derrida's infinite movement of hyper-totalizing can only achieve the economy it seeks (in order to take place in the finite space of a text) by means of "translating figures into one another."[67] This approach draws on the principle of substitution, which is one of the most potent resources of what Deleuze calls "interpretation" (it is not for nothing that a translator is sometimes called an "interpreter"). Even though Derrida's project is not to be confused with classical hermeneutics, the gesture of substitution is in the end one of demonstrating the relevance of one thing to another by means of reading that thing as something else (Derrida calls it the unsubstitutable substitution): reading literature as archive, as law, as economy. His work is not as hostile to interpretation as is often suggested by the scholars who want to prevent an understanding of Derrida in the vaguely deconstructivist, Yale school context. Derrida himself resists this latter reading of his work: "I have never 'put such concepts as . . . the stability of interpretive context radically into question' if 'putting radically into question' means contesting that there *are* and that there *should be* . . . stable contexts of interpretation."[68] Nonetheless, this leaves open the possibility of interpretation and reinterpretation, even if not "radical" reinterpretation. (It is perhaps useful here to take the word "interpretation" as referring to its Latin, rather than Greek, antecedent [*hermeneuin*], which suggests a more totalizing search of signification or meaning.)

If we agree on this, then Deleuze's famous summons to the institution of French literature—"[e]xpérimentez, n'interprétez jamais"[69]—could also be taken to apply to Derrida. In the essay in which those words appear, Deleuze attributes the superiority of the Anglo-American literature to its having liberated itself from what he calls the "diseases of the earth": "signifiance and interpretosis,"[70] where these neologisms mark instances of attempting to say one thing by saying something else. (In France, Deleuze says, on the contrary, *il faut toujours que quelque chose nous rappelle autre chose, nous fasse penser à autre chose. . . . Depuis qu'on a inventé le "signifiant" les choses ne se sont pas arrangées.*) Even though Deleuze's critique of "la manie du sale petit secret, . . . la cochonnerie laborieuse, ponctuelle, enchaînée d'écrivains français"[71] seems to be aimed primarily at the more hermeneutic models of interpretation, which presuppose one interpretive horizon (one "secret"), it might also have some bearing on the aspect of Derrida's work that we are discussing here. The scope of this chapter does not allow for any more detailed discussion of the respective differences in the perceptions of literature presented by Derrida and Deleuze. Without wanting to suggest that these perceptions are irreconcilable, it should be noted that quite often Deleuze's critique is applicable to certain aspects of Derrida's enterprise. Deleuze distinguishes between the domain of the gods, the city, the king (with its interest in the code, the archive [*le cadastre*], and economy), and the nomadic—the latter being the subject of his interest. By contrast, Derrida seems to fit much better into the description of the former (namely, the code, the archive, and economy). To the Deleuzian flight from code Derrida opposes a multiplicity of codes. Perhaps the most obvious point of disagreement comes to light when Deleuze criticizes French authors for their interest in history.

The French are too . . . historical, too concerned with the future and the past. . . . They do not know how to become, they think in terms of historical past and future.[72]

If indeed Derrida's gathering of "everything" takes place, as he himself puts it, "by translating all figures into one another," then precisely what Deleuze calls interpretation is an instrument of this gathering. It should be emphasized here that Derrida's gesture of gathering is different not only from the absolute Hegelian gesture (as I noted in Chapter 1) but also from classical hermeneutics, which, even though radically finite, presupposes a unitary horizon of meaning.[73] No translation is final or exhaustive; instead, they are all provisional, temporary, and partial. (That is not to say that all readings are equivalent to each other, just that no one reading is exhaustive in such a way that it could subsume all others.) "Interpretation" has a very specific meaning here; it no longer signifies a subsumption of all figures under one meaning but their (always provisional) mutual substitutability.

It is because Deleuze rejects interpretation that he contrasts two visions of writing: one focused on *une vitesse d'événement* and one that takes recourse to *une économie des moyens* (the latter involving archiving). Deleuze tells us that characteristic of "true novels" (*les vrais romans*),[74] just as for *le télégramme* (an example quite relevant to Derrida's thinking of *envois*, telephone and gramophone), is "une vitesse d'événement, pas une économie des moyens."[75] In other words, for Deleuze, a "true novel" is not an "archive"; it does not have an ambition to gather.[76] On the contrary, a "true novel" has "killed interpretation" (*tué l'interprétation*), to the effect that (and here Deleuze quotes Henry James) "*il ne restait qu'une lumière crue,*"[77] a light in which an experiment, stripped down to bare essentials, can take place.

The "telegraphic" quotation above is illuminating for the relationship between Derrida and Deleuze, and in particular for the difference in the way they perceive literature. For Derrida, events of literature require interpretation—in virtue not only of economical necessity (containing the infinite in the finite; writing as an act of infinite gathering presupposes an *économie des moyens*) but also of juridical necessity: like the law, literature is something to be interpreted (or translated). A reading of a literary work is a pursuit of the law governing that work, and "*the law is not to be seen or touched but deciphered.*"[78]

For Deleuze, a literary experiment is indifferent to interpretation because, like everything else in Deleuze's framework of thought, literature participates in the "univocity of Being."[79] From the perspective of the univocity of Being, not only is the issue of mediation (and hence also the gesture of the deciphering provoked by the ubiquity of mediation) not a real concern, but it is also explicitly rejected. Badiou is faithful to the spirit of Deleuze's thought when he notes, "Deleuze's method rejects all recourse to mediations."[80] Rather (and granting that this reading is contentious), Badiou pursues in Deleuze's thought the idea that the unique intuition of being traverses "in a single circuit" every thinkable opposition.[81] That is why Deleuze opposes a "single voice" of Being to the "two paths" (affirming respectively Being and "Non-being") of Parmenides.[82] The same thought feeds Deleuze's critique of Heidegger.[83] According to Deleuze, by needlessly positing an analogy or a "hermeneutic convergence"[84] between the visible and language, Heidegger failed to take the notion of the univocity of Being far enough.[85] Deleuze argues that since Being is univocal, it does not require thinking in terms of analogy or convergence. From his perspective, the writer who, like Spinoza's God, exhausts himself in a (literary) "becoming" follows the same uninterrupted path of a single voice and a single intuition. This means that as a process of mediation (including the possibilities of substituting figures for one another, or gathering economically under one or more figures, like the yes in Joyce), writing itself is literally the least of the writer's concerns. Gathering is not so much opposed as considered unnecessary in Deleuze's literary pantheism. Whereas Derrida's gesture of substitution can be seen as a radicalization of the characteristic of the structuralist pursuit of "correspondences without resemblance,"[86] Deleuze makes it a point to distinguish "becoming" from the structuralist operation of gathering (which organizes its subject matter by means of substitution). He writes: "[T]o become is not to progress or regress along a series. . . . [B]ecoming is not a correspondence between relations."[87] Rather than of "exhaustion," Deleuze speaks of the "athleticism" of the artist, an "athleticism of becoming"[88] (where the psychosomatic aspect of the project is preserved). Deleuze's "artist-becomer" creates "beings of sensation" (i.e., percepts and affects) or "sensation as being."[89] If percepts and affects are indeed "beings," then writing is an ontological activity to which putting marks on paper is quite secondary. "[T]he writer's position is no different from that of the painter, musician or architect."[90] The whole metaphorical network of notions like "deciphering," substitution, and archiving is thereby rendered unnecessary.

After Deleuze's death, Derrida described him as "more than anything else" "the thinker of the event" and of singularity. So, too, we might add, is Derrida—except that where Deleuze's event, anonymous like the nomads, "travels light" ("indefinite"), Derrida's event carries with it a huge baggage of archives (names, dates, and secret meanings that make it "hyper-" rather than "indefinite"). For Derrida, the preservation of "a certain zone of disacquaintance" in a text is a question of "donner à lire" and of "hospitality."[91] A totally intelligible text is not hospitable to another's reading. The event of a text can only "have a future" on the condition that it possesses "a reserve" that is capable of "engendering new contexts."[92] Thinking in terms of "giving to read" or giving to "decipher" always presupposes a consciousness or subjectivity that reads or writes it. This is a second way in which Derrida's perception of literature is opposed to that of Deleuze, for whom the purpose of writing is "to get *out* of the black hole of subjectivity, of consciousness and memory."[93] For Deleuze, creative activity is in conflict not only with any kind of mediation but also with subjectivity. Deciphering presupposes a deciphering subject—for Deleuze, a relation of knowledge that must be abandoned. This seems to be what the exemplary assemblages like the wasp and the orchid[94] are to make us appreciate: they form a functioning singular assemblage that does not require the mediation of a consciousness (they are indifferent to our knowing of their existence). Writing, Deleuze seems to suggest, is an activity that produces this kind of nonhuman interaction. We might ask whether in a world like this the principle of iterability still applies.[95]

Perhaps the most striking difference between Derrida and Deleuze in their perception of literature is the issue of memory. The baggage of history that is intrinsic to Derrida's notion of iterability (and thereby to virtually all of his thought) can be contrasted even to the early Deleuze of *Proust and the Signs* (1964). There the latter calls "superior" the signs that "cause no memory, no resurrection of the past to intervene," and insists that the search must be oriented "to the future." In *A Thousand Plateaus,* when discussing Proust's *A la recherche,* Deleuze is even more explicit. "The narrator munches his madeleine: redundancy, the black hole of involuntary memory.... It is, above all, something one has to get out of, escape from. Proust knows that quite well, even if his commentators do not."[96] Deleuze is quite clear: memory must be overcome. Memory is directly related to archiving—and about archiving, Deleuze is quite explicit:

[T]he art of the novel . . . is the source of a misunderstanding: many people think that novels can be created with . . . our memories and archives, our travels and fantasies, our children and parents.[97]

Moreover, memory is shown to hang together with "interpretation." After all, Deleuze argues, this is how Proust makes "the face, landscape, painting, music, etc. resonate together"—through the feature of "Swann's aestheticism," in virtue of which "a thing must always recall something else." "Recall" is the key word here. Even with respect to Proust, Deleuze does not hide his feeling that Anglo-American literature is in this respect superior, because instead of giving in to the contemplation of memory and history, it undertakes to "get out of the black hole of involuntary memory." "They (the Anglo-American authors, 'from Hardy to T. E. Lawrence, from Melville to Miller') know how difficult it is to get out of the black hole of . . . memory."[98]

But Deleuze drives his point still further: he claims that "becoming is an antimemory"[99] (again, it has to be kept in mind that for Deleuze, "literature" is, precisely, "becoming"—i.e., literature is an antimemory). And, what might explain Beckett's infatuation with music: "[T]he musician is in the best position to say: 'I hate the faculty of memory, I hate memories,' . . . because he or she affirms the power of becoming."[100] The exhausted is an "amnesiac witness":[101] his memory is exhausted too. (Being able to recall belongs still to the realm of being tired. The exhausted person "can no longer stir even a single memory.") This means that the exhausted person ends up beyond the repetitive stage of the ritornello: "the rocking chair is still imperfect in this regard: it must come to a stop."[102] Repetition is only a stage of transition in the becoming of Being.

Deleuze's readings of literature all seem to be begging a question—namely, in what way can a literary experiment, in focusing on the "speed of event" rather than on the "economy of means," avoid being always tainted by the latter? How is it possible to avoid the economical effect of language? "It is not only that words lie," Deleuze says when commenting on Beckett,

> they are so burdened with calculations and significations, with intentions and personal memories, with old habits that cement them together, that one can scarcely bore into the surface before it closes up again. It sticks together. It imprisons and suffocates us.[103]

To be able to experiment with "pure intensities," we must get rid of all this mental baggage. Both Beckett and Deleuze think that music comes closer to achieving this task than words will ever do.[104] Deleuze shows that whereas initially Beckett exhausted "words, voices and images," with time he found words increasingly difficult to work with. It is possible, as Bergson has shown, to think images "before" a consciousness, and in the same way, it is possible to think space and sounds—but not words. Words are always bound with the particular or the general, which makes it impossible for them to reach the visible as it is in itself. It is thereby easier to exhaust images, space, and voices because they have less "materiality" ("materiality" referring here to "the burden" of "intentions . . . memories . . . habits").[105] Writing as flight signifies precisely a process of discarding this "materiality." At its extreme point, writing as flight is the radical extenuation of all subjectivity (the "non-personal power"[106]), a flight from consciousness to the point where everything, including iteration, is brought to a stop and images can interact freely in the "sharp light" of a "non-human life."[107]

In what way does Deleuze's reading of Beckett through the notion of exhausting differ from Derrida's understanding of literature as gathering? Exhausting can to an extent be seen as parallel to archiving: whatever their gesture, they are both in a sense concerned with "everything + n." The one who archives, archives everything, including himself; the one who exhausts, exhausts everything, including himself. It might be argued that Beckett's exhausting himself in his work is the same as leaving his signature in that work: that in both cases, haunting—the return of the author—is taking place. The author's return (Derrida's *revenir*), his re-inserting himself into his work, his attempt to recapture his work, would equally be his becoming (Deleuze's *devenir*).

Certainly, it might be said that archiving fails to address the psychosomatic (and ontological, since we speak of "being" as percepts and affects) aspect of the writing process: that the work requires the dissolution of the self not only as a (quasi-) transcendental condition. To limit our understanding of the literary work to the latter condition would be to assume that all it needs is the "necessary possibility" of the death of the author. But the possibility of the death of the author is the condition on which all writing depends in general. This would not account for writing as experimental for an individual (even as de-subjectivizing) artistic innovation. Similarly, insofar as archiving can be seen as producing an archive, it is not becoming: it is neither becoming a cockroach as in Kafka, nor becoming exhausted as in Beckett. Becoming is a much more extreme process because it conceives the work as that into which the author translates himself physiologically and ontologically (whereas the signature is only a matter of structure of "law"). (Looked at from the perspective of writing as a process of becoming, Deleuze's aesthetic is expressive—or, rather, since we are talking about exhaustion, the negative, "depressive.")

It might be retorted that whether we consider the self's dissolution as empirical or merely transcendental, the result will be the same: the "ashes," the haunting of the negative. There are nonetheless some differences worth pointing out. More than anything else, archiving indicates a different attitude to the complex of consciousness and the unconscious. Archiving presupposes an instance that, consciously (the self) or not (the unconscious), either keeps the archives or makes use of them.[108] The archives presuppose the necessary possibility of the death of the subject, but this is a structural possibility that does not preclude in the absolute sense the return of the author (as haunting or signature). Deleuze and Beckett alike push further than this, unraveling the self—exploring its decomposition. In fact, Deleuze says, "many authors are too polite, and are content to announce the total work and the death of the self. But this remains an abstraction as long as one does not show 'how it is': how one makes an 'inventory,' errors included, of how the self decomposes, stench and agony included."[109] The examples of the undoing of the self (or, as Deleuze calls it, "the center of indetermination") that can be found in

Beckett include the flight from memory, from choice, and from "the personal or the rational."[110]

First, exhausting—unlike the archives that are irreducibly linked to memory—attempts to go beyond the redundancy of (both voluntary and involuntary) memory. Beckett's "amnesiac witness" is an example of this: forgetting is a necessary part of the process of shedding all aspects of subjectivity. To indicate how deeply rooted Beckett's commitment to this process of leaving the self is, it should suffice to recall Beckett's confessions of love for certain stones that he explained by way of a "fascination with the mineral, with things dying and decaying, with petrification." Beckett's biographer, James Knowlson, recalls that Beckett "linked this interest with Sigmund Freud's view that human beings have a prebirth nostalgia to return to the mineral state."[111]

Second, where Derrida's gathering relies on the continuous necessity of making choices, exhausting takes place on the condition of absolute indifference. Deleuze often speaks, in the context of Beckett's work and outside of it, about the "renouncing of any order of preference" as well as of "privileged instants" (this renouncing turns every instant into "any-instant-whatever," and every space into "any-space-whatever").

We might attach to it a conclusion that whereas the philosophies of both Deleuze and Derrida can be described as affirmative, it is a different kind of affirmation. Where Derrida says yes, Deleuze says with Bartleby, "I would prefer not to." It is not an opposition of yes and no as might, too easily, be surmised. Rather, whereas the iterability of the yes affirms the general and the particular and thereby takes recourse to a self, the inclusive disjunction of Bartleby's expression (that effectively means "I would prefer not to prefer," "I would prefer not to choose") takes place "before" the particular and the universal, in a flight from the self. Bartleby is, strictly speaking, not a human subject. It is for this reason that whereas Derrida's archiving is hospitable to the particular and the universal, Deleuze's exhausting, in being a flight from the archives is also the flight from the universal and the particular. The singular in Deleuze, which he addresses with the indefinite article, is that which, like "pure images, retain[s] nothing of the personal or the rational."[112]

For Derrida, as the notions of authorial signature and "hauntology" suggest, writing presupposes both the death and the return or the survival of the author—for example, in a private idiom. Deleuze, by contrast, argues for the ultimate dissolution of the author in the work, which entails a loss of anything resembling the private idiom in favor of any-idiom-whatever. The supreme moment of subjectivity is the ultimate dissolution of the subject in the work. What Deleuze seems here to be rightly sensitive to in Beckett is that his work should not be seen as writing, strictly speaking, but as a pantheism (*devenir*) that is coextensive with the loss of self.

5

Singular Points of Transaction (I): The Subject

> For me the great question is always the question who.
> —Derrida, *A Taste for the Secret*
>
> what? ... who? ... no!
> —Beckett, "Not I," *Complete Dramatic Works*

If, as the preceding chapters should have made clear, Derrida's understanding of literature as archive and critique is (despite some tensions I have indicated) not irreconcilable with Beckett's project, then staging what Derrida calls "points of transaction" between these two discourses should be possible. In the following three chapters I will confront the main foci of Beckett's project with Derrida's notion of literature as archive and as law, and present three such points of transaction, as well as their limits. The present chapter will deal with the extent to which it is possible to speak about a human subject in Beckett and Derrida. More specifically, I will argue that in addition to there being no doubt that both deconstruct the self-present human subject, Beckett and Derrida both institute the delay of self-presence as the source of the authorial "I." This "I" might no longer be called the subject but the subjectile—the singular signature of the subject. This is the first and also the least problematic point of transaction.

I have chosen this subject as a point of transaction because the exploration of certain effects of subjectivity is one of Beckett's most enduring concerns. I could hardly do justice to Beckett's work without addressing it. On the other hand, this choice requires, at least at first sight, a quite substantial bending of Derrida's discourse. Derrida, for reasons that will soon become clear, almost always tries to circumvent the word "subject." Despite this, as we shall see, under different names and granted specific precautions, the "effects of subjectivity" are an enduring concern for Derrida, too. In this chapter, I will start with an introduction to Derrida's position on the subject, then move on to an analysis of the functioning of the subject in Beckett's novel *The Unnamable*. This, in turn, will prepare the ground for the discussion of the ethical and political implications of these two positions.

The Perturbations of the Subject in Derrida

I have mentioned before that Derrida's interest in literature was originally phenomenological in nature. Derrida's first Ph.D. thesis proposal, in 1957, had as a provisional title "The Ideality of the Literary Object." Its objective was to develop, with the help of Husserl's transcendental phenomenology, a "new theory of literature, of that very peculiar type of ideal object that is the literary object."[1] In fact, in an interview given in 1992, Derrida indicated that the phenomenological way of looking at literature remained relevant for him. When addressing the literariness of a text with the help of phenomenological terms (like *noesis*, the "real" side of intentional acts; and *noema*, the "ideal" side of sense), he comments: "I believe this phenomenological-type language to be necessary, even if at a certain point it must yield to what . . . puts phenomenology in crisis as well as the very concept of the institution or convention."[2]

I recall here Derrida's early involvement with the work of Husserl to remind the reader that Derrida's formative period was focused on a philosophy that posited a pure and constitutive consciousness not only as the genesis or "origin of the world" but also as its own starting point. In order to see how Derrida moved on from the philosophy that granted absolute privilege to consciousness (whether empirical or transcendental) to the thought of iterability—where the notions of the subject, ego, and consciousness hardly ever make an appearance—we need first to answer the question of what it is that Derrida thinks puts phenomenology in crisis.[3]

It is not, as might be thought, the complicity of phenomenology with the metaphysics of presence. This argument of Derrida's early texts still holds, but it is not enough to shake the foundations of phenomenology.

In fact, this complicity is even necessary: "[p]henomenology can only make sense if a pure and primordial presentation is possible and given in the original."[4] Paradoxically, it is precisely a certain imperfection of this complicity that puts phenomenology in crisis: the fact of the irreducible unity of presentation and representation, which makes a "pure and primordial presentation" impossible.[5] This unity, called by Derrida "re-presentation,"[6] precedes the first step of phenomenology—namely, reduction.

The argument of the unity of re-presentation is important in a twofold manner. Not only is what Husserl called "the principle of all principles" (of evidence in the form of original presentation) hereby brought into crisis; in a very subtle way, while using the Husserlian terminology of consciousness and auto-affection, Derrida gives it quite another content, one that no longer, or at least no longer necessarily, addresses consciousness. The "experience" of the irreducible unity of "re-presentation" (in the form of the irreducible unity of parallels, "the pure psychology of consciousness," and "the transcendental phenomenology of consciousness") is defined by Derrida not only as "life" but also as "*self-relationship, whether or not it takes place in the form of consciousness.*"[7] The self-relationship is thus no longer conceived as necessarily a property of consciousness; this is a step in the direction of Derrida's later work on the originary iterability of signs (we might speak of the sign's "self-relation" or "re-presentation").

It is because this "experience" of "re-presentation" is always constitutive of consciousness (or rather and more precisely, they are mutually constitutive) that Derrida's texts address notions like the singularity and iterability of a (subject's) signature rather than notions of consciousness or of the subject (transcendental or empirical) itself. "I would keep the name [subject] provisionally as an index for the discussion, but I don't see the necessity of keeping the word 'subject' at any price, especially if the context and conventions of discourse risk re-introducing precisely what is in question."[8] Derrida's discussion of the quasi-constitutive role of re-presentation with respect to the phenomenological subject prefigured and would later develop into the notion of iterability, the necessary condition of nonidentical repetition. After arguing for this co-constitution, Derrida did not engage in discussions of the subject-related issues (consciousness, existence, man) unless explicitly prompted. However, he also did not stop recognizing the necessity of a certain notion of the subject. "The subject is absolutely indispensable. I am not destroying but situating it. At a certain level of experience and philosophical or scientific discourse it is impossible not to use the notion of the subject. The question that remains however is where it comes from and how it functions."[9]

Not only is the subject not rejected by Derrida, but a certain notion of a subject is even strongly linked to his engagement with literature. When expressing his interest in the meaning "Kierkegaard . . . gives to the word 'subjectivity,'" Derrida says that his own interest in literature

> stems from the same gesture. It is not that I find literature desirable for its own sake, but that for me it also represents this singularity of experience and of existence in its link to language. In literature what interests me is essentially the autobiographical.[10]

In order to underline that the subject is constituted by the effects of inscription (including "re-presentation" and iterability), Derrida employs other terms to bypass this problematic notion. As mentioned previously, "the autobiographical" is one of those terms; others are "the signature," the "subjectile," and even "circumcision." (Circumcision is the "moment of signature" that marks the "birth of the subject.")[11] Event, signature, and subject are united here, but again the "birth of the subject" is dependent on the event of "re-presentation" through the signature. It is with the institutive signature of circumcision—and not with the physiological birth—that the autobiography of the subject begins.

The importance of the subject to Derrida can be seen from his often-repeated acknowledgment that his original interest was, strictly speaking, neither in philosophy nor in literature, that he hesitated between the two, and that the name he gave to this hesitation is "autobiography."[12] Derrida characterizes what he calls the "autobiographical" dream as three questions: "Who am I? Who is me? What's happening?"[13] It is a certain experience of the "link to language" of subjectivity—that is, of "autobiography"—that drew Derrida to literature. (And not only to literature—Derrida insists that philosophy, too, "has always been in the service of this autobiographical design of memory.")[14]

If literature is understood as autobiography, then everything that we have addressed as gathering or archiving is the gathering of a subject in a double sense. On the one hand, there is the traditionally understood constitutive subject as the one who gathers, the one who has mastery and control over the gathered archive. On the other hand, and more importantly, lies the constituted subject as the effect of the gesture of gathering. This side of the subject originates in total passivity and loss of mastery, as "the gathered." Returning to Derrida's reading of the subject's signature as the "sponge,"[15] the subject (or, more precisely, the signature) is the one who sponges and what is being sponged. They mutually presuppose each other, and hence neither is absolute. There is no mastery over the gathered archive.

The "gathering of a subject" in its double sense is what takes place in Beckett's novel *The Unnamable*.[16] In the following pages, I will focus on Beckett's inquiry into the problem of the self in this novel. Questioning the picture of the subject inherited from philosophical tradition (and also manifested in language)[17] *The Unnamable* records a struggle between the Cartesian (constitutive) subject (or even a stronger, Hegelian, totalizing version) and the sheer passivity of its other. The Unnamable is this "between."

The "Unnamable" Subject in Beckett

The Unnamable addresses the issues that Derrida identified as determining, from the very beginning, his intellectual pursuit. The novel is "autobiographical"[18] in the sense ascribed to the term by Derrida. *The Unnamable* is a tour de force of a fragmented self, who is "desolate," "obsessional," and "irradiated with flashes of last-ditch black humor" (so described by a critic upon its first appearance in print). In its distinctive "prattle," it asks the questions earlier attributed to Derrida: "Who am I? What's happening?" Or, in the Unnamable's words: "Am I animal, human or divine, awake or dreaming," "perhaps it's a dream, all a dream, that would surprise me, I'll wake, in the silence, and never sleep again, it will be I, or dream, dream again, dream of silence, a dream of silence, full of murmurs."[19] Derrida's professed "obsession with the *proteiform*"[20] would find its equal here. The Unnamable "writes" itself—or, rather, it is being "written"—in multiple voices, without a hierarchy or even a consistent distribution among them. There is no way to ascertain whether the "I" is in fact a person, for, without interrupting its discourse, it undergoes a series of incarnations, some of them animalistic, some god-like, and (with the possible exception of Mahood) none of them decidedly and consistently human. We might try to identify the speaking subject with the "thing told,"[21] but what if a number of contradictory things are "told"? We do not know who is speaking in *The Unnamable* (Malone's soul,

Mahood, Worm). Indeed, it is this enigma that keeps us reading on: Who is speaking, and can this speech be interrupted? In this sense, the text could almost be read as a simple "whodunit," were it not that the element of satisfaction in the form of an answer or a solution is denied right from the beginning; the implausibility of information provided by the narrator makes it clear that no solution is to be expected. Undeniably, we are told by the Unnamable itself, "I am all these voices," but that can easily be doubted in a discourse that perfects the practice of self-contradiction. Rather than an all-encompassing, unified self-reflection, the effects of the subjectivity of the Unnamable (if it is still possible to speak about subjectivity) originate in a multivoiced writing without hierarchy, which by definition cannot be mastered. (In due course, as the notion of the subjectile becomes clear, I will give up the vocabulary of the Cartesian subject.) The "I" (that does not so much speak as merely open its mouth) is overpowered by its own words. "I am afraid, afraid what my words will do to me."[22] This creates a sphere of confrontation between the "I" (the one who appears to utter) and the mutually subversive multiplicity of voices that overpower the "I." It is a case of enforced ventriloquism; the one who appears to speak, does not.[23] The Unnamable is explicit about this: "[D]o they believe I believe it is I who am speaking? . . . It is not mine, I have none, I have no voice. . . ."[24]

This "autobiographic" but also *proteiform* nature of *The Unnamable* allows it to question the nature of subjectivity from a position different from that of the subject. The Unnamable, as I have already said, is the "between"—precisely that which precludes naming and thereby subjectification (hence its being called the Unnamable). As the "between," the Unnamable is not a subject in the traditional sense but what Antonin Artaud, and Derrida after him, called a "subjectile." I will return to this later.

Let us look more closely at the discourse of the Unnamable, which concerns speaking and the impossibility of halting the flow of words. The motive behind this incessant speech is the desire to fall silent. The inability to control and overcome the voice is the essence of the "I"'s complaint:

It issues from me, it fills me, it clamours against my walls, it is not mine, I can't stop it, I can't prevent it, from tearing me, racking me, assailing me. (303)

Since the "I"'s objective is to discontinue speaking, to cut short the comedy of ventriloquism, it focuses on how this could be attained: What is the condition of the possibility of its own interruption?

There are two sorts of options to choose from. They describe in a nutshell two lines of inquiry that Beckett alternately pursued in his work. We might call them "passive" and "active." The "passive" options are grouped around the idea that the "I" should "renounce all," including the pronoun "I." "But enough of this cursed first person, it is really too red a herring. I'll get out of my depth if I am not careful. But what then is the subject? . . . Bah, any old pronoun will do, provided one sees through it. Matter of habit" (345). "I shall not say I again, ever again, it's too farcical. I shall put in its place, whenever I hear it, the third person, if I think of it" (358). The gesture of "renouncing all," in which the "all" indicates the interest in a certain totality, was discussed in the previous chapter. Deleuze's reading of Beckett in terms of exhausting the possible shows that the apparent "passivity" of this gesture conceals a pantheistic self-transformation.[25] What the "passive" options ascribed to this gesture have in common is that the "I" seems not to be in any state to master the situation. Instead, it exhausts itself in trying to influence the situation in its favor. And, paradoxically, in its exhaustion—or, rather, exhaustivity—is its power.

The other option that would allow the Unnamable to terminate the flow of speech is one of mastery and control. To silence the clamor of voices, the "I" should become the owner of those voices, to thereby saturate the flow of words with its (the "I"'s) own intentions. Should the "I" identify itself, reject that which is its other and therewith take full possession of the speaking voice—should it say "I"—it would be free to go silent. In other words, the possibility of going silent requires becoming a speaking subject in the sense determined by philosophical reflection.

It is between those two options that the Unnamable, as the "between," is situated. We will see later on that this "between," having "no thickness," is in fact situated in the same way that the subjectile is—between an inside and an outside in general. But in order to render the picture complete, let us consider the second of the options the Unnamable has at its disposal to fall silent: the possibility of its becoming a subject.

How can this happen? Being a subject in the sense of a foundation requires a self-present existence, as in the expression "the speaking subject," in which the present participle indicates a synchronic, self-present action on the part of the subject. In other words, the subject is the subject while speaking, in virtue of its being self-present to itself in the moment of speaking. If a perfect immediacy is not possible, at least a perfect return might be; the subject hears himself speak and takes possession and control of everything that is said. The assumption that spoken words, heard by the one who utters them, return to their origin—thus completing a full circle—is central to the notion of subject identity examined by Beckett. In his analysis of the voice, Beckett engages in a dialogue with phenomenology, showing that the voice, even in a solitary position, is never immediately present to the "I" that utters it. It must be noted that this is precisely one of the conclusions of Derrida's own exchange with Husserl, to the extent that some of the passages of *Speech and Phenomena* can be read as an elucidating rewording of the Unnamable's enigmatic statements. In his reading of Husserl, Derrida is in this sense rewriting and reaffirming Beckett's project of the investigation and critique of the self-present subject.

In his reading of the first of Husserl's *Investigations,* Derrida has shown not only why it is essential for Husserl that the "I" is present to itself in the immediacy of a conscious act but also how Husserl is trying to ensure it. The answer to the first of these questions is that "[p]henomenology can only make sense if a pure and primordial presentation is possible and given in the original,"[26] and this presentation can only be given to a self-present instance that is capable of receiving it "in the original." In answer to the second question, Husserl's discussion of the case of "solitary mental life" serves primarily to stabilize the otherwise precarious "essential distinction" between indication and expression.[27] (He writes that "expressions function meaningfully even in isolated mental life."[28] That is, solitary life is the only situation that definitively dismisses indication as "purposeless" and presents itself as a realm reserved for expression alone.) On Husserl's account, the "solitary mental life," in virtue of being the realm of expression (and hence of the type of sign that can "function meaningfully" without recourse to signs, as a pure, unmediated transfer of sense "indifferent" to words), provides a situation in which the subject can be present to itself in the moment of "hearing-itself-speak." This nonmediated self-relation, called "auto-affection," is constitutive of the subject's relationship to itself. In the "hearing-oneself-speak," which requires no detour through an other, the Husserlian subject experiences its self-presence as evident. The "meaning of 'I' is essentially realized in the immediate idea of one's own personality."[29] Derrida has argued that this structure is "constitutive of the metaphysical privilege of speech. In the system of hearing-oneself-speak, the exteriority of the vocal signifier is experienced as effacing itself entirely in the very moment of its utterance, with the effect that the subject of uttering comes into an immediate relation with the full meaning of his speech."[30] It is only at a cost of this metaphysical penchant that Husserl can arrive at the subject's self-identity,[31] which is a necessary presupposition of phenomenology.[32] In solitary speech, the speaking subject exists simultaneously with its speech; in other words, the subject is able to hear the spoken words at the very moment of their being uttered and so accompany them as a subject. That being the case, the subject would demonstrate its own identity just by saying "I" and establish itself as the unquestioned source of the intuitive constitution of the world.[33]

This is precisely what Beckett questions, insisting on the irreducible difference that makes it impossible to say "I." (This position is perhaps even more radical than that of Derrida, for whom the difference is both the condition of the impossibility and the condition of the possibility of saying "I.") The Unnamable's insistence on the impossibility of hearing or seeing itself, of return, or of "closing the circuit" addresses this originary difference.

Shall I come upon my true countenance at last, bathing in a smile? I have the feeling I shall be spared this spectacle. At no moment do I know what I'm talking about, nor of whom, nor of where, nor how, nor why, but I could employ fifty wretches for this sinister operation and still be short of a fifty-first, to close the circuit, that I know, without knowing what it means. The essential is never to arrive anywhere, never to be anywhere, neither where Mahood is, nor where Worm is, nor where I am. . . . The essential is to go on squirming forever at the end of the line.

I am he who will never be caught . . . , I knew it, there might be a hundred of us and still we'd lack the hundred and first, we'll always be short of me.[34]

The question in the above fragments can be rendered as: "Can I reach my self with my voice while speaking? Can I grasp my own subjectivity through this monologue? Shall I come upon my true countenance at last?" And the answer is negative: "I am he who will never be caught." At the moment I speak, I do not hear myself; and the moment I hear myself, the "I" that had once uttered what I hear has already passed away.[35] Rather than an empirical observation, an irreducible difference lies at the bottom of this reasoning. This difference should be seen as a constitutive delay (a temporal one but also one of coding and decoding, of re-presentation), an in-between, which accounts for the fact that when we start listening to ourselves speak, we seem to lose the ability to speak. The Unnamable's confession, "at no moment do I know what I'm talking about, nor of whom, nor of where, nor how, nor why," sounds farcical (and justifiably so) but should also be taken in all its literality.

In order to identify itself, in order to give itself presence, the "I" must overcome this predicament; it must succeed in hearing itself speak and know that it is the "I" that speaks. This is why the Unnamable tries to rid itself of its alter ego, the "voice [that] continues to testify for me," in the hope that it could then experience a moment of self-presence and self-containment, of identity, in which "I" am "me." "Hear me! Be yourself again!" are the words of the voice that the Unnamable experiences as coming from a distance and thus mourning the impossibility of its return to the state of self-presence and immediacy. Yet the "I" does not give up easily; it will use prosthesis if needed—the telephone line—to close the circuit. To no avail: "I could employ fifty wretches for this sinister operation and still be short of a fifty-first, to close the circuit." And, "there might be a hundred of us and still we'd lack the hundred and first, we'll always be short of me." Unable to close the circuit, not even by prosthesis, the Unnamable is doomed to end up "squirming forever at the end of the line."

This impossibility of "closing the circuit" testifying to the intransigent pursuit of difference marks the radicality of the Unnamable, which even Derrida, despite being guided by similar insights, cannot afford: Derrida needs both identity and difference to assure the minimal stability of his argument. His demonstration that, in Husserl, hearing-oneself-speak in solitary speech requires the exclusion of difference[36] does not mean that, since it is impossible to radically exclude this difference, we cannot let ourselves be guided by the opposed notions of presence or identity. To believe that auto-affection comes full circle is to idealize its movement, to make a circle from what is almost a circle, but this idealization is necessary. In the transmission of meaning from consciousness to itself (the situation of "solitary speech"), the place of the "return" of meaning will necessarily be different from the place of "departure" (in time if not in space). Consequently, the transmission never comes full circle. Yet the movement posed therein must remain recognizable as circular so as to hold a minimal identity. The different must appear as the same. The ambition to produce a *proteiform* discourse that would dispense with the minimal requirements of identity, even an identity that is prosthetically established (via a detour, by letting an other speak, a provisional and partial identification), is not one to which Derrida is able to commit himself unreservedly. (At the end of the day he remains, unlike Beckett, a philosopher, and so is ultimately constrained in the extent to which he feels able to experiment.)

Not only does the Unnamable not succeed in excluding the difference, required to hear oneself speak, but stronger even, the difference succeeds in excluding (almost) everything else. In a sense this is the novel's strength: the movement of difference is the necessary condition of all experience and thus of thought, speech, writing. Without this movement, the "I" would know, think, and say nothing. From the moment the "I" has started to experience, it has left behind the position of identity. What happens when the differential movement is excluded can be seen in the example of Worm. Worm is one of the Unnamable's avatars, although even this fact is not left uncontested: "[I]f I were Worm I wouldn't know it, I wouldn't say it, I wouldn't say anything. I'd be Worm."[37] Worm is one of the two main incarnations of the "I" in *The Unnamable*. Let us have a closer look at them.

The voice, which guides us through *The Unnamable*, is most often attributed to either Mahood or Worm. It is between them that the "I" shifts, in its vain attempt to establish its own identity. "[I]f I am Mahood, I am Worm too" (340). Both names are meaningful for Beckett's project of questioning the conditions of the possibility of the subject.

"Mahood" is the embodiment of the gesture of substantialization that produces the subject, subject as substance, "my selfhood," or "minehood." (The suffix "hood," added after the substantive, indicates the essence of the former substantive: the motherhood as the essence of mother, manhood as the essence of man. Thus, "Mahood" might denote the essence both of man and of my[self].) Mahood, contemplating "truth," "time," and "identity," is "*me whom they have reduced to reason*" (340, emphasis mine). Mahood's first name, Basil, evokes "base" or "basis"—that is, that which underlies or supports, like "sub-stance" or "sub-ject." In other words, it is the cognitive subject, and it is possibly more powerful than just the Cartesian *ego cogito*. Through the association with the Hegelian "Meinung," Mahood's "minehood" and his "time-abolishing joys of impersonal and disinterested speculation"[38] point the way to the absolute, totalizing speculation of the *Phenomenology of Spirit*.

The Worm is the opposite of Mahood. It is a nonreflective, silent "body" (Badiou calls it "le corps idiot")[39]—a living, spatially extended thing. I suggest that one read the name "Worm" as a calque, a loan translation from the Latin *ubi sum*, since it sounds like the "where'm" in "where'm I?" fashioned after the quest for the self, whose existence the Worm places in doubt.

Yes, let us call that thing Worm, so as to exclaim, the sleight of hand accomplished, Oh look, life again, life everywhere and always, the life that's on every tongue, the only possible! Poor Worm, who thought he was different, there he is in the madhouse for life. *Where am I?* That's my first question, after an age of listening.[40]

Taking into consideration Beckett's fascination with homonyms (in this case, homophones), Worm (*where'm, ubi sum*) is the name of the singular place that could hold something of a self-identity, the place without reflection, without difference: a "where I am" without an "I." "Where?" is the first word of *The Unnamable*, the text that prepares and questions the arrival of the Worm. In this sense, the novel can be read as an attempted passage from "where" to "where am," from just any place to the place where subjectivity originates. "[O]ne day I simply stayed in, in where, instead of going out, in the old way, out to spend day and night as far away as possible, it wasn't far. Perhaps that is how it began" (293). "[I]f I were Worm I wouldn't know it, I wouldn't say it, I wouldn't say anything. I'd be Worm" (350). In other words, "if I were the unmediated 'where I am' (without the mediation of the 'I') I wouldn't know it, I wouldn't say it, I wouldn't say anything. I'd be where I am." Worm is thus the pure identity of a substance in space, incapable of reflection or communication. It cannot attain the position of the subject for it is not capable of being aware of itself (a minimum of difference would be necessary for this). It is for this reason that we read in *The Unnamable* that the Worm cannot get born: "Mahood I couldn't die. Worm will I ever get born? It's the same problem" (355).

The problem with Mahood's speculative constitution is not that he cannot return to himself, but that in the infinite movement of self-reflection he returns to himself absolutely and eternally, which makes him unable to stop speaking—that is, "die." The Worm does not relate to itself at all. It thereby renounces from the beginning any possibility, however remote, of becoming aware of itself and thus getting "born." These two figures are actually, therefore, two sides of the same coin—the coin of self-reflection. But this is not where the story ends.

130   *The Subject*

Piercing the Subjectile

Appearing as both all and none of its avatars, the Unnamable reveals itself as the constitutive difference that makes them possible: the "between." (We will see that this too is a temporary identification.)

[A]n outside and an inside and me in the middle, perhaps that's what I am, the thing that divides the world in two, on the one side the outside, on the other the inside, that can be as thin as foil, I'm neither one side nor the other, I'm in the middle, I'm the partition, I've two surfaces and no thickness, perhaps that's what I feel, myself vibrating, I'm the tympanum, on the one hand the mind on the other the world, I don't belong to either, it's not to me they're talking, it's not of me they're talking. (386)

The "I" speaks about itself as a "partition" with "no thickness," "thin as foil" (all those words belong, and not accidentally, to the semantic field to which Derrida repeatedly takes recourse; think, for example, of the tinfoil, the "tain" of the "mirror," in *Psyché*,[41] and also the hymen, the "between" [*entre*], the tympanon). In addition, for Beckett, the hymen and the tympanon are substitutable "partitions": *Molloy* (the first part of *The Trilogy* that ends with *The Unnamable*) examines the possibility of "conceiving through the ear." This "partition" is neither the "mind" nor the "world," neither the subject nor the object, neither Mahood nor Worm, and does not "belong to either" (because it is constitutive of them). It can be placed everywhere. The "subjectile"—the word used by both Artaud and Derrida in a text on Artaud[42]—means precisely this: a universal partition. The latter text will turn out to be helpful in our reading of *The Unnamable*. For, indeed, via his reading of Artaud, there is a sense in which Derrida might be said to be reading Beckett.[43]

The subjectile is . . . not a subject . . . nor is it the object either, . . . nothing . . . but a solidified interval *between* above and below, visible and invisible, before and behind, this side and that.[44]

The subjectile is "unnamable," we cannot say what it is; moreover, Derrida rightly poses the question whether "the question of 'what' ha[s] any meaning for what is *between* this or that, *whatever it is?*"[45] There are nonetheless things to be said about this partition. "[M]yself vibrating, I'm the tympanum"; the Unnamable appears to be a "membrane," which seems to bring us closer to the hypothesis that the Unnamable is indeed the "subjectile."[46]

Being neither the subject nor the object, the "partition" does, however, address certain effects of subjectivity. It functions as the intermediary between the subject and the object in a way similar to the functioning of language in verbal expression or the functioning of the canvas (or any other sort of surface) in drawing or painting.[47] It is the ground, the "support" for the work—or (although this term does not appear in the text on Artaud) what Derrida would call the "signature." The subjectile so understood is not a work yet; the latter has to be produced by "perforating" the subjectile (also a word that Beckett and Derrida share).[48] As Derrida puts it, the "singularity of the event made work" has to be marked in the "body" of the "subjectilian wall."[49] As the "neutral" "support of a representation," the subjectile must be "traversed, pierced, penetrated in order to have done with the screen, that is, the inert support of representation."[50]

If it is the case that the subjectile is merely a neutral surface, waiting to be pierced by the (subject's) signature, the hypothesis that the Unnamable "I" is the "partition" appears now to be insufficiently precise; rather, the Unnamable is that which must penetrate the partition. Indeed, the whole adjacent rhetoric of the "violent obstetrics"—"difficult birth," "forceps," etc. (Derrida on Artaud)[51] (as well as the vocabulary of the "marriage" that is the hymen, be it with a characteristically Beckettian impotent bent)—is pervasive in all of Beckett's work of that period.[52] It seems at first as if exactly this, a perforation, is going to take place in *The Unnamable*. The "I" fantasizes that its membrane is going to be pierced, that it will get an opening, a mouth:

I have no mouth . . . I'll grow one, a little hole at first, then wider and wider, deeper and deeper, the air will gush into me, and out a second later, howling.[53]

But then a doubt enters the picture: "but is it not rather too much to ask, . . . is it really politic?" (387). This does not mean that the project is abandoned but that it begins to reveal itself as impossible for "substantial" reasons: toward the end of *The Unnamable,* the membrane of representation turns out to be significantly transformed, into a solid ("wooden," in fact) "door" that remains "bolted" and thus cannot be "traversed or penetrated."

"It's the door that interests me, a wooden door, who bolted the door," says the Unnamable in a hilarious story that, as we shall see, only appears to stand in no connection to the rest of the discourse.[54] Significantly, this story begins with a "marriage"—that is, with a "hymen"—and ends with an impenetrable "wooden door." However, the story, or rather the door in it ("it's the door that interests me"), is more than just an intermezzo; the motif of the door so introduced will guide the rest of the novel. A few sentences further, the Unnamable compares words to doors:

> I use them all, all the words they showed me, there were columns of them, ... they were on the lists, with images opposite, I must have forgotten them, ... these nameless images ... these imageless names, these windows I should perhaps rather call doors. (411)

There is a continuity between the story and the rest of the Unnamable's discourse. After telling the story in which the house doors are bolted after a man has hanged himself inside ("when she got back from the station she found the house-door bolted, who bolted it, he the better to hang himself or the mother-in-law the better to take him down" [411]), the story-telling "I" reasons further as the hangman. In this role, he says, "find the door, find the axe, perhaps it's a cord, for the neck, for the throat ... perhaps it's a drop, find the door, open the door, drop, into the silence, it won't be I" (416). These are the final pages of the novel, with the Unnamable's pursuit becoming more and more urgent, and the door motif returns here with rhythmical precision. It opens "to have them [i.e., "the words that remain"] carry me into my story, ... through the door, into the silence," and continues insistently: "perhaps it's the door" "perhaps I'm at the door" "it's I now at the door" "what door, what's a door doing here?" (All of these citations are taken from page 418, the last of the book, where Beckett writes: "it's the last words.") The closing statement runs:

> perhaps they have said me already, perhaps they [i.e., "the words that remain"] have carried me to the threshold of my story, before the door that opens on my story, that would surprise me, if it opens, it will be I . . . I can't go on, I'll go on.

That it was not possible to traverse the subjectilian wall must be the conclusion of this reading. The surface of the canvas (of language) did not give way. The door remained bolted. In Derridean terms, this is to say that the subjectile has not been marked by the "singularity of the event made work." We witness a confession of failure at the end of *The Unnamable* that says something like "I have not marked the subjectilian wall. I have left no signature" (but also a proof of courage: "I'll go on"). Whose confession is it? Did Beckett doubt his ability to "perforate language"? That this had once been his ambition is unquestionable:

> To bore one hole after another in [language], until what lurks behind it—be it something or nothing—begins to seep through; I cannot imagine a higher goal for a writer today.⁵⁵

Beckett is known to have given up this idea with time. We might conclude from this that the last words of *The Unnamable* pronounce a verdict on the novel itself: *The Unnamable* is a failure because it is unable to become what Derrida calls the "singular signature" of the author. However, whether this conclusion is construed as a case of unaccountable modesty or a firm persuasion about the nature of representation, the story of Beckett's interest in the subject, subjectile, or subjective effects has not thereby come to its end. It remained an issue that occupied Beckett for the rest of his life and yielded quite different linguistic experiments, not least in his last prose work, *Worstward Ho*.

The reading of *The Unnamable* as the expression of the failure to leave a personal signature on the surface of the novel's language has one notable consequence. When Derrida says that for him "the great question is always the question who," the question matters to him because without it we could not address the issues of responsibility: "responsibility cannot be other than the responsibility *of someone*,"[56] and responsibility is a matter of signature. The "risk of irresponsibility in literature"[57] lies precisely here:

> Literature may call for the highest responsibility but it is also a possibility of the worst betrayal . . . and dispossession. . . . Fundamentally, it's not me who signs, from the moment it has been launched on the literary market it no longer comes from me.[58]

What happens to responsibility in *The Unnamable*? In what way can the subjectile without a signature be responsible?

Gathering and Responsibility

To address this issue, we must turn to an analysis of responsibility in Paul Ricoeur's *Time and Narrative*, a work that reserves a special place for Beckett's oeuvre to the extent that Beckett's name stands for the limit case of Ricoeur's argument. Beckett's work functions there as the counterexample that must somehow be refuted or neutralized for Ricoeur's argument to remain valid.

Let us retrace the relevant part of Ricoeur's reasoning. As a part of its overall project of demonstrating that the configuration of time by a (fictional) narrative permits a better understanding of temporality, the second volume of *Time and Narrative* is devoted to substantiating the claim that every narrative relies on some minimal formal principle of configuration (the quasi-plot, the quasi-event, and the quasi-character).

[T]he modern novel teaches us to extend the notion of an imitated or represented action to the point where we can say that a *formal* principle of composition governs the series of changes affecting beings similar to us—be they individual or collective, the bearers of a proper name as in the nineteenth-century novel, or just designated by an initial (K) as in Kafka, or even, at the limit, unnamable as in Beckett.[59]

Similarly, when—in the conclusion to the three-volume work as a whole—Ricoeur returns to this claim, insisting on "the persistence of *the same formal principle of configuration even in those forms of composition of the novel apparently most inclined towards schism*" (3:242, my emphasis), it is enough to return to the pages of the second volume of *Time and Narrative* to realize that in the above passage Ricoeur is referring specifically to Beckett as the author whose works most powerfully challenge every possible formal principle of configuration. Whereas "for the older forms of modernism" (Pound, Yeats, Eliot, Joyce), Ricoeur argues (relying on Kermode) that "the past remains a source of order, even when it is rallied against and decried," for the newer, "schismatic" form of literature, "order itself is what must be denied." Samuel Beckett's work is here invoked to "illustrate" this "shift towards schism." Beckett is "the perverse theologian of a world which has suffered a Fall, experienced an Incarnation which changes all relations of past, present, and future, but which will not be redeemed."

Ricoeur turns this apparent problem in favor of his argument by concluding: "in this respect, Beckett preserves an ironic and parodic tie to Christian paradigms, whose order, even when inverted through the author's irony, preserves its intelligibility," and (Ricoeur cites Kermode again) "whatever preserves intelligibility is what prevents schism."[60]

In other words, according to Ricoeur, no work of fiction has been able to dispense with the tie to the paradigm of a quasi-plot. Even when we think that it is not there, it is, merely because of its "ironic or parodic" form that nonetheless continues to function as a paradigm itself (for example, the "parodic tie to Christian paradigms" in Beckett). On the one hand, it is difficult to disagree with Ricoeur; what he is saying here is actually the quite common observation that there cannot be a schism unrelated to what preceded it. On the other hand, we should perhaps be vigilant, given both Kermode's warning that Beckett's schism was not ordinary but "perverse" and his insistence that Beckett's world "will not be redeemed."

This view presents us with two related problems: the problem of the validity of Ricoeur's interpretation of Beckett, and the problem of the conclusions attached to this interpretation. Let us have a look at the interpretation first.

In including, even in a marginalized way, *The Unnamable* in his set of literary examples, Ricoeur seems to suggest that it is possible to establish a self on the basis of the Unnamable's monologue (for the moment, I am leaving the questions regarding what Ricoeur will later call "*ipseity*" aside).[61] One way of forming an identity when we have only a "perverse" narrative like that of the Unnamable is, according to Ricoeur, by recourse to psychoanalysis (especially to the so-called re-working—Freudian *Durcharbeitung*—of "case histories"). The goal of this recourse would be to "substitute for the bits and pieces of stories that are unintelligible as well as unbearable, a coherent and acceptable story, in which the analysand can recognize his or her constancy."[62] The Unnamable can hardly be said to be unprepared for this suggestion:

> [I]t's all part of the same old irresistible baloney, namely, But my dear man, come, be reasonable, look, this is you, look at this photograph, and here's your file, no convictions, I assure you, come now, make an effort, at your age, to have no identity, it's a scandal, I assure you, look at this photograph, what, you see nothing. At your age, no human shape, the pity of it, look, here's the photograph, you'll see, you'll be all right, what does it amount to, after all, a painful moment, on the surface, then peace, underneath, it's the only way, believe me, the only way out.[63]

The Unnamable clearly describes the prospect of substituting something "coherent" and "acceptable" for that which is "unintelligible" and "unbearable" as an assault on himself: "I too have the right to be shown impossible" (379). It should be noted that what the Unnamable sees as its "right" is not merely to *be* impossible but also to be shown as such. Its impossibility should not be redeemed by the organizing function of mimesis. A sense of identity can hardly be derived from an existence that takes place in different frequencies, or in different temporal dimensions, switching at random from one to another: "Mahood is silent, that is to say his voice continues but is no longer renewed" (327). Furthermore, Ricoeur's suggestion that dates or historical evidence allows us to correct our narratives finds a response in the Unnamable's discourse: "[t]hat's one of Mahood's favorite tricks, to produce ostensibly independent testimony in support of my historical existence" (321). The novel is precisely about that which resists the ambitions of coherence and acceptability (but which, as the subjectile, as the originary difference, indeed stands at the basis of such notions).

The Ricoeur of *Time and Narrative* does not fail to recognize that "narrative identity is not a stable and seamless identity."[64] Nonetheless, his use of the term "identity" (as in "narrative identity") must have led to the objection that the Unnamable, in its struggle to be "shown impossible," is perhaps not really a "being similar to us." It is perhaps for this reason that in the subsequently published *Oneself as Another*, Ricoeur felt the need to clarify his argument by emphasizing the distinction between ipse- and idem-identity (or selfhood and identity, or self-constancy and "character") and by dividing the narrative identity into one of "character" (where ipse and idem are coextensive) and one of "self-constancy" (where they are separate). Of the two, only the second would be identity in the traditional sense of an "unchanging core of the personality."[65]

However, the importance of the decision about whether or not we can find "narrative identity" in Beckett lies somewhere else: to his thesis about the prevalence of a formal principle of configuration in all narratives, Ricoeur attaches certain conclusions regarding the way we make ethical decisions. For among the conclusions of *Time and Narrative* we find the claim that by narrating one's own life (rather than by mere self-reflection) one produces one's (narrative) identity and that this identity so defined enables us to make ethical decisions. According to Ricoeur, one's life-narrative functions not only as the matrix of identity but also as the starting point and the ground in any moment of choice. In making decisions, we remain faithful to our narratives in accordance with what Ricoeur calls "self-constancy."

Even if we assume that we can speak of a minimal narrative identity of the Unnamable, the question remains as to what extent we can link this claim (about narrative identity in Beckett's work and in literary works in general) to ethical considerations. Furthermore, an argument that the reading of the Unnamable as the subjectile provides such a formal principle of identity would be unjustified, since the subjectile is said to be precisely that which resists the idea of identity.

Ricoeur's claim that "reading also includes a moment of impetus"[66]—that is, a moment of gathering together all past experience and making a decision: "here I stand"[67]—is coextensive with Derrida's understanding of the signature as that which gathers (albeit always provisionally, never absolutely) and which tends to indicate its signatory as the one who is responsible. (For Derrida, the signature calls the signatory to his responsibility.) It is not a matter of choosing between the conception of an ethical decision as (1) a discrete event that depends solely on a singular sensibility to a singular case and (2) one that somehow issues from the self's reworking its narrative history (in a gathering gesture). Rather, it is both. In other words, whether or not we think that an ethical decision presupposes a subject who constitutes himself through gathering (archiving), the decision itself—iterable as every event—multiplies itself in its iterability and gathers its own iterations. There can be no genuine decision without this kind of hermeneutic operation of sorts, which Derrida calls the "signature."

If decision presupposes gathering, then literature, understood as gathering, is also a relevant field for addressing the issues of ethical decision—but in a sense different from Ricoeur's. As opposed to Ricoeur's "moment of impetus," which becomes the source of the responsible self, Derrida's "signature" is not responsible in a straightforward way. It involves writing, with all its consequences: death, disappropriation, and irresponsibility, among others.

My signature is the moment of highest responsibility in a deep irresponsibility.... usually interpreted as one's very own mark, it is instead what I cannot appropriate, cannot make my own.[68]

In literature as "hyper-totalizing," everything and more—"everything plus n"—can be gathered. At stake is always literature's overflowing, exceeding the totality. In this sense, analogously to the notion of "hyper-totalizing," Derrida says that literature is "hyper-responsible":

I insist in general on the possibility of "saying everything" as a prerogative granted to literature in principle, not in order to emphasize the irresponsibility of the writer, of whoever signs literature but his *hyper-responsibility*, that is the fact that his responsibility is not responsible to the already constituted instances.[69]

In other words, the responsibility of literature, entering the scene "before the law," consists in being responsible to the instances that are not yet there but only remain to be set up. This can be read in a double way: literature is responsible to the laws that it itself creates and constantly modifies; but in a more general sense, literature is responsible to the law of the future that is constantly deferred, its role being one of an unappeasable critique. In the latter sense, literature's role is coextensive—and Derrida never fails to underline this—with that of democracy (a democracy that is also constantly deferred as the "democracy to come" in the double sense of *avenir* and *à venir*, "always still to come"):

[T]he institution of literature in the West, in its relatively modern form, is linked to an authorization to say everything, and doubtless too to the coming about of the modern idea of democracy . . . , it seems inseparable to me from what calls forth a democracy.[70]

Entrusting the future to this "authorization to say everything"— common to Derrida's thinking of literature and democracy—means living "in a promise" that is not free of risks. To expect responsibility from literature without accepting its prerogative of possibly deceiving us in the worst way (*la pire trahison*) would be to limit its critical function. In order to respond to the law that is not yet constituted, literature must be able to "say everything" (*tout dire*), not only in the sense of freedom of speech required by the institution of democracy but also in the sense of hyper-totalizing (and "hyper" also means "beyond"), of exhausting the resources of what can and cannot be said. The hyper-responsibility of which Derrida speaks in referring to literature, as well as the gesture of hyper-totalizing, can only take place as the gesture that never ceases to be iterated: one must go on saying everything. It is only in this sense that we can speak of responsibility in Beckett's *Unnamable:* "I can't go on I'll go on."[71]

In this chapter, I have tried to show that there is a sense in which Derrida and Beckett alike destabilize the notion of the subject in order to address that unnamable difference (the subjectile as language or as other surface that must be pierced), which is constitutive of the subject. However, whereas Derrida believes that it is possible to revive the subjectile that is "neutral" and "without life"[72] by perforating it with a singular event of the signature, the Beckett of *The Unnamable* does not allow for any such possibility.

This reading demonstrates how extraordinarily close the discourses of Derrida and Beckett can be, and how true it is when Derrida says that Beckett is almost "too close" for him to be able to respond to. On the other hand, it has reinforced my initial presupposition that Beckett and Derrida differ significantly on the issue of singularity (the signature, the date, the singular event—these are all the things that Beckett contests) and that, were Derrida ever to read Beckett, he could not circumvent this issue. Since Derrida's readings often consist in showing a blind spot in a literary work, such a reading would perhaps have to demonstrate that the hidden effects of the signature, denied by Beckett, are nevertheless haunting Beckett's work.

6

Singular Points of Transaction (II): "What Are Poets For?" The Authority of Literature

The Iterated Authority in *Molloy*

We have seen that on Derrida's account, in the singular literary work, archiving and critique occur in one and the same gesture. The singular marks gathered in a work obey (i.e., organize themselves according to) the singular law that they produce themselves. To employ the words of Derrida's essay "Force of Law," each of those events is potentially an "ungraspable revolutionary instant" that produces a law by "inscrib(ing) iterability in originarity, in unicity and singularity."[1] "Force of Law," Derrida's rereading of Benjamin's *Zur Kritik der Gewalt*, explores the grounds of legal and state authority, rather than of literature. (Benjamin's *Gewalt* can be rendered as "authority," but also as "force" and "violence.")[2] Yet by repeatedly referring here to his earlier essay on Kafka and literature,[3] Derrida invites an analogy between his analysis of the authority of the law and that of a literary work. One of Benjamin's findings in *Zur Kritik der Gewalt* is that it is impossible to distinguish clearly between instances of law-making violence (*rechtsetzende Gewalt*) and law-preserving violence (*reschtserhaltende Gewalt*). Benjamin finds it difficult to accept this. (He needs to arrive at an unalloyed phenomenon of law-making violence—which has, in his eyes, a more originary and singular relationship to justice than its law-preserving counterpart—in order to be able to determine its relation to that which is beyond the law and violence, namely justice. Only by doing this does he feel entitled to draw a distinction between the just and the unjust law, as well as between the just and the unjust force.) While Benjamin searches for further criteria of justice in the distinction between mythical and divine violence, Derrida takes the inseparability of law-making violence from its law-preserving counterpart to confirm his own conviction about the necessary repetition, or iterability, of every foundation (including, therefore, the ground of law).

In the framework of that reading, every element of a literary text—while, in principle, conforming to one particular interpretation of the text—may be seen as opening a series that will give rise to a new law, a subversive interpretation. The same counts for the status of the literary work as such with respect to the institution of literature: a subversive work of literature enters the literary institution in an act of institutive, law-making violence. This act cannot be absolutely singular; the violence committed must be iterable (i.e., law preserving and not just law making) to be able to sustain itself. At stake here is the question of the authority of both the existing law and the subversive moment that overthrows that law and produces its own: What is it that gives the subversive literary work its "right" to enter into and modify the literary institution?

The institutive, revolutionary violence cannot be entirely distinguished from the conserving, law-preserving violence, which enforces the former in a gesture of repetition. In the end, the distinction between a singular break with tradition and a gesture of conforming to that tradition is difficult to make, since they both share the effects of iterability:

Rigorously speaking, iterability precludes the possibility of pure and great founders, initiators, lawmakers—including "great" poets.[4]

The authority of the law (and the ground of the claim a literary work can make on the community of readers) cannot thereby be sought in the moment of its origin (*Setzung*). Yet Derrida does not conclude from this that authority is in any straightforward way unfounded. On the contrary, in his essay on Benjamin, Derrida pursues what he, following Montaigne and Pascal, calls "the mystical foundation of authority."[5] "Mystical" means "neither apparent to the senses nor obvious to the intelligence"[6]—hence, neither (purely) sensible nor (purely) intelligible. While the expression appears in a discourse on the revolutionary *coup de force* that initiates a new law, its definition is just as relevant for the phenomenality of a subversive literary work.

No justificatory discourse could or should insure the role of metalanguage in relation to the performativity of institutive language.... Here the discourse comes up against its limit: in itself, in its performative power itself. It is what I here propose to call the mystical. Here a silence is walled up in the violent structure of the founding act. Walled up, walled in because silence is not exterior to language.[7]

The analogy with Derrida's discourse on literature is here quite clear; whereas in the "institutive language" of revolution "the discourse comes up against its limit," the subversive works of literature "make the limits of our language tremble." With respect to Beckett's "institutive language,"[8] Derrida hereby declares "metalanguage" to be just as powerless as it would be in the face of, for example, any general strike. But, more significantly, the fragment quoted above indicates what for Derrida functions as the "mystical foundation of authority": a "silence ... walled up in language," the spacing of originary language—in other words, what Derrida elsewhere calls *différance*. This original division of any singular moment precludes the possibility of any pure origin, but at the same time, in virtue of the same self-reproductive division, a law-making movement of iteration is put in motion. The latter allows the non-originary beginning to repeat itself and, in this way, to set up its own authority. In other words, authority is an effect of the impossibility of its own pure origin.

The main interest guiding Derrida's examination of the "mystical foundation of authority" is, as he repeatedly states, his interest in "power" or "force." But it should be clear by now that when referring to "power" and "force," just as when using the term *Gewalt*, Derrida returns to the question of différence ("*différance* is a force *différée-différante*").[9] The phenomenon of *Gewalt* is in the end always a function of a differential and formalizing force, the gathering force that is at the same time the force of law.[10] So understood, difference is for Derrida the "origin" of (i.e., that which is presupposed by) every phenomenality. When we keep in mind the almost tautological relation between "force" and phenomenon ("by its very articulation force becomes a phenomenon"),[11] Derrida's interest in "the force of the event" of a singular literary work turns out to be at the same time an interest in the phenomenality of the literary work—or, rather, in the deferral of its phenomenality (*force différée*). The authority of both law and literature is directly linked to their deferred phenomenality.

Just as "the Law" in Kafka's parable is always deferred, so the "force" of the work is never present as such. But this deferral is at the same time a condition of its authority. Analogously to the man from the country who aspires to be admitted to the law, the literary text that we attempt to enter in reading defers the phenomenality (of both the referent and the meaning) of what it promises, urging us instead to go on reading. In this way, the deferred phenomenality—the deferred foundation—of authority produces effects of responsiveness and responsibility.

It is because of this deferral that we can speak of the responsibility of the man from the country—and of the reader. If the law were something immediately present and given as such, there would be no need for responsibility. The latter presupposes distance. Living "in the presence of law" would paradoxically mean parting with responsibility. The greater the possibility of irresponsibility (in the situation of the deferral of the law as much as in the situation of the deferral of meaning), the greater the need for the ability to be responsive. In demanding responsiveness (deciphering, interpretation) even at the risk of the worst betrayal ("la pire trahison"),[12] literature calls for something that resembles the highest degree of responsibility ("hyper-responsabilité").[13]

If indeed it is the case that the work of literature can be seen as the singular producing its own law (by gathering its iterations), then we come to a certain conclusion about the production of authority in the literary work: the work comes to appear to us as a literary phenomenon by repeatedly eliciting affirmation or responsiveness. While all texts may be said to demand a response from us, the texts that "make the limits of our language tremble" demand a "hyper-responsibility," in view of the absence in them of any immediately recognizable grounds or laws to which we might respond. This hyper-responsibility requires a response that generates its own grounding principle. Having shown how the iterations of the always already divided singular produce effects of authority in literature, I now turn to reexamine the effects of authority in Beckett's work. In Chapter 1 I argued that the task of the gathering of the singular in Beckett seems to be subordinated to, and even overridden by, issues of authority. I suggested that since the archiving aspect of literature both presupposes and clouds the relation of power, destroying or overlooking the archive permits one to emphasize what is under scrutiny, precisely, authority—or, in other words, phenomenality, the subversive literary work's coming to appear as such.

Beckett's novel *Molloy*, in which the mysterious Youdi summons his "agent," Jacques Moran, to set out on a journey in search of the tramp

Molloy, can be read as a novel about writing and authority. In the first part of the novel, the wandering of the tramp Molloy brings the (representatives of the) law to a state of exasperation. This provides the background for the setting of part 2, in which Youdi (through the messenger Gaber) orders "agent" Moran to find Molloy and write "a report."[14] I suggest reading this novel as a playful allegory—a pastiche on the medieval parable, where the characters are the personifications of agencies involved in the process of writing. Molloy is the recalcitrant presence of the sensible that has to be captured in language; Youdi is the source of the obligation to write; Gaber is a transmitter of Youdi's absolute authority. Moran is (initially) the blind force charged with the execution of orders that Blanchot calls the "hand holding a pencil."[15]

In each case of its utterance, Youdi's name—glossed by Martha Nussbaum as a conjunction of "you" and "die"[16]—makes an announcement that, while being equally true of whomever it addresses, nonetheless singles out whomever it addresses. Hence it is both singular and universal. "You die" (cast back at Moran by Gaber "*with corpse fidelity* to the letter of [Youdi's] message")[17]—this is where Moran's duty to find Molloy and to write a report comes from. The transcendental relationship between death and writing seems here to be both phenomenological and existential-ontological. On the one hand, the death of the author (understood as his necessary separation from the effects of his work) is always presupposed as a necessary possibility of writing (as has been argued by Foucault, Blanchot, and Derrida, among others). This necessary possibility forms a part of the intentional attitude of the author to his work. On the other hand, the necessity to face one's own mortality is (as in Heidegger's *Sein und Zeit*) also at the source of responsibility, of the "ought," here in the sense of the obligation to write. Derrida indicates death and finitude as a source of responsibility and writing (writing understood as assuming one's responsibility) in very similar terms:

> I keep recommencing the same story differently. . . . Each time I take the responsibility I can. For this injunction to discontinue would be nothing but an arrest of death. . . . This is what causes one to write, it is this which both makes possible and threatens everything.[18]

This reading of Youdi's name as the singularizing authoritative moment can be extended in an analysis of the role of the messenger Gaber (who

The Authority of Literature   145

transmits the orders issued by Youdi). Gaber's function, similar to that of the doorkeeper in Kafka's "Before the Law," is to stand in the opening of the unique door of responsibility "meant only for you,"[19] with the difference that Gaber actually comes to Moran instead of just waiting to receive him. It has been repeatedly pointed out that Gaber may mean the "giver" (taking into account the possibly German provenance of the name) and that his name bears resemblance to that of the archangel Gabriel (the carrier of annunciation, who, as Moran stipulates, made Mary "conceive through the ear"). In both senses, Gaber's name might suggest that he brings some God-like inspiration, with writing as the moment of conception.[20] However, there is a shift in emphasis here with respect to what writing is: what Gaber brings is not so much any content ("inspiration") as a mere obligation (he does not bring anything except an order, a demand). "I was looking for what was wanting to make Gaber's statement complete. I felt he must have told me what to do with Molloy once he was found."[21] In the text, Gaber, "the giver of death," is that authoritative instance (whose force is sustained by the highest authority of Youdi) that both initiates and completes the process of writing: Gaber's appearances are the punctual encounters with death that gather the novel and give it form. If Moran is the "hand holding a pencil," described by Blanchot in his passage on "Tyrannical Prehension,"[22] then Gaber is the other hand. Moran, just like "the hand holding the pencil" that cannot let go because it is not really in control, will compulsively continue his pointless wandering until he is ordered to stop. In his function of the Blanchotian *arrêt de mort*,[23] Gaber not only made Moran set out on his journey but also, in the end, summons him to give up his search. The full entry in Gaber's notebook on that visit reads: "Moran, Jacques, home, instanter." Like all other entries, this one reiterates Youdi's order, namely for Moran to return home immediately, yet the repetition has a singular effect here. On an earlier occasion we are told that Youdi uses the prophetic present. In other words, his utterances function in two tenses simultaneously: the future and the present merged into one. If this is the case, then the phrase "Moran, Jacques, home, instanter" can be read in two ways: not only as an order to be realized in the future but also as a present-tense description. We must not forget that the first time Gaber utters those words is in response to Moran's question: "you recognize me?" The answer sounds like an entry in a census record (last and first name, address, profession) and therefore has an automatic token of recognition: "Moran, Jacques, home, instanter." If this reading is plausible, then Moran is not only an "agent"—the "hand holding a pencil"—but also someone with the curious profession of "instanter"— the performer of instants, of singular moments or raptures, that are at the same time instances (in the sense of "institutions") of law. This is the essential characteristic of the writer, and Moran, despite his protests ("it is not at this late stage of my relation that I intend to give way to literature"), became one.[24]

Gaber is the giver of death. We might call it Beckett's reference *avant la lettre* to Derrida's *Gift of Death,* an essay on (among other things) the story of Jahweh, Abraham, and Isaac.[25] It has been observed that the figures of Youdi, Moran, and his son mimic the Old Testament story and evoke the same motif of paternal authority.[26] But as usual with Beckett's works, the interpretative gestures of identification between characters are at best approximate (quite in agreement with Beckett's well-known warning that "the danger is in the neatness of identifications"). For if indeed Gaber, bringing the message from Youdi, is the "giver of death," then Moran, even though to his son he is the authoritarian father (Abraham), is also the one who is to die (Isaac). Moran's own words confirm this: "I was my father and I was my son." Not for nothing the son's name is identical to the father's name: Jacques Moran.[27] When we take into account that the couple of Abraham and Isaac is the paradigmatic father and son couple for both the Old and the New Testaments, both the superior authority of Youdi and the minor characters like that of Moran's son begin looking like iterations of one agency. They all collectively bear responsibility for the report, as a singular authority that keeps iterating itself.

The mirror play between the characters of *Molloy* is put into operation. Here, too, as in Kafka's story, there are two mirrors: a *mise en abyme* and a *contre-abyme*. On the one hand, the figure of Gaber functions as a mirror that reflects to Moran his own mortality. Youdi is then simply a reflection *en abyme* of Moran himself. On the other hand, Moran's report can also be seen as a mirror that reflects and corrupts (*mise en abîme*) the essence of Youdi's order. We expect a report to be truthful, but Moran's is an antitestament because it is false. It is through an interaction of these reflecting and corrupting mirrors that the novel is organized and disorganized at the same time: Gaber's orders gather the whole work, but Moran's failure to obey them corrupts the work to the point of self-cancellation.

The Authority of Literature 147

The report literally vanishes into itself, having been corrupted by Moran's disobedience. It opens up with the words "(i)t is midnight. The rain is beating on the windows,"[28] only to annul itself at the end: "(t)hen I went back into the house and wrote, It is midnight. The rain is beating on the windows. It was not midnight. It was not raining" (176). In this way, the "now" from which Moran speaks—and on which the rest of the narration hinges—effaces itself, and the whole temporal extension of the novel is contracted to this point of self-cancellation. Yet even though it annuls itself as a truthful account of anything, at the same time it marks the birth of fiction, the final overcoming of Moran's earlier declaration of "not intend[ing] to give way to literature" (152). The silent space dividing the true from the fictive resembles the "deferring and deferred" force that functions as the mystical foundation of authority of Beckett's novel.

As so often in Beckett, a chain of authorities is thereby suggested. Moran's confession "I was my father and I was my son" permits us to see in him an embodiment of both God (Youdi's absolute power) and the sacrificial victim.[29] What can be seen from the above reading is that the singular moments of authority in Beckett are always dispersed: both inside the novel (Who is responsible for the report? And to whom?) and outside it. The authoritative characters in Beckett echo one another, Hamm, Moran, and Pozzo, to name but a few. Similarly, the tramps form a chain of iterations: Molloy, Mercier and Camier, Watt, Malone, Vladimir, and Estragon. Authority in Beckett is dispersed most visibly in *How It Is,* where it becomes the authority of an identification number. Here, again, it is this dispersal that seems to produce the effects of authority and responsibility. It is also in this work that we can see most clearly that, paradoxically, the position of the passive victim and of the "tormentor" is substitutable. It is impossible to gather all those iterations conclusively into one singular moment; their role is rather to reinforce each other, producing a kind of punctual—or, as Derrida calls it at another place, "contrapuntal"—force, by way of which Beckett's work affirms its own authority.[30]

Molloy read in this way is a parable; it does not have philosophical pretensions. And yet we might say that it has what Derrida calls a "philosophical *dunamis,*" in that it provokes us "to think phenomenality":[31] it incites a reflection on the phenomenality of the literary medium. What is reflected on is not just the phenomenality of the fictive world given to us by literature but also the phenomenality of the literary medium itself—its law—where the authority of this law is the result of an indefinite iteration.

Badiou on Beckett

Beckett's project of impoverishment can be seen in essence as a phenomenological project; a guiding principle of Beckett's oeuvre ("[c]'était ma chance d'être plus pauvre")[32] echoes the opening words of Husserl's *Cartesian Meditations:* "I have thereby chosen to begin in absolute poverty."[33] This is not the only coincidence that suggests that the impoverishment emanating from Beckett's work is methodical; the phenomenological method would be a perfectly logical next step after Beckett's earlier reflections on Cartesianism. In his reading of Beckett's "testamental" and "recapitulary" text *Worstward Ho*, Alain Badiou proposes reading Beckett's work as an exercise in phenomenological reduction.[34]

Fundamentally, Beckett's method is like Husserl's *épochè* turned upside down. Husserl's *épochè* consists in subtracting the thesis of the world, in subtracting the "there is" in order to turn towards the movement of the pure flux of that interiority which is directed at this "there is." Husserl's lineage originates in Cartesian doubt.... Beckett's method is precisely the opposite: it is a question of subtracting or suspending the subject so as to see what then happens to being.[35]

At first sight this phenomenological point of view seems to permit an easy realignment with the Derridean reading of Beckett and of literature in general. After all, from the very beginning of his career, Derrida repeatedly links his interest in literature to his engagement with phenomenology. Not only does he propose to read Joyce as Husserl *à l'énverse,* but he also plays with the idea of a reading of Husserl upon which "the whole phenomenological enterprise . . . becomes a novel"[36] (it should be noted that Derrida does not succumb to the temptation of such a reading) and reasserts Husserl's own statement that fiction in general is "the vital element of phenomenology" (45/29). However, Badiou—who makes a point of sharply distinguishing his philosophical project from those of the "modern sophists" (including Derrida)—proffers a view of literature that conflicts with Derrida's own.

On Badiou's reading, *The Unnamable*—generally considered to be the apex of Beckett's pursuit of his own signature—is a cul-de-sac in Beckett's work, a solipsistic crisis resulting inevitably from Beckett's earlier Cartesian itinerary. Instead, the major achievement of that work is its subsequently developed focus on "the event" (the latter is not the only term that Badiou's vocabulary confusingly shares with that of Derrida). At first sight, it looks as if Badiou's reading of Beckett would provide precisely what is missing from my reading (namely, an account of the operation of the singular in Beckett) and thereby make possible a full transaction between Beckett and Derrida. However, Badiou's reading presupposes a quite different understanding of the phenomenality and authority of literature.

Rather than being self-reflective, Badiou insists, Beckett's work is primarily focused on naming events and on exploring what Badiou calls "the generic." Prima facie, Badiou's claim that in Beckett—with a lapse in the main *Trilogy*—we encounter a shift toward thematizing the event seems quite plausible. One can see this shift in considering Beckett's works in terms of the questions that they ask. The questions pertaining to the disintegrated human subject posed in the *Unnamable*—"Where now? Who now? When now?"[37]—can be opposed to the event-related questions "What?" "Where?" and "How?"[38] posed in the later works. Yet Badiou's sharp distinction between, on the one hand, the *Trilogy*, which he condemns as an impasse in Beckett's work because it is "folded upon itself" ("plié vers lui même"),[39] and, on the other hand, the remaining works that he praises for "opening onto the other" ("s'ouvre à une altérité . . . la voix de l'autre interrompt le sollipsisme")[40] is not innocuous. This diagnosis has its parallel in the way Badiou sees literature in general and the singular event in particular.

Badiou's thinking about literature begins with poetry, construed by him as the highest form not only of literature but also of art in general.[41] According to him, this perception of poetry is generally held by philosophers: "since Nietzsche, all philosophers claim to be poets, they all envy poets, they are all wishful poets or approximate poets, or acknowledged poets, as we see with Heidegger, but also with Derrida or Lacoue-Labarthe."[42] Poetry as Badiou sees it appears to have two forms, which we might call "self-reflexive" and "nominative." The general objective of poetry is nomination—that is, to capture in language the singularity of the sensible. In the period that Badiou calls the Age of Poets—a period that Badiou loosely associates with the modernist project of self-reflection and that he considers to have been completed with Celan—this objective has been modified. Instead of pursuing the singularity of the sensible, the poem was to capture its own singularity. Thus, in the Age of Poets,

> [t]he singularity that the poem has to account for is in the end the singularity of the poem itself! It is this element of turning back onto itself [*torsion sur soi-même*] of the language's summoning of absolute singularity that will be taken as the singularity by which the poem nourishes itself: from here we get the Mallarmean thesis of a sonnet that does not point at anything else than itself, that is itself an echo of the Flaubertian thesis of a novel about nothing; this is modernity. But this nothing, this void, is nothing else but a void surrounded by a torsion of an artistic object upon itself, a self-reference of a poem to itself.[43]

The self-reflective form of poetry of the Age of Poets is "immediately recognizable as a work of thought."[44] But to conceive poetry in these terms is, according to Badiou, an anachronism: the phenomenon of poetry "recognizable as a work of thought" belongs to the past.[45] (It should be noted that Badiou thereby suggests that Derrida's enterprise, as poetic in nature, also belongs to the Age of Poets.) That poetry of that period appears to be a work of thought is due to the failure of philosophy. "[B]y the absence of free play in philosophy," the writing of the Age of Poets was forced into a position where it had to attempt to replace philosophy, was "sutured to philosophy."[46] Here Badiou reapplies to modernism Lacoue-Labarthe's and Nancy's diagnosis of the origin of romanticism (in a philosophical crisis), but in order to direct it against them. According to Badiou, rather than the first genuine interaction between philosophy and literature, the philosophical dimension of the literary (and, vice versa, the literary dimension of philosophy) must be seen for what it is: a philosophical and literary cul-de-sac, a course that must be abandoned. Badiou reads Celan's work as an "avowal, that poetry no longer suffices to itself; that it requests to be relieved of the burden of the suture; that it hopes for philosophy relieved of the crushing authority of the poem."[47] As Badiou admits, this reading is exactly inverse to Derrida's project, which "pronounces the ineluctable suture of philosophy to its poetic condition." Celan's poetry, Badiou says, wants to be relieved of the burden to reflect on itself. "The most profound sense of his poetic work," Badiou says of Celan, "is to . . . free the poem from its speculative parasites, to restore it to the fraternity of its time, where it will thereafter dwell side by side in thought with the matheme, love and political invention."[48] What Badiou might mean by "free[ing] the poem from its speculative parasites" and "restor[ing] it to the fraternity of its time" can be glimpsed when we consider another passage.

> Everything hinges ... on the sense we give to the encounter between Celan and Heidegger, a quasi-mythical episode of our epoch. Lacoue-Labarthe's argument is that the Jewish poet survivor could not, what? Tolerate? Support? In any case, overlook the fact that the poets' philosopher kept in Celan's presence—and in every presence—the most complete silence about the Extermination. I do not for a second doubt this to be the case. But there is also the fact, and necessarily so, that to go see the philosopher was to experience what the ascent "upward and back" toward the sense of the epoch could expect from him, in the element of the outer-poem. Yet, this philosopher referred to the poem, precisely in such a way as to make the poet feel more alone in his presence than ever before. It has to be seen that Heidegger's question "what are poets for?" can become for the poet "what are philosophers for?" and that if the answer to this question is "for there to be poets," the solitude of the poet is redoubled. Celan's work makes an event of this solitude by asking, from the position of the poem that an end be put to it.[49]

The above fragment seems to suggest that the de-suturing of poetry from philosophy that Badiou pleads for entails more than just that the poem must be released from the task of inquiring about the nature of its own medium—or from thinking tout court (since this task was only a necessity of the Age of Poets). It also means that the philosopher (in this case, Heidegger) owes some answer regarding this issue to the poet. But what is the nature of this answer? Badiou seems to be suggesting here that the essence of Celan's disappointment was that his somewhat idiosyncratic poetic project failed to find its conceptual fulfillment, completion, or closure in Heidegger's response. The de-suturing that Badiou says Celan demands implies not only that philosophy must no longer mistake its role for that of poetry (the latter now taking on the place of one of the four starting points, or "conditions," of philosophy) but also that philosophy is expected to take poetry a step further, toward the reconciliation of poetry's findings with those of what Badiou calls the "fraternal" disciplines.

But that necessarily reduces the role of poetry. No longer, as in the Age of Poets, "burdened" with the philosophical task of thought—that is, with the duty of self-reflection—poetry is left with one remaining task. This task—in Badiou's eyes, the essential task of poetry—is nomination. No longer self-centered, sutured to philosophy, or self-reflective, this poetry is focused on naming the singular event. This naming is one of the conditions of philosophy. On Badiou's reading, naming is necessary for the philosopher, whose "ethical task of thought" is to formalize the laws of the singular. In other words, formalizing the laws of the singular that the poem names is no longer the task of the poem. Instead, the "speculation" from which the poem is "freed" returns to its proper realm, namely, philosophy: "for a philosopher, a certain type of a poem guides or orients the speculation."[50]

Badiou reads Beckett's work as at least in part a poetic enterprise: "ses dernières proses sont plutôt comme l'effet d'un poème latent,"[51] "il s'agit d'une entreprise . . . à demi gagnée par le poème."[52] Yet Badiou refrains from classifying Beckett's work as a phenomenon of the Age of Poets, hence as an exercise of thought that, however valuable and inspiring for philosophers, has lost its fruitfulness and must be considered an anachronism. He also refrains from classifying the work as nomination without the exercise of thought. What is it that saves Beckett from either of those unattractive alternatives? To answer this question, we need to examine Badiou's reading of Beckett in more detail.

Badiou's reading of Beckett focuses on the question of whether—and, if so, in what way—Beckett's work allows room for affirmation of meaning, freedom, or outright happiness. To the widespread perception of Beckett's work as being primarily a reflection on human misery,[53] Badiou's remarkable *L'increvable désir* opposes an image of "another Beckett . . . — one expressive of giving and the happiness of existence."[54] It is a little strange that among Beckett critics, the book has gained a reputation as one that "effectively summarizes ideas about Beckett's output which have been making themselves heard more forcefully over the last decade or so."[55] The originality of Badiou's input in the reception of Beckett, understated by the above comment, lies in his focus on chance (encounters, happenings, occurrences, and events)—in what had previously seemed to be the totally predestined world of Beckett's fiction—and in his thinking affirmation precisely in terms of the affirmation of the aleatory. By dealing with the notions of chance and event, Badiou's book is essential for the understanding of Beckett's attitude toward the unique.

Badiou's starting point is indeed not very new: he evokes the somewhat outdated (but still widespread) reception of Beckett's work as of a nihilist project in which the imagery of bareness, impotence, and destitution is tacitly assumed to represent the human condition. Man's existence is beset by obstacles such that it becomes marked by an overwhelming sense of impossibility. This could be the impossibility of knowledge and meaning at the cognitive level, of justification at the level of values, or of freedom and happiness at the existential level. As long as Beckett's prose is seen as mimetic—that is, aiming at the representation of the actually existing world—such an interpretation is a more or less direct consequence. The indisputable tendency of Beckett's work toward increasing immanence, its focus on inability (for example, the inability to move, to stop speaking, or to die) and on other negative features of the human condition, has facilitated the particularly persistent perception that Beckett is a "painter of misery." (There is an analogy here with the expression "painters of impediment," which Beckett coined for his favorite painters, the brothers van Velde.) This reception was widespread, despite early essays by Bataille and Blanchot (in the 1950s) that demanded we abandon the "humanist" approach to Beckett, as well as Wolfgang Iser's insistence that "Beckett's texts . . . cannot . . . be reduced to the representation of a given reality."[56]

In his *L'increvable desir,* Badiou offers an explanation for this persistence in seeing Beckett as the author whose main aim is to deprive his readers of illusions about human existence. The reason, Badiou claims, is our having confused *cette ascèse méthodique, mise en scène avec un humour tendu et volubile* with "je ne sais quel pathos tragique sur le dénuement et la misère des hommes."[57] In other words, Beckett's method of detraction, negation, and unsaying, so well captured in the title of *Worstward Ho,* has been mistaken for the message. The "real message" of Beckett's work, Badiou argues, is, on the contrary, that of affirmation. On Badiou's account, affirmation is a response to the desire to welcome "tout ce qui arrive,"[58] whether by assigning a sense to it (the hermeneutic approach, characteristic of Beckett's earlier work) or by giving it a name (the poetic approach, roughly starting with *How It Is,* 1961). The "yes" of affirmation is directed ahead, toward the possible, toward that which arrives, toward the event. (It is quite natural to define the event as that which arrives, since, etymologically speaking, it is a tautology: "event" means *arrivant.*) Hence, affirmation involves the expectation and hope of producing a truth.[59] If affirmation points toward that which arrives, it focuses on accounting for an event.

That this kind of change in our approach to Beckett would result simply from our giving up the mimetic reading of his work is by no means evident. Even if we succeed in extricating ourselves, completely and for good, from the overwhelming image of Beckett as a writer of the "human condition," it does not follow that his work will present itself to us as affirmative. In the very criticism that opposed the reading of Beckett's work as mimesis, it is not difficult to find statements to the effect that "Beckett's work offers nothing affirmative"[60] and that "[i]f one looks for affirmation in Beckett, all one will find is the deformation of man."[61] We might blame the critique for not being radical enough and not drawing the ultimate conclusions of its analysis. However, a more probable explanation seems to be that the interpretation of Beckett's work in terms of affirmation does not emerge as a direct consequence of parting with the mimetic reading. Neither does it directly follow from conceiving Beckett's work in terms of a methodical inquiry. It is difficult to find a sufficient reason for the radical revision in the reading of Beckett's work suggested by Badiou unless a totally new aspect of this work is put into focus. For Badiou, this new aspect is Beckett's interest in the event.

The emphasis on the event, and not the (perhaps less original) insistence on Beckett's work not being mimetic, is the true novelty of Badiou's reading of Beckett. There is a difference between reading Beckett as a master of black humor, for whom repetition is an inexhaustible source of hilarious one-liners, and reading Beckett as an enterprise driven by hope—for hope is inextricably linked to the unpredictable. (For a sample of Beckett's black humor, consider the following citations: "there is rapture, or there should be, in the motion crutches give";[62] "to see yourself doing the same thing over and over again fills one with satisfaction."[63]) Whereas a totally predestined world would not have to be characterized by misery alone, it is not conducive to hope or freedom. Consequently, Badiou reads Beckett's work not merely as a simple methodical suspension of mimesis but as a methodical inquiry that aims at being able to account for the unpredictable.

When Badiou claims that "tout le génie de Beckett tend à l'affirmation, de façon presque aggressive,"[64] when he discovers a *bizarre énergie* in Beckett's texts, and when he calls Beckett's style "affirmatif, presque violent,"[65] the "affirmation" in question stands for a vigilance and openness toward that which comes as a radical surprise. This surprise is "so singular that it has already disappeared at the very moment of its taking place" ("si singulier que ça a déjà disparu quand ça a eu lieu").[66] Badiou formulates the objective of his own philosophical search as a step further: the ethical task of thinking ("une question d'éthique de la pensée")[67] is to formulate a "system" to receive the unpredictable that poetry attempts to name.

But when we think about Beckett, we might ask ourselves: What is being affirmed, precisely? After all, there are very few surprises in Beckett's narratives. His remark about *Endgame* testifies that Beckett conceived at least some of his work as free of chance: "there is no accident . . . , all is based on analogy and repetition."[68] Badiou interprets Beckett's work as affirming "events," with examples oscillating between "freedom," "love," "truth," and "language." Beckett's affirmation gains here the status of an unreflected (nonspeculative) and yet "methodical" nomination.

Badiou contests the claim that in Beckett's work there is no room for the singular event by arguing that the whole corpus gradually opens up so as to account for the possibility of such an event. "We turn towards event." "Bit by bit, not without hesitations and regrets, the oeuvre of Beckett will open itself to the accidental, to the sudden modifications of the given."[69] In particular, Badiou perceives Beckett's early novel *Watt* as the "interrogation of the event" (*l'interrogation sur l'événement*). One of those (extremely rare) incidents more than others—the famously puzzling incident of the tuning of the piano in *Watt*—corresponds perfectly to Badiou's definition of the unpredictable: it has "no [material] thickness" ("aucune épaisseur").[70] The sound-event of *Ill Seen Ill Said* captures Badiou's attention too: "During the inspection a sudden sound. Startling . . . the mind awake. How explain it? And without going so far how say it?"[71] This central function of the event has, according to Badiou, been forgotten in the most famous works by Beckett—including *Waiting for Godot* and *The Trilogy*—but has resurfaced again in the so-called second trilogy (a triptych consisting of *Company, Ill Seen Ill Said,* and *Worstward Ho*)—in particular, in *Ill Seen Ill Said* and *Worstward Ho*.

I return now to the vexed question of how to locate Beckett's work in Badiou's system. Badiou not only credits Beckett's work after the 1960s as a way out of the solipsistic impasse but also argues that there is a typically poetical move to "nomination" in Beckett's work after the 1960s,[72] and that Beckett's later work has a poetic quality. According to Badiou, the essence of poetry is naming the singular. In virtue of this poetic quality, should we read it as a case of pure nomination or rather as a poetic, self-reflective effort to practice philosophy? In other words, does Badiou read Beckett as one more exemplification of the Age of Poets, a poetic writing chasing "the disappearing singularity of the poem itself"?[73] Or does he think Beckett's writing to be one that names, where the poem is the privileged means of welcoming the unpredictable in the realm of language, thereby preparing the way for philosophy?

Poetry is that, which in language—other arts do it otherwise than in language—summons to the absolute of singularity.[74]

In Badiou's *Conditions*, the chapter on "Beckett's Generic Writing"[75] is the only one that is not titled in terms of a relationship between philosophy and one of its conditions (the other chapters deal with philosophy and poetry, philosophy and mathematics, philosophy and politics, philosophy and love, and finally philosophy and psychoanalysis). This chapter on Beckett, which closes the book, could therefore be read either as a transition—a radicalization, a step beyond the argumentative pattern of the whole—or as a supreme gathering, completion, and exemplification of the defended thesis. In the former case, this would imply that Beckett's writing somehow escapes the system propounded by Badiou (the system in which it would function as a condition of philosophy, with philosophy retaining its separate function). In the latter case, Beckett's writing would function as an exemplification of Badiou's system. In calling Beckett's writing "generic" (while also insisting that generic procedures are conditions of philosophy),[76] Badiou makes clear that Beckett's writing also belongs to the category of the conditions of philosophy (the conditions that must nevertheless remain separate, "de-sutured" from philosophy). The exceptional quality of Beckett's writing, according to Badiou, resides in its being a perfect exemplification of the system. Whereas the poem is only one of the four conditions of philosophy (the other three are the matheme, the political, and love—each of them with its own "truth procedures"), and whereas the Age of Poets is now over, Beckett does more than explore the poetical alone; he explores each of the four conditions about which Badiou speaks. In other words, Beckett's writing is a kind of superior nomination that opens the way for philosophy's task of thought, exceeding the Age of Poets by giving up its speculative task. At the same time, it exceeds any mere nomination focused on naming "this particular sunset"[77] by coming up with a method, a "technique, and an 'experiment' comparable to those of Descartes and Husserl."[78] But, in nomination (where each of the multiple generic truths has a content), it will never reach the task of philosophy that is "the thinking of the generic as such."[79] Strangely enough, Badiou accords Beckett's last, recapitulatory text *Worstward Ho* the status of "a short philosophical treatise, a treatment in shorthand of the question of Being."[80]

It seems that Badiou is right in insisting that Beckett's way of impoverishment (including humor, which tends to disappear in Beckett's later works) is to be seen as a method of inquiry and not as a reflection on the human condition. He is also right in his observation that in Beckett's later texts, this method of inquiry is directed toward the event. What is striking in Badiou's reading of Beckett is that it falls short of accounting for the qualities of the *Trilogy*, a work considered by many a tour de force but that, in Badiou's reading, gains the label of the impasse in Beckett's work. This goes together with his complete lack of interest in the issues of authority, force, and law, which seem central to Beckett's work—not least as exemplified in Beckett's famous couples of tormentor and victim, a motif that persists from Pozzo and Lucky in *Waiting for Godot* until the very last works. Badiou would perhaps condemn an emphasis on this motif either as a speculative—and hence "modernist"—reading of Beckett, or as a pure sophistry that focuses on rhetoric instead of truth.[81] This is a measure of Badiou's originality but also leaves Beckett somewhat amputated.

In Badiou's eyes, the works that make up Beckett's "pivotal" period (the *Trilogy* and *Waiting for Godot*) fail to open themselves toward the event. The fact that waiting for something to happen is an ever-present theme in Beckett seems to contradict this claim. The difference is rather in the successfulness of the pursuit. While the Unnamable's approach is, as Badiou puts it, "solipsistic"—so that despite waiting for something to happen, nothing does happen—the approach of the later works is not solipsistic and is therefore rewarded. In other words, the *Trilogy* is a failure because it bears the consequences of the self-reflective concern of Beckett's literary enterprise. Yet how could Beckett have come up with what Badiou calls a "method" of pursuing the event if he did not first examine the phenomenon of pursuit itself? In fact, Beckett undertook several experiments in method in the *Trilogy*. Some of them concern the arrival of the event, a passive "waiting for it to happen"—for example, in Moran's receiving of Gaber, his avoiding of him, and his being surprised by him. Some of them look more like active attempts to capture the event: the search for Molloy and the writing of the "report" of this chase, for example. In *Molloy*, Beckett might be said to have kept note of these experiments. By ignoring this, Badiou's reading fails to account for the possibility that, over and above accounting for an event, Beckett's work explores itself, the literary work, as the event of accounting. Insofar as this event is shown to examine its own conditions, Beckett's work can be said to deal with the structural possibility of an event. However, contrary to Badiou, this does not necessarily make Beckett's work purely self-centered and closed on itself. The divergence that comes to light here, between my own reading of Beckett's work as the exploration of the principles of its own law or authority and Badiou's reading of it as the phenomenological quest for the event (a quest that results in naming), says something about the contrasting implicit conceptions of literature in each case.

No longer supported by an authoritative unifying intention of the author, what makes the work appear to us as a singular unity? Badiou invokes the authority of truths (about the "human") and of what he calls Beckett's courage (it appears to be something like the scientific courage of a researcher.) For Badiou, a work like *Worstward Ho* is the record of an experiment where, in successive detractions, Beckett exercises his ability to name—in the hope of eventually naming the utterly new, until now indiscernible (but not unnamable) event. Writing is a "truth procedure." Not surprisingly, Moran's untrue record in *Molloy* had to be excluded from this appreciation of Beckett's work. This novel, with respect to which Badiou was forced to observe silence, shows that in contrast to Badiou's system, Beckett does not leave the notion of writing unchallenged. A record (of which a work is one example) establishes its own law and is capable of reflecting on it.

For Badiou, the law-producing aspect of literature is not relevant because for him, a literary work must appeal to a different kind of authority: the authority of truth to underscore the accuracy of the record. In the modernist conception of literature, the work produces its own authority by reflecting upon itself as a medium and thereby upon "the law." By contrast, when literature is conceived as nomination, it has an external goal: to say "the truth." Now, whereas both Derrida and Badiou agree that literature is more than self-reflection—that literature is open to its exteriority—there is a significant difference between their views. Derrida insists that the literature's openness to alterity and its capacity for self-reflection must coexist. Badiou, utterly disregarding the possibility that the institution of literature may not want to give up the intellectual autonomy it had gained in the Age of Poets, considers the literary work's self-reflection a burden and an unnecessary task, of which literature should be relieved. Whereas they both posit a link between literature and the phenomenological method, Derrida accords literature a far higher status. According to the latter, rather than merely extending and imitating the method of phenomenology, literature would provide, at least in its potentiality or *dunamis,* the possibility of questioning the phenomenological point of view (in particular, by putting in question the complicity of phenomenology with the metaphysics of presence).

The authority of the work—the "power" or the "force" of the work—cannot be traced back to a single source. With the author having effaced himself, we may speak of "ghosting" or of permutations of authority. (An early interpretation of Beckett's *How It Is* speaks about "authorité de nombres,"[82] which might be thought analogous to the "law of the number" that Derrida describes in "The Deaths of Roland Barthes" [295/304]). The source of authority is thereby rendered undecidable and vacillating, but its dispersed state produces at the same time the law of the work, giving it a sense of unity.

In the end, for Badiou, literature seems to derive its authority from philosophy: not only is the pursuit of truth staged in literary works situated as a condition of philosophy (one of the four) but the successfulness of this pursuit is to be retrogressively recognized (or not) by philosophy. This leads to the paradoxical situation in which, after vindicating the de-suturing of literature from philosophy and declaring the completion of the Age of Poets, Badiou chooses as his literary example what he will later praise as a "philosophical treatise": Beckett's *Worstward Ho.* Perhaps the de-suturing of literature and philosophy is better completed in Derrida after all. The status of literature in his thought seems to be more respectful of the distinctness of the literary phenomenon (and institution) than the status that Badiou grants to it in his reading of Beckett—namely that of mimicking philosophy by performing an operation of phenomenological reduction.

Should literature feel threatened by Badiou's attempt to relieve it of the tasks he considers properly philosophical? His overt intention is to protect the distinctness of literature. Yet it is very uncertain whether this distinctness could stand without literature's reflecting on its own phenomenon. This reflection, despite Badiou's assertions to the contrary, was Beckett's preoccupation from his early parable on writing (*Molloy*) to his "testamentary" reflection on the nature of language—the medium of literature—in *Worstward Ho.* In the latter, Beckett adopts a procedure of negative theology to explore the originary silence from which language derives its force: the mystical foundation of its authority.

7

Singular Points of Transaction (III): "Wanting in Inanity." Negativity, Language, and "God" in Beckett

This chapter investigates the resemblance of Beckett's discourse to negative theology. It is my contention not only that can we speak of such a resemblance but also that the understanding of its function might yield new insights into a vital aspect of Beckett's work, namely his interest in "nothingness" and his commitment to thinking in the negative.[1] At least from *Watt* onward, Beckett experimented incessantly with the rhetoric of negation, a practice that culminated in his last prose work, *Worstward Ho*. A fascination with "nothingness" and various attempts to capture it by staging the failure of language typified this endeavor. Beckett expressed this characteristic trait of his writing in the (already mentioned) letter that he wrote to Axel Kaun: "[m]ore and more my own language appears to me like a veil that must be torn apart in order to get at the things (or the Nothingness) behind it."[2] Beckett's remark is a quintessential expression of the idea that motivates negative theology—perhaps not least because the name of God does not appear in it. According to the doctrine of the *via negativa*, God—who cannot be named and is, strictly speaking, "nothing"—can only be reached by tearing away the veil of language.

Negativity and God

In the concluding passages of *Beckett's Fiction: In Different Words,* Leslie Hill indicated the importance of negativity in reading Beckett in the following way:

> The questions of Beckett's writing are questions of negativity, and the fate of Beckett's texts hangs, quite uniquely, on the issue of how the power of the negative in his work is understood. Indeed, the history of reception of Beckett's texts could be written in terms of the different interpretations put forward as to the force and significance of the negative. It leads one to believe that the single most important reason for Beckett's success, with critics and audiences alike, is in the questions his work raises as to the shape and character *of the negative, the different, the other, the something without name* that haunts not only the words and rhythms of Beckett's writing, but also the words with which audiences, too, strive to pattern their lives.[3]

What is the meaning of "the negative, the different, the other, the something without name" in Beckett? The idea of God seems not to be very distant from the idiom of this phrase. Hill must have realized this affinity, for in a later paper[4] he qualifies his own position by insisting that the "use of negative constructions" is "not the admission of God by the back passage." In other words, here Hill severs the link between negativity and God, the possibility of which had been opened up by his suggestive words in *Beckett's Fiction.*

I would argue that there is more to the link between negativity and God than Hill's denial implies, because the reliance of mystical discourse upon negativity is by no means accidental. They are mutually dependent, which is well captured by Derrida when he says that the reading of "God" as "*that without which* one would not know how to account for any negativity . . . will always be possible."[5] While sympathizing with Hill's intention to keep negativity and God apart, I would suggest that this intention reflects just one certain way of thinking about God, namely as presence. The tradition of negative theology permits such a reading. However, there is more than one possible way to think about God in accordance with this tradition.

The other possible approach is to resist lapsing into thinking God as presence. On this reading, God would be a name of a certain void and of a process that is propelled by this void. In this chapter, I want to consider the possibility that Beckett's work was an example of such a discourse, namely a discourse focused on articulating God as absence.

The discourse focused on articulating God in the negative has a long history. The procedure was known to the Stoics, to the neo-Pythagoreans, and to the Neoplatonists. It appears in the hermetic texts of the Hellenistic Gnostics and in the texts of the Judeo-Christian authors.[6] Within the Christian tradition, the first known adherent of speaking about God in the negative was Dionysius the Areopagite (fifth century), whose work was translated into Latin by Scotus Eriugena in the ninth century. This prepared the way for other apophatic discourses in which the Neoplatonic and, after Aquinas, Thomistic influences prevailed alternately—for example, those of Meister Eckhart; Nicholas of Cusa; or, as late as the seventeenth century, Angelus Silesius.

Recently, the discourse of negative theology has drawn renewed attention, especially since the philosophical project of Jacques Derrida (most notably, the part accompanying the introduction of the notion of *différance*) has been repeatedly identified with apophatic discourse.[7] This comparison brought about a number of responses from Derrida,[8] which in turn provoked a substantial critical discussion about the rapprochement between philosophy and theology[9] and the way other discourses hinge on the apophatic. As a result, the quasi-apophatic thought of Derrida that both engages and questions this tradition cannot be ignored when addressing the topic of negative theology. It is partly in the wake of this discussion that negative theology should be taken no longer to indicate merely an immensely rich yet obsolete, esoteric tradition, but to stand for a kind of rhetoric from which we might draw new insights about the functioning of language and representation. It is this latter content of negative theology that I want to address when examining the resemblance of Beckett's discourse to it. The echoes of the *via negativa* in Beckett go beyond epigonism. They do not testify to a certain nostalgia for a remote tradition, but employ a strategy characteristic of this tradition in an experimental way—to let certain effects become apparent in its working.

Negative theology begins with the insight that predicative language (i.e., the language of formulations of the type S is P) is inadequate to the task of speaking about God. In the words of Meister Eckhart, "God is neither this nor that, that man can say" (*Got inist noch diz noch daz, daz man gesprechin mac)*.[10] This insight of nonadequacy that as such already indicates an alternative to predicative language in the form of negative attribution is the first step of the *via negativa*.

The next step is from negation to subtraction. The negation of the *via negativa* is not dialectical and is thus irredeemable. (A dialectic would promise a third moment in which the positive element [i.e., the first moment] after being negated in the second moment, is finally recuperated via a synthesis, or *Aufhebung*, in the third.) That which is excluded by negation is excluded for good and cannot be reintroduced; herein lies the characteristic radicality of the *via negativa*. Since that which is negated is therewith elided from discourse, there remains less and less to be said—or rather to be unsaid. As a consequence, the discourse evolves toward unsaying everything—that is, toward silence. As Pseudo-Dionysius says in his "Mystical Theology,"

> my argument now rises . . . and the more it climbs, the more language falters, and when it has passed up and beyond the ascent, it will turn silent completely, since it will finally be one with him who is indescribable.[11]

By rarefying the discourse, negative theology moves toward a void, which can only be filled up with a mystical experience—or so the proponents of negative theology surmised. The favorite image with which to illustrate this void is of the desert. It is not only in virtue of the geographical setting of biblical narrative that the desert is the place of encounters with God. The desert was the ultimate image of renunciation, of self-denial, which by its negative aspect paved the way to the direct intimation of God. The deserted spaces of Beckett's stage settings reflect this climate of renunciation.

It might be concluded that the discourse of negative theology eventually recuperates the presence of God. After naming everything that God is not, it would somehow be possible to experience his sheer presence in the created linguistic void or desert. Yet a careful reading of the texts of Pseudo-Dionysius and Meister Eckhart clearly demonstrates that the *via negativa* can only endlessly approach the threshold of the promised revelation without being able to step over it. The experience of the presence of God is simply not built into its procedure.

Derrida's radical reading of the *via negativa*, in which he refrains from conceiving the final goal of the apophatic discourse in terms of an experience of presence, allows him to assign it to a larger domain. After detracting the final moment of God's presence, the *via negativa* can be approached as a textual practice proper to many discourses, a procedure of address constructed on the principle of negation. As Derrida says, negative theology is a "language" or an "attitude toward [it]," and

[b]y a more or less tenable analogy, one would thus recognize some traits, the family resemblance of negative theology, in every discourse that seems to return in a regular and insistent manner to this rhetoric of negative determination, endlessly multiplying the defenses and the apophatic warnings.[12]

This is a reading of apophasis in which that to which the address directs itself is effaced. The discourse empties itself in order to arrive at an empty place. Even though empty, or maybe precisely in virtue of being such, this place is of great interest to modern philosophy and theology—and, as I argue in this chapter, to Beckett's "writings." This space, which can no longer accommodate the presence of God and which, therefore, is home to an originary absence, is perceived by Derrida as the locus of that which he calls "writing," *différance*, or the "trace"—a quasi-transcendental principle governing our experience. The purpose, then, of the thus modified negative way is to address something that cannot be isolated in its presence but can only be discerned in its working. This emptying kenosis of discourse is the place where the interests of Beckett, negative theology, and Derridean reflection on it come together.

The Negative Way in Beckett

Historically, the negative discourse so often stigmatized as heresy was, in fact, the most critical, consistent, and uncompromising way of speaking about God. It is not surprising that it appealed to Beckett. Several critics stress the relevance of the mystical tradition to his writing. It is known that Beckett read the work of mystics in his youth, that he was familiar with the writings of Meister Eckhart (he discussed them in 1977 with Charles Juliet), and that he quoted the fifth-century mystic Pseudo-Dionysius in his 1931–1932 "Dream" notebook and subsequently in the *Dream of Fair to Middling Women*. The same notebook contains references to St. Augustine, John of the Cross, Thomas à Kempis, and Julian of Norwich.

The content of what has been widely referred to as Beckett's "revelation" or "mystical experience" reflects the mode of renunciation so characteristic of negative theology. Beckett restates this experience in the following words: "I realised that my own way was in impoverishment, in lack of knowledge and in taking away, in subtracting rather than adding."[13] It would be an oversimplification to treat this revelatory moment (which took place in the summer of 1945—and thus after *Watt* and before *Waiting for Godot*) as a sharp caesura, indicating a radical and unexpected change in Beckett's work. On the other hand, it is undeniable that it anticipates a direction that Beckett's later work pursued, and that one aspect of this direction was the radicalization of its apophatic nature.

It is not difficult to observe that Beckett's miming of the discourse of negative theology is often playful—it has the nature of an experiment designed more to test the tenacity of language than to bring about its rarefaction. This is especially true of the early texts, which tend to mimic the *via negativa* in its rhetorical patterns (various modes of "unsaying")[14] rather than in its inevitable consequence (silence). True, Beckett's silence is never far away, but only from a certain point in his work is language deliberately thinned down in order to expose it in its working, rarefaction becoming an instrument of inquiry. I will discuss two cases of such playful early "unsaying"—one in Beckett's early novel *Watt*, and one in *Waiting for Godot*.

At first, the "unsaying" in Beckett's work consists not in a retraction but simply in speaking backwards, in the reversal of spelling and syntactic order. This kind of situation takes place in *Watt*, which also functions as a humorously mystical account of the perambulations of the titular character, including the description of his stay in the house of the unfathomable Mr. Knott. The "nicest" examples of the *via negativa* in Beckett can be found in *Watt*, even though they are surrounded with red herrings and even though their function is not as clear as in later writings. *Watt* could be, after all, just a parody—of negative theology, among other things—and still be as good a book. Yet the element of the mystical is undeniably there. Watt starts speaking back to front, as Shira Wolosky reminds us, "in pursuit of Mr. Knott's Nothingness," and in this he imitates "the linguistic breakdown of an apophatic prayer."[15] The breakdown thus described is not incurable; even though this "unsaying" renders the speaker apparently incomprehensible, there is a code to it. An example of the negative way of thinking from *Watt* illustrates this:

Lit yad mac, ot og. Ton taw, ton tonk. Ton dob, ton trips. Ton vila, ton deda. Ton kawa, ton pelsa. Ton das, don yag. Os devil, rof mit.[16]

By following the narrator's instructions (in this case: "invert . . . the order of letters in the word together with that of the sentences in the period"), this could be translated into something like "So lived, for time. Not sad, not gay. Not awake, not asleep. Not alive, not dead. Not body, not spirit. Not wat/Watt, not Knott. Till day came, to go." The narrator's comment is, appropriately, "This meant *nothing* to me" (165, my emphasis), for the objective of the *via negativa* is, precisely, to express the "nothing."

The other mode of "unsaying"—by undoing language irreversibly—can be found in *Waiting for Godot*, written a few years after *Watt*. The incomprehensibility of Lucky's monologue is all the more tragic, as its meaning can no longer be restored—this time, the code is missing. If the essence of negative theology can be said to consist in provoking a linguistic breakdown in order to address God, then Lucky's soliloquy is an extreme case of such an experiment. Wolosky points out that this monologue breaks down while playing with the idea of God "outside time without extension" and with scholastic terminology ("conating"). This links the discourse on God to a linguistic breakdown known as aphasia. Among other possibilities, this might suggest that only through aphasia is it possible to speak about God—or that speaking about God leads to aphasia.

Such expressions as "unwording," "unsaying," and even "leastward on" testify to the interaction of Beckett's work with the discourse of negative theology. Mary Bryden mentions the "apophatic" characteristic of Beckett's work and the "kenotic" mode in which Christ is depicted in *Waiting for Godot*. Precisely apophatic kenosis—the draining from language of all content by means of "unsaying"—is the essence of negative theology. Wolosky even goes so far as to insist that "the premises and practices of negative theology act as a generative condition of Beckett's books" and that, for example, "The Unnamable openly parades this impulse" in stating the procedure to be followed. "'First I'll say what I'm not,' declares the narrator, 'that's how they told me to proceed, then what I am.'"[17] "The way of negation—of passing to true reality by progressive denial and reduction—is here declared the Unnamable's very method."[18]

Yet if this mimicking was applied as a method, its function has not been sufficiently elucidated. We are familiar with Beckett's ambiguous but mainly negative attitude to religion, which many commentators qualified as agnostic, as well as his denial of having "religious emotions" or "the least faculty or disposition for the supernatural."[19] Derrida, too, says of himself, "I quite rightly pass for an atheist," while also reminding us of the possibility that "the extreme and most consistent forms of declared atheism will have always testified to the most intense desire of God."[20] But, then again, if it is true that the propensity of Beckett's discourse to the rhetorical practice of negative theology testifies (just as does the negative discourse itself) to the "most intense desire of God," how is this God to be thought? How is it possible to think God without lapsing into the metaphysical trap of thinking him as presence or being?

Thinking God as Language

In its most radical gesture, the *via negativa* addresses God without ever hoping to reach him in his presence or being, without conferring on him the status of being. Addressed in the negative way, God would be, in Jean-Luc Marion's formulation, a "God without being" (*Dieu sans l'être*).[21] According to this discourse, "God" "is" not; the word "being" does not apply in any discourse on God. About God so thought, nothing can be said—except maybe what Hamm says in *Endgame*: "The bastard, he doesn't *exist*."[22] Or what we learn about Mr. Knott in *Watt*: "Not that Watt was ever to have any direct dealings with Mr. Knott, for *he was not.*"[23]

This God of questionable origin who "doesn't exist" can be addressed in prayer, but to no avail. The only thing that can be evoked in this prayer is "God's place which is not God."[24] In that place, that which we call "God" is visible in its effects. According to the tradition of negative theology, God's place, the place where God appears, is the origin of language; as Angelus Silesius put it, *der Ort ist dass Wort* (the place is the Word).

Der Ort ist dass Wort.
Der ort und's Wort ist Eins, und wäre nicht der ort
(Bey Ewger Ewigkeit!) es wäre nicht das *Wort.*

The place is the word
The place and the word is one, and were the place not
(of all eternal eternity!) the word would not be.[25]

The God without being and, arguably, his favorite place—language[26]—are interdependent, and neither can be thought without the other. Thus, God cannot be thought outside language. To this extent, negative theology addresses language and the fact that language cannot point outside itself. In other words, negative theology is a rhetorical practice that addresses its own "rhetoricity." I suggest that Beckett's gesture toward it is prompted by the realization that all that we can say about God are his effects in language, and that God is, strictly speaking, "nothing," but a "nothing" that "happens," that has the status of an "event." This was "(w)hat distressed Watt": that "nothing had happened, with the utmost formal distinctness, and that it continued to happen, in his mind."[27]

Thought about God, both in its positive and negative modus, originates in and through language. This is the questionable origin of God, the reason for Hamm to call him a "bastard": God is the consequence of the way our language is. And our language is such that "any expression of an abstract idea can only be by analogy"[28]—to an expression denoting something particular and tangible. Only by an analogy that obliterates the tangible, "primitive" referents does a new, universal, and abstract concept enter language. In the words of *Watt*,

the only way one can speak of nothing is to speak of it *as though* it were something, just as the only way one can speak of God is to speak of him *as though* he were a man, which to be sure he was, in a sense, for a time, and as the only way one can speak of man, even our anthropologists have realised that, is to speak of him *as though* he were a termite.[29]

It is not inconceivable that the principle of analogy "engendered" or "yielded" a couple of abstract ideas, including the idea of God. Our language's ability to express abstract ideas would in this case be the origin of the idea of a transcendent being. This being, by analogy, would be capable of explaining the world.

HAMM. We're not beginning to . . . to . . . mean something?

CLOV. Mean something! You and I, mean something! (*Brief laugh.*) Ah that's a good one!

HAMM. I wonder. (*Pause.*) Imagine if a rational being came back to earth, wouldn't he be able to get ideas into his head if he observed us long enough. (*Voice of rational being.*) Ah, good, now I see what it is, yes, now I understand what they're at![30]

As mentioned before, Beckett's project of experimenting with the rhetoric of "unsaying" may be said to have culminated in his last prose work, *Worstward Ho*. This remarkable text might be read as a reflection on the human condition, a phenomenological study of experience, or an account of the persistence of artistic inquiry, which goes on "till nohow on." The quest of *Worstward Ho* might plausibly be interpreted as directed toward "God," understood as the condition of the possibility (and impossibility) of meaning and language.

In this reading, I will try to avoid reading "God" either as presence or as substance (including the *hyperousia,* excess of presence that Derrida argues is the *telos* of various negative theologies). It has been demonstrated (against Mikel Dufrenne) that Derrida's project is not that of theology and (against Marion) that it does not eliminate God either. Rodolphe Gasché shows that in addressing God, Derrida pursues the law (in the form of the quasi-transcendental structures of referral) that "regulat[es] the exchange between different types of discourse on the Other."[31] It is in virtue of thinking this law that Derrida can say that God is an effect of the trace. The "theological trap" consists in the fact that even when we try to keep in mind that "the dream of full presence is not possible without a trace," the full presence always takes over from the trace. The trace's being "erasable" results in a "structural occultation and oblivion [of the trace] by the idea of God." Gasché's argument stems from the conviction that "[b]rutally put, God is not God if, even as *absconditus,* He cannot be said somehow to exist."[32] Without denying that this is a possible reading of "God" in Derrida (cf. "the name of God, at least as it is pronounced within classical rationalism"),[33] I suggest a different reading of "God." Thus, God would be understood as a figure (or as a name that Derrida wants to "save" [*Sauf le nom*]), yet not as a figure of presence that occludes the trace. Instead, I would urge that God should be read as the figure of an originary, quasi-transcendental difference "before" it has been occluded by an appearance of presence. I would draw attention to what Derrida says on this topic in his essay on Levinas:

God is *nothing* (determined), is not life, because he is *everything*[,] and therefore is at once All and Nothing, Life and Death. Which means that God is or appears, is *named*, within the difference between All and Nothing, Life and Death. Within difference, and at bottom as Difference itself.[34]

Accordingly, God will be understood here as a figure of difference, one that is "older than Being itself," hence beyond (distinct from) the ontico-ontological difference—"a difference still more unthought than the difference between Being and beings."[35] But is it then still possible to speak about God? "Such a *différance* . . . upsets . . . all theology."[36] There remains nothing except (*sauf*) the name—the figure of God.

From its very first word, *Worstward Ho* addresses Being: "on" is in Greek the very word of being.[37] But which side of the ontico-ontological difference is at stake here: Being (the Being of beings) or the beings (i.e., entities) themselves? Introducing the question of Being in *Sein und Zeit*, Heidegger quotes Thomas Aquinas: "An understanding of Being is already included in conceiving anything which one apprehends in entities."[38] Heidegger's commentators distinguish three senses of the notion of Being: identity stipulates that something is what it is; existence, that something exists; and truth, that something is the case.[39] Heidegger appealed to all three of these senses to distinguish his notion of Being from that of an "entity." "The Being of entities 'is' not an entity."[40] God as the Supreme Being, hence also an entity, must be distinguished from "Being." To conceive of them as equivalent would mean to give in to onto-theology, to neutralize the ontological difference between "Being" and beings (in making the former appear simply as a variation in degree of the latter). It is in order to protect the ontico-ontological difference that Heidegger insisted on a clear-cut distinction between Being (the Being of beings) and God as the Supreme Being.

At the same time, Heidegger was, paradoxically, inclined to think of God in terms parallel to those of Being—namely, by exclusion of "being" (supreme or not). In his own words, were he "to write a theology, as [he was] sometimes tempted to do, the word 'being' ought not to appear there."[41] In his "How to Avoid Speaking: Denials," Derrida addresses this remark and points out, first, that in virtue of this exclusion of being from both "Being" and "God," they become indistinguishable. He then observes that addressing both God and Being presupposes a detour through being (in virtue of his argument that the universal, the ontological, the ideal, cannot be separated from the particular, the ontic, and the real).

Heidegger says . . . that if he were to write a theology, he would avoid the word *being*. . . . But didn't he write it? And in it did he avoid writing the word *being*? In fact, since Being is not (a being) and in truth is nothing (that is), what difference is there between writing *Being*, this Being which is not, and writing *God*, this God of whom Heidegger also says that He is not?[42]

Consequently, *Sein und Zeit* can be read as a "theology with and without God," the latter understood as Being or as being. This was Heidegger's testimony, in Derrida's words: "he was not there without leaving a trace of all these folds."[43] What is the import of this "Heideggerian hope," this "metaphysical," "affirmative" part that Derrida discerns in the "The Anaximander Fragment"?[44] Can we speak of (an inflection of) such hope in Beckett? In Derrida?

The Function of Subtraction in Beckett

Negative theology, while it addresses God, is in the end a self-interrogation of language. The interrogation of itself was for Beckett the function of art (and thus the function of art is, in a sense, epistemological): "[a]rt has always been this—pure interrogation, rhetorical question less the rhetoric."[45] In her *Unwording the World: Samuel Beckett's Fiction after the Nobel Prize*, Carla Locatelli concludes from the above passage that in Beckett's view, a "'pure interrogation' can only be structured as a subtraction (of rhetoric from the rhetorical question)."[46]

Hence, subtraction, earlier shown to be an essential phase in the *via negativa*, functions in *Worstward Ho* as an "epistemological instrument" (Locatelli's expression, but confirmed by Badiou's diagnosis that here Beckett applies the method of epochē). According to Locatelli, the notion of subtraction stands for a process of emptying language to see what remains in its absence. Yet it might also refer to the process of emptying for its own sake. Indeed, the primary concern of *Worstward Ho* is that language empties itself:

The words too whosesoever. What room for worse! How almost true they sometimes almost ring! How wanting in inanity!⁴⁷

The words seem to be "wanting in inanity"—they invite, provoke us to empty them—because they "ring" "true," or appear to offer a full presence of meaning. However, this "true ring" (as Derrida demonstrates with respect to Husserl in *Speech and Phenomena*) is always intertwined, *Verflochten*, with absence, death, deferral. The function of negative representation in Beckett comes to light here: it is to address the originary division and delay inherent in language that both keeps up and subverts the "true ring" of words.

Language and God in Beckett

The relationship between language and God in Beckett may also be determined by the latter's reception of Dante, of whom he was an avid reader. Dante's idea was that the fall in paradise was semantic in nature.⁴⁸ Part of the first man's disobedience was the trespass of a linguistic sign. The punishment was appropriate to the misdemeanor: Adam, and with him the whole of mankind, experienced a fall from unmediated knowledge and communication with God to a state of imperfect mediation by means of (mutable) signs.⁴⁹ This meant that the direct intimation of God was no longer possible, with all experience becoming mediated. *Worstward Ho* reads as a report of the failure of representation (the failure of which the Fall in paradise is a figure): "Ever tried. Ever failed. No matter. Try again. Fail again. Fail better."⁵⁰ Granting that *Worstward Ho* is an "epistemic novel,"⁵¹ and taking into account Dante's reading of the mediation of language as the result of the Fall, the failure addressed above consists in an inability to overcome the Fall, to overcome the mediation of signs. "Failing better" cannot undo the Fall, but it is nevertheless inevitable. This has always been the problem that faces negative theology: "how to talk properly of God when language can only improperly signify Him."⁵² As such, the purpose of negative theology is to unsay the distance created by the Fall. This was how Beckett perceived the function of his discourse in his letter to Axel Kaun:

More and more my own language appears to me like a veil that must be torn apart in order to get at the things (or the Nothingness) behind it. . . .

Language is most efficiently used where it is being most efficiently misused. As we cannot eliminate language all at once, we should at least leave nothing undone that might contribute to its falling into disrepute. To bore one hole after another in it, until what lurks behind it—be it something or nothing—begins to seep through; I cannot imagine a higher goal for a writer today.[53]

The idea of representation that Beckett expressed in this letter (but that he later discarded) was that it should "perforate" language in order to get beyond it to the "thing behind (it)."

The acceptance of the position that there is no "beyond" language calls for a rethinking of the role of negative theology. While in certain strains of negative theology, negations served to function as "investments," "expended in order to yield the higher return of the *hyperousios*,"[54] this function is no longer available. The act of the emptying of language would no longer serve the purpose of revealing what is "behind" it but would focus on language itself. The purpose of "failing better" would no longer be to undo the Fall but to address the principle, the law of failing itself: the silence dividing every sign from itself. Saying is failing: "How try say? How try fail?"[55] The function of Beckett's negative discourse in *Worstward Ho* would be to address the saying by unsaying it.

Original Affirmation as the Source of the Obligation to Express

The motif of obligation recurs throughout Beckett's writing, manifesting itself in various forms of compulsive behavior, of which the most characteristic is the dutiful or fearful obedience of Beckett's characters to what is often no more than a name (Godot, Mr. Knott, or Youdi, for example). With time, the names gradually disappear, making the obligation even more prominent. The obligation to express is omnipresent in Beckett's work. Next to the renowned fragment from the "Three Dialogues"—to which I will return—it is especially strong in the *Trilogy*, in *How It Is* (manifested as an obligation to quote), and in *Worstward Ho*. To my knowledge, Beckett has always refrained from speaking about the source of or the reason for this obligation. Nonetheless his "obligation to express" bears a certain resemblance to the expression "creative exigency," which Bergson uses when discussing the sources of moral obligation in his *Two Sources of Morality and*

Religion.[56] This might suggest that Beckett's "obligation to express" appealed to all three senses of "exigency" in Bergson (creative, moral, and religious).

As Derrida reminds us, language is dependent on a kind of original affirmation: the affirmation of the precarious identity of the sign, and of both its power and its weakness. Using language requires a minimal element of faith, in virtue of which one assumes that something means/is "what one thinks it means/is."[57] The affirmation of meaning, in the face of the sign's vulnerable and imperfect identity (for one can never be absolutely certain that something means "what one thinks it means"), coincides with the acceptance of the "obligation to express." Once we have started to "speak" by acknowledging the mediated nature of all experience, it is impossible not to express or to be "silent"—in other words, to leave the mediation. In his reading of Joyce's *Ulysses*, Derrida compares the interpretive gesture that allows us to experience "the world" to a gesture we make when receiving a phone call: "in the beginning was the telephone."[58] The "yes" uttered into the receiver acknowledges that the mediation is there and that it is successful. This "yes, I receive you," indicates also a certain commitment (and thus faith again): It means "yes, I will. I will respond to what you say next. What you are going to say will not remain without response." In other words, in every interpretive gesture (which might extend to include all experience), we have said yes, and in saying yes, we have promised. It is in this promise that the "obligation to express" is rooted. "Thought is fidelity to this promise," Derrida says.[59] But this thought should be aware that the promise at stake is not simply docile. (Derrida repeats Paul de Man's pun on Heidegger's famous phrase "die Sprache spricht": "die Sprache verspricht"[60] and later "die Sprache verspricht sich.") "[L]anguage or speech promises . . . but also goes back on its word, becomes undone or unhinged, derails or becomes delirious, deteriorates, becomes corrupt just as immediately and as essentially."[61]

The imperative "say on" in *Worstward Ho* reflects this obligation, arising from being thrown into language. It means "you have (always) already said (even if only in silence). Go on saying." "One starts speaking as if it were possible to stop at will," laments the Unnamable.[62] Once we have started to speak, everything we say addresses what has already been said. In Beckett's words, language is "preying on foresaid remains."[63]

Beckett's famous dictum from the "Three Dialogues" indicates the impossibility to express—or so it seems, for the observation that there is nothing to express does not entail that no expression is possible. With this observation, Beckett, rather than dismissing the possibility of expression, indicated impossibility (*empêchement*) as the field calling for artistic investigation. The paradox is well known to Beckett readers, who are repeatedly reminded that a condition of the possibility of discourse (and of meaning, truth, reference, etc.) is rooted in its impossibility. It is for this reason that Beckett pursues silence without ever actually falling silent.

There is nothing to express, nothing with which to express, nothing from which to express, no power to express, no desire to express, together with the obligation to express.[64]

The statement that there is "nothing with which to express" may reflect a conviction that expression is not possible (and so it is commonly read). Yet it can also mean that the true expression cannot be of something, or with something, or from something. (This reading would pursue the path of Beckett's "relentless Spinozism.") Alternatively, it can also mean that that which must be expressed is not a thing—that it is not something that "is" but, depending on how we name it, "Being," "God," or some quasi-transcendental principle. In this case, the "subject" (the "nothing from which to express"), the "tool" (the "nothing with which to express"), and the "object" of expression (the "nothing to express") are an effect of one process. The "tool" becomes indistinguishable from the "object" of expression and from its "subject" (I have shown this in my discussion of the "subjectile" in Beckett's *Unnamable*). The obligation is then to express the impossible. We might say that all experience begins with this impossibility or impasse, with what Watt called the "nothing" that "happened" and that "continued to happen."

But if he could say, when the knock came, the knock become a knock, on the door become a door, in his mind, presumably, in his mind, whatever that might mean, Yes, I remember, that is what happened then, if then he could say that, then he thought that then the scene would end, and trouble him no more.[65]

What "troubled" Watt was the irrepresentability of this experience due to the unbridgeable gap, the difference between the knock as it was and its becoming "a knock" to him. Watt's "mystical" experience related to the visit of the Galls consisted in the impasse produced by this difference, the (temporary) impossibility to express. Beckett seems to have indicated precisely this impasse as the object of the obligation to express, when, in the "Three Dialogues," he criticized the art that "never stirred from the field of the possible."[66] To Duthuit's question, "What other plane can there be for the maker?" Beckett's response was "logically none." This illustrates Beckett's urge to investigate the impossible—and there is no better way to express and explore the impasse that results from such an investigation than through the negative way that takes this impasse as its starting point. (In the words of Angelus Silesius, "go there where you cannot; see where you do not see; Hear where nothing rings or sounds.")[67] In this sense, Beckett's statement could be interpreted as attempting, through negation, to reach the most radical conditions of experience, language, and knowledge—conditions that are not transcendental but codependent on the very things they bring about. And these conditions arise out of an impasse. Consequently, the impasse is not the end; it is not a black hole out of which nothing emerges, for despite the fact that "the artist" is "helpless to paint"—since "there is nothing to paint and nothing to paint with"[68]—in *Worstward Ho* we read:

Nothing to show a woman and yet a woman.[69]

Nothing to show a child and yet a child. A man and yet a man. Old and yet old. Nothing but ooze how nothing and yet. (115)

In *Endgame,* Beckett signaled the feeble nature of the sign, which is also its strength. In line with Heidegger's metaphor of language as "the house of Being,"[70] the linguistic house inhabited by Hamm and Clov is said to be made only out of "hollow bricks"—constructed only from pieces of vacuum. But it does not collapse. Despite, or maybe because of, this hollowness of the sign, representation is omnipresent. This precarious status of language that originates from "nothing," from "impossibility" (or from God so defined), is addressed in *Worstward Ho.*

The Unnamable Source of Authority

The first word of *Worstward Ho* is not only "the very word of Being" but also an *imperative* to continue with something that apparently started without us. This injunction to go on might address the Heideggerian notion of *Geworfenheit* (a state of "thrownness," of "being thrown" into Being, or, as Locatelli puts it, the state of being caught in a "hermeneutic circle").[71]

It echoes the Mexican poem by Manuel Gutierrez Najera that Beckett translated as "To Be":

We crave a single instant of respite / and a voice in the darkness urges: "On!"[72]

Much of *Worstward Ho* is written in the same imperative mode, indicating that it comes from some higher yet unidentifiable and absent authority. The modus of authority is already there in language, conferring obligation and hiding its origin in one gesture. "The words too whosesoever."[73] "On. Say on" (89). This is an obligation to speak, but who or what says these words?

All of old. Nothing else ever. Ever tried. Ever failed. No matter. Try again. Fail again. Fail better. (89)

In the above fragment, the demanding yet absent other (speaking in the imperative) is indistinguishable from the one who is called on to obey (speaking in the constative). They speak in a single voice—the demand speaks through the voice of the demanded. Heidegger defines the voice of conscience in a similar way: the call of conscience is from Dasein to Dasein. On this reading, "on" would be the voice of conscience summoning Dasein "to its ownmost potentiality for being its Self"—in other words, to authentic existence.[74] "Ever tried. Ever failed" is no excuse: "No matter. Try again. Fail again. Fail better." The uttering of the injunction "Say on" and the performance of the duty it confers (to speak, to express) are one. This is not only an act of "saying"; the saying itself is shown, or "said," here.

Worstward Ho is a portrait of the "saying," a portrait of language in its working, a self-portrait of language. Language speaks here itself (compare Heidegger's expression "die Sprache spricht"), as through a medium in an oracle, for the origin of the words remains unknown. This near autonomy of language reflects the position of God. As Derrida says, "Language has started without us, in us and before us. This is what theology calls God, and it is necessary, it will have been necessary, to speak."[75] Yet that origin from where language comes cannot be named:

Whose words? Ask in vain. Or not in vain if say no knowing. No saying. No words for him whose words. Him? One. No words for one whose words. One? It. No words for it whose words.[76]

The above passage addresses that which engenders words, the "language into which we are thrown." Can it be called "God"? That which engenders words is anonymous. Similarly Heidegger says about conscience: "if the caller is asked about its name . . . it . . . refuses to answer."[77] (The functioning of conscience in Heidegger can be understood as relying on a temporal deferral, *différance*.) Negative theology might be helpful here: "in negative theology . . . that which calls forth speech is called 'God.'"[78] "Whose words? Ask in vain." The question about the identity of the voice is of no avail—unless you know the negative way: "Or not in vain if say no knowing." The only way God can be addressed in his singularity is by negation: "no words for it whose words." The pronoun "it" functions here as it does in Heidegger's "es gibt," which is to say that it is something that "gives" (i.e., produces certain effects) rather than "is." In this it displays a similar structure to Derrida's "*différance*." "It" lies at the origin of language and representation.

In *The Prayers and Tears of Jacques Derrida*, John D. Caputo insists that God is not *différance*. However, the main force of his argument is directed at the God of negative theology, who, as Derrida has shown, must somehow be permitted to partake of being (whether by relation or by degree—beyond being or more than being). Having drawn this distinction between God and *différance*, Caputo qualifies his position as "*sous rature*, with a measure of *sic et non*,"[79] in order to say that "[*d*]*ifférance* is altogether too meagre and too poor a thing to settle the question of God, as if there were only one question instead of *a mise en abîme* of questions spreading in every direction."[80] But is it not precisely the working of *différance* to permit this *mise en abîme* to "spread in every direction"?

Say a body. Where none. No mind. Where none. That at least. A place. Where none. For the body. To be in.[81]

On the other hand, again, it is impossible to think "it" as an origin independent of what it originates. "It" can only be made visible in its effects, that is, in language: in words. The words are all we have to express their origin:

Worsening words whose unknown. . . . Dim void shades all they. Nothing save what they say. Somehow say. Nothing save they.[82]

In *Worstward Ho*, a sphere of secrecy protects the anonymous source of authority. The way to express the "it" is, just as in negative theology, by renunciation: images are rarefied, and words are banned ("pox on bad"). A sphere of secrecy surrounds the origin of words and images. The productive "dim" is described as a "grot" or a "gulf" in the void, in which "shadows" appear. Both "grot" and "gulf" carry mystical associations: "grot" is also a "crypt" (from Italian "grotto"), and "gulf" can be both a "vault" and an "abyss."

Whence no knowing. (96)

At all costs unknown. (101)

According to Derrida, the negative discourse is inseparable from the notion of the secret.

There is a secret of the denial and the denial of the secret. The secret, *as secret*, separates and already institutes a negativity; it is a negation that denies itself. It denegates itself. This denegation does not happen to it by accident; it is essential and originary.[83]

Significantly, Derrida has also confessed that he has a "taste for the secret."[84] At the beginning of my argument, I discussed Derrida's preference of the secret by linking it to the *secrétaire*, a container for gathering. On the other hand, I have also shown how in Derrida the force of law relies on that which is secret because endlessly deferred, the "mystical foundation of authority." In the figure of both the secret and the *secrétaire* that harbors the possibility of the secret, the "essence" of literature now returns, showing itself to take part in the same economy as any discourse on God.

I have been trying, with the help of Derrida, to approach Beckett in the way that Derrida approaches Heidegger when he gives a theological reading of the latter in "How to Avoid Speaking: Denials" and in *Of Spirit*. In other words, my intention was not to give an apodictically theological reading of Beckett that would present itself as a necessary truth, but to demonstrate that under certain conditions such a reading is possible, and to see what this would entail for the understanding of the whole corpus of Beckett's work. It is possible to read certain aspects of Beckett's work from within the context of negative theology. In mobilizing a corpus of semantic resources through which one might make sense of the Beckettian desire for the "least" that propels *Worstward Ho*, I do not pretend to assign to it an exhaustive explanatory power. I do not wish to claim that Beckett's work is all about negative theology, even less that his work is about religious experience, which for Beckett, "in the only intelligible sense of that epithet," would have to be "at once an assumption and an annunciation."[85] If religious experience so understood were to be addressed by Beckett at all, it would rather be in its impossibility. Rather, in this chapter, some aspects that either are or can be associated with religion—like faith, obligation, and its impossible and unnamable source—are shown to permeate language and representation. And this means that *Worstward Ho*, since it is about language and representation, also addresses "religion." It is true that God addressed in this manner loses all specificity. But since, as Derrida says, his name is all we have, and it is the name of a mortal that in the end addresses the "tout autre est tout autre,"[86] it is, on a certain reading at least, a very nonspecific name—one that gathers.

In the tradition of negative theology, kenosis is supposed to lead to a silence that enables the faithful to experience the ineffable. Needless to say, this is not the intention of Beckett's gesture. Beckett's insistence on the obligation to express precludes interpretation of his work as a plea for silence. Rather, silence is investigated here in the sense of its being ineffable; as the secret that is the source of obligation, as that which is affirmed by language but that at the same time resists any mediation by it and cannot be represented by it. (The ineffability of *différance* is not a mystifying gesture but a structural necessity; language, which is always a language of identity, tends to occlude difference, which it nevertheless presupposes.)

What is left of God in Beckett cannot be understood as an absolute, whether linguistic or epistemic—not least because Beckett's work does not allow us to think in terms of an absolute "beyond." In a consistently developed discourse of negative theology, God becomes "a name that no longer names *anyone* or *anything*."[87] At most one might call it a productive absence at work in language, an absence that never fails to manifest itself and that in this way is both inside and outside language. If we assign to this absence the status of the source, it is only provisionally, for this "source" is always already embedded in language. The analysis of the discourse of negative theology demonstrates that when language becomes the object of inquiry, it can only empty itself and show its original desertlike quality. I suggest that when Derrida, while referring to the kenotic procedures of negative theologies, says that "'God' 'is' the name of this bottomless collapse, of this endless desertification of language,"[88] he is moving beyond a simple commentary to proffer his own point of view.

"It was on the key issue of pain, suffering and death that Beckett's religious faith faltered and quickly foundered," writes Knowlson in Beckett's biography. At the same time it is difficult to disagree with Christopher Ricks when he observes that "Beckett . . . felt twinges of the quondam believer, as in a phantom limb."[89] Was God a limb that Beckett discarded? Paradoxically, from the point of view of negative theology, this would constitute the most profound experience of God—the desired end of the *via negativa*, according to which only by getting rid of God can we understand his real nature. In the words of Meister Eckhart's confession: "I pray God to rid me of God."

Concluding Remarks

As a part of his crusade against sophistry and for the vindication of the question of truth, Alain Badiou has accused philosophy of confusing its task with that of literature and pleaded for their neat separation.[1] In light of this attack, the periodically returning questions of the relationship between philosophy and literature—how the different disciplines stand in relation to one another, what they might mean to each other, and whether (and in what way) they might supplement each other—have once again been raised. Among the thinkers interested in these issues, Jacques Derrida has given the question of the relation of philosophy and literature particular credit and attention—not least because it is intimately connected with his other pursuits: the singular event, iterability, and *différance*. Given this, and when we consider the multiplicity of written and oral responses to literary works that he has delivered over the years, Derrida's brief but courteous refusals to comment on the "both too close and too distant" works of Samuel Beckett remain a telling moment of silence. I have attributed this silence to Derrida's difficulty with Beckett's refusal to address the unique and with the latter's refusal to archive or to gather—gestures that for Beckett were equivalent to the exercise of control or authority. Beckett repeatedly denounced this proper-to-writing pursuit of control or mastery and at the same time always dreamt of an "ill-seen, ill-said" writing that would place itself beyond this pursuit.

I started my argument by showing that Derrida tends to read literary works in terms of the relationship between a singular event and a general law. The two literary gestures that capture the poles of this relationship—the archiving and the juridical—are shown by him to be impossible without one another. On the one hand, the singular could never appear without dividing itself at the origin—that is, without effacing itself as a singular mark in order to become iterable (which is the first condition of the possibility of its authorizing a law). The juridical, on the other hand, would be devoid of force without appealing to the originary silence of the singular, which has thus effaced itself: the "mystical foundation of [its] authority." Derrida demonstrates the necessary coexistence of these two movements in his essay on Roland Barthes, wherein a singular event (of death) is shown to stretch itself into a "terrifying and endless series," which in turn becomes an implicit law governing Barthes' attempt to establish a "science of the singular." Throughout this reading of the position of literature in Derrida's project, Beckett's gesture of emptying the archives and his refusal to gather remained opposed to that project.

I consequently mobilized three philosophical motives to account for Beckett's reluctance to gather: his perception of the failure of meaning, analyzed in a discussion of ordinary-language philosophy; Deleuze's "exhausting"; and Badiou's "methodic subtraction." Reading Beckett through the focus of ordinary-language philosophy means taking his work at face value, emphasizing the literal and the banal side of Beckett's language (nothing more is meant than what is said, or even less is meant than what is said). It is a legitimate gesture, taking into account Beckett's preoccupation with the worn-out character of our language. For Marjorie Perloff, Beckett's exploration of literal language is diagnostic in nature; in her view, Beckett's work consists in wondering about the functioning of language, experimenting with situations at the limit of meaning. Cavell, in an early essay on Beckett, went further, offering a quietist interpretation according to which the failure to mean is not the object of exploration but the desired goal of the whole enterprise. According to Cavell, the "literalization" of language in Beckett is a way of "undoing" it and, together with this gesture, undoing the "curse of meaning," "belief," and "knowing"[2] that haunts humanity. In other words, Beckett is not about "the failure of meaning" but about its "total, even totalitarian, success—our inability not to mean what we are given to mean."[3] And about an attempt to undo this "curse."

Read through this last insight, Beckett represents the functioning of our language as the little comforting games Vladimir and Estragon play with each other to pass the time. "Will you not play?" "That's the idea, let's contradict each other." "Let's ask each other questions."[4] Pozzo exemplifies here a man who simply cannot function without recourse to the right context and grammar:

> POZZO. I'd like very much to sit down, but I don't quite know how to go about it.
> ESTRAGON. Could I be of any help?
> POZZO. If you asked me perhaps.
> ESTRAGON. What?
> POZZO. If you asked me to sit down.
> ESTRAGON. Would that be a help?
> POZZO. I fancy so.
> ESTRAGON. Here we go. Be seated, sir, I beg of you.
> POZZO. No, no, I wouldn't think of it! [*Pause. Aside.*] Ask me again.
> ESTRAGON. Come come, take a seat, I beseech you, you'll get pneumonia.
> POZZO. You really think so?
> ESTRAGON. Why it's absolutely certain.
> POZZO. No doubt you are right. [*He sits down.*] Done it again! [*Pause.*] Thank you dear fellow.[5]

From Beckett's perspective, the games like those played in *Waiting for Godot* make clear that a narrowly conceived realm of language games, even though successful in refraining from essentialist gestures, presupposes the same recourse to mastery (as opposed to freedom) as any essentialist equivalents. Theirs is just a mastery of the real rather than of the ideal, of mundane repetition rather than of any essence to which such repetition might give access. Given that this mastery precludes freedom (here mastery of language is equivalent to being mastered by language), it is a truly miserable world in which these three play language games while waiting for Godot. (Again, these are not language games of the sort that Wittgenstein envisaged, but an oversimplified perception of them, feeding Perloff's analysis of the ordinary in terms of "context requirements.") The impoverishment of this world is not yet purely and simply "methodical"; the mastery is denounced but without an alternative, quietist or other. The language games fail to give comfort because they do not bring about any change; in the end, as before, "nothing happens." In other words, the fact that language can still be depended on does not change anything about the lack of prospects that the characters have to endure. The functioning of the game is not nearly enough without an attempt to account for the unpredictable that transcends the scope of the game. Beckett on the one hand denounces the omnipresence of mastery in language and writing—including his own—and on the other hand dreams of a kind of writing that, through assuming radical poverty, would release itself from this gesture of mastery.

It is rather in this sense that Beckett's enterprise is directed at trying to capture the breakdown of a language game and not in the sense Perloff ascribes to it. Perloff's explanation of the breakdown of language in *Watt* (as demonstrating what happens when words are used out of context) in no way accounts for the later Beckett's passion for what he calls "ill-saying." In this respect, Badiou's astute reading of Beckett's later work is more helpful. In *Worstward Ho* it becomes clear, if it was not yet so in *Watt*, that "ill-saying" is the *telos* of Beckett's artistic enterprise and does not denote a failure that has to be overcome or avoided. "Becket's fundamental thesis is that *the saying that is adequate to the said suppresses saying*. Ill saying is the free essence of saying."[6] Badiou interprets Beckett's ill-saying as the opening of language toward the unpredictable: a "new" language that will be able to name events that remain invisible in the framework of prevailing language.

Cavell's reading was not unaware of its possible quietist implications. Toward the end of his essay, Cavell recalls Beckett's reply to a suggested contradiction between his pursuit of not having to mean on the one hand and his continuing to write on the other: "Que voulez-vous, Monsieur? C'est les mots. On n'a rien d'autre."[7] This seems to suggest that Beckett's pursuit of silence should not be taken too literally—or that it is not his only pursuit.

I then considered one possibility of approaching Beckett's gesture of emptying the archives that was suggested by Deleuze's reading of Beckett. According to this reading, the goal of Beckett's writing can be seen as analogous to that of Spinoza's God: to exhaust himself in his creation. Thus, Beckett's gesture of hollowing out (of emptying language of words and words of their content)—the "exhausted" nature of his writing—can be seen not merely as a desire to turn silent and embrace the void but as a reflection on Beckett's role as the author of his work. What Perloff's reading took to be the evacuation of meaning turned out in Deleuze to be the evacuation of the self. (Under certain conditions, this reading appears to be analogous to Derrida's Joyce-inspired hyper-totalizing project. The "total exhaustion" functions then as a negative flip side of Derrida's attempt to account for a totality.)

The third reading of Beckett I considered, that of Badiou, seems to license a distinction in Beckett's negative gesture between two quite separate stakes. Beckett's terms "unsaying" and "ill-saying" can no longer be used interchangeably since subtraction and failure become two independent pursuits. Whereas "unsaying" (subtraction) should be seen as a gesture of *epochē* (a gesture proper to thinking), "ill-saying" ("failure") is a poetic gesture of artistic production. In other words, the negativity in question is not to be seen as an evacuation of any sort; the thinking subject asserts itself through procedures of subtraction (reduction to the essential), and (innovative) meaning comes to be through artistic ill-saying. This is the most affirmative of the existing readings of Beckett, but it is also the one in which Beckett's own desire to elude the position of sovereignty dictated by language and by the position of the author is wholly ignored.

I also proposed three points at which Beckett and Derrida might meet. I chose these three singular transactions not only because they were the most opportune meeting points for these two authors in particular, considering their interests and intellectual itinerary, but—more importantly—because they denote three foci through which contemporary philosophy looks at literature: its unique signature, the conditions of its appearing for us as such (variously addressed as the phenomenality, authority, or autonomy of the literary object),[8] and the status of its language.

The first of these foci was the subjective signature, or what Derrida (following Artaud) calls "the subjectile." This reading seemed to bring the two authors as close together as they could ever be, yet they remained separated by the ultimate impenetrability of the "subjectilian wall" in Beckett. This impenetrability once again confirmed the latter's disbelief in the possibility of a singular institutive event. On the other hand, it would be too simple to conclude univocally that the impenetrability of the subjectile in Beckett is univocal. The event of the signature in *The Unnamable*, which, as we have seen, fails to take place, is described as passing over a limit or a threshold (the "threshold of my story") and also as an aporia ("aporia pure and simple").[9] Analogous to the singular that produces its own law in disappearing, aporia, even though it "can never be endured as such," remains, in virtue of some "contaminating contraband," "the law of all decisions."[10] Derrida's deconstruction, if we rely on his own statement, is located in this partition ("[d]econstruction is explicitly defined as a certain aporetic experience of the impossible").[11] Beckett's *Unnamable*, evoking "aporia" in its opening sentences and insisting that a similar status of impossibility be granted to it ("I too have the right to be shown impossible"), is a discourse on this partition. This means that the (im)possibility of penetrating the "wooden door" of words, of death, of "the threshold of my story," remains, in the end, undecidable. After all, even though the Unnamable describes its enterprise as impossible, this does not result in silence: the "contaminating contraband" keeps seeping through. The threshold is shown to be impassable, but, nevertheless, the phenomenal authority of the literary work establishes itself precisely as a function of this impassable threshold.

In my analysis of the *Unnamable*, I noted that, just like in Derrida's reading of Artaud, the subjectile stands at the same time for the subject-producing gesture of artistic production as for what happens to the medium of that production: the point in which the hand touches ("pierces") the canvas. I have retraced the rhetoric of partitions in Beckett's *Unnamable:* the "tympanum," "membrane," the "doors," and "windows." The "I" and the "words" (i.e., the linguistic "canvas") turned out to function within this rhetoric in exactly the same way. At first it is "me" who has to traverse the doors of my story (or, in the words of the letter to Axel Kaun, it is me who has to pierce the words), but at the same time I am this ossified partition myself (at first a membrane, a tympanum, later a (trap)door fallen above the hangman). The subjectile is precisely this coincidence of the subject and the work. Consequently, if "I" am charged with the task of "perforating" language ("the words"), then perforating "myself" is a part of this task. That which must be pierced is at the same time that which must do the piercing. (Or, putting it in semi-Beckettian vocabulary, "there is nothing to pierce with," and yet it must take place.) Badiou calls this acrobatic attempt at self-piercing, in which the "subjectile" and language are one, a "torsion du sujet"—a torsion of the subject. (A literal example of this can be found in Beckett's *How It Is* in the form of the bizarre image of "that extreme eastern sage" growing nails through the palms of his clenched fists.)[12] This self-aggressive gesture in Beckett is one of the many in which the subject is turning both against and toward itself. That is the meaning of Beckett's *Company*: one is company to oneself but never without prostheses in the form of stories, characters, and words. In this sense, Beckett's work is all about closing the circuit.

The claim here is not only that one is company to oneself; the other part of it is that literature is "for company." Literature performs the prosthetic function of closing the circuit (stories told for company, for comfort, like the one about the heroic Joe Breen in "The Calmative").[13] In the end, unless one finds a way to escape the position of mastery, one always ends up, in the closing words of *Company*, "as you always were. Alone."[14]

Beckett alternates between the acknowledgment of his sovereign position as writer and language user and the desire for release from this sovereignty (in silence, forgetting, the loss of self). Deleuze's interpretation of Beckett via "exhaustion" is perhaps most successful in presenting itself as a limit case in this choice: the supreme sovereignty through the supreme loss of sovereignty.

Epilogue: Without Writing

In one of his last published texts,[15] Derrida quite explicitly identified writing, including his own, with a desire for mastery: "[W]riting dreams of sovereignty, writing is cruel, murderous. . . . A crime against humanity, the genocide itself, and the crime against *generation*."[16] This "silent lesson" (which he draws from his rereading of Jacques Trilling's book on Joyce) makes Derrida contemplate a certain "nostalgia of retreat" in the shape of a dream of another writing:

[T]o begin to love life, to know birth. Including my own. . . . A new rule of life: to breathe without writing, from now on, to breathe beyond writing. . . . [W]ithout writing, without phrase, without murder. . . . Beyond the instinct of death, beyond the instinct of power and mastery. Writing without writing. Another writing, the other of writing, the altered writing, the one that has always traversed mine in silence.[17]

These words are not simply recalling, as so often in Derrida, the gesture of negative theology (e.g., in the expression "writing without writing"). The "new rule of life" evoked here is "to breathe without writing." Would this constitute a reappraisal of Derrida's reading of Husserl in *La voix et le phénomène,* the essay that for the first time brought Derrida fame and recognition? In that essay, Derrida argued that Husserl privileges voice over writing—voice that, as breath, "simulates" life and presence—in order to protect what he took to be our unmediated access to the ideality of meaning. (Husserl's fallacy here would be to think of the meaning of the written word as mediated by a sign in a way that the meaning of the spoken word is not.) And now, thirty-five years later, Derrida announces his desire to "breathe without writing"—"beyond the instinct of death, beyond the instinct of power and mastery." This overtly recapitulatory reference to the beginning of Derrida's career as a philosopher ends with a parenthesis—"signé Ulysse"—that announces Derrida's return to the point of origin, the end of a circular journey that started with Husserl.

Derrida's essay addresses both the desire to and the impossibility of releasing oneself from one's origin—one's "mother"—by killing her ("matricide"). Thereby he poses an analogy, in psychoanalytic terms, between paternity and maternity. The return to Husserl considered here would be a return to the "mother." The desire of matricide—attributed to Joyce on the basis of the autobiographic motives in the opening pages of *Ulysses,* and via Joyce to writers in general (hence the title of Trilling's book: *James Joyce ou l'écriture matricide*)—is interpreted by Derrida as a gesture of sovereignty. To kill one's mother means to stop the possibility of birth—that is, to arrest time: Joyce, Derrida's example, is reported to have wanted to be "father and son of his works."[18] (Moran's words in Beckett echo this desire but with a significant subtraction, in which "the works" disappear: "I was my father and I was my son.")[19]

Renouncing this gesture is perhaps the most explicit gesture Derrida has ever made toward Beckett: "beyond power and mastery." On the other hand, this reading of matricide as a gesture of sovereignty that arrests time sheds light on Derrida's old, inexplicit gesture toward Beckett. Without mentioning Beckett's name, Derrida inserts Molloy's words in his *Glas*:[20]

> I called her Mag, when I had to call her something. And I called her Mag because for me, without my knowing why, the letter g abolished the syllable Ma, and as it were spat on it, better than any other letter would have done. And at the same time

I satisfied a deep and doubtless unacknowledged need, the need to have a Ma, that is a mother, and to proclaim it, audibly. For before you say Mag you say ma, inevitably.

This quotation is accompanied by a reference to Ivan Fónagy, a Hungarian linguist inspired by Freud, who links the *g* sound to "the pharyngeal contraction that accompanies a refusal of nourishment" and to a "phantasy of the *vagina dentata*." Suddenly in one gesture Derrida shows Beckett to be an accomplice, sharing with him the phantasm of matricide, of arresting time, of mastery or of sovereignty (just as much as they, only a moment ago, turned out to share the desire for a nonviolent, nonsovereign writing—writing "without matricide").

Notes

When two page locations are given for a single quotation, the first refers to the English source, the second indicates the location of the corresponding fragment in the French version.

INTRODUCTION

1. Jacques Derrida, "This Strange Institution Called Literature," in *Acts of Literature,* ed. Derek Attridge (New York and London: Routledge, 1992), 60–61.
2. André Bernold, *L'amitié de Beckett: 1979–1989* (Paris: Hermann, 1992), 85–86.
3. Derrida, "This Strange Institution Called Literature," 61–62.
4. "[N]on seulement mais en particulier en raison de mon incompétence, d'écrire quelque chose qui soit digne . . . de Beckett," in "Beckett in France," special issue, *Journal of Beckett Studies* 4, no. 1 (1994): 85.
5. Anthony Uhlmann, *Beckett and Post-structuralism* (Cambridge: Cambridge University Press, 1999), 3.
6. Peter Murphy, "At Beckett's Grave (or Why Jacques Derrida Has Given Up on Writing in the Direction of Beckett—for the Moment)," *Textual Studies in Canada/Etudes Textuelles au Canada* 6 (1995).
7. Jacques Derrida, *Signéponge/Signsponge,* trans. Richard Rand (New York: Columbia University Press, 1984), bilingual edition, 22/23. "In this respect, from the edge on which it takes place, his [Ponge's] signature will have foiled those excessively loose or crude machines which are as much those of biographical and psychological criticism (or literature), whatever their refinements or modernization may be, as those of formalist or structuralist criticism (or literature) which encloses itself too quickly within what it takes to be the inside of the text, leaving the signature on the outside and sheltered from its being put on stage, into play, or into the abyss."
8. John Pilling, ed., *The Cambridge Companion to Beckett* (Cambridge: Cambridge University Press, 1994), 222.
9. Georges Bataille, "Le Silence de Molloy," *Critique* 7 (1951): 387–96; Maurice

Blanchot, "Où maintenant? Qui maintenant?" *Nouvelle Revue Française* 2 (1953): 678–86; Cavell (1958) in Stanley Cavell, "Ending the Waiting Game: A Reading of Beckett's Endgame," in *Must We Mean What We Say?* (Cambridge: Cambridge University Press, 1976); Adorno (1961) in Theodor Adorno, "Trying to Understand *Endgame*," in *Notes to Literature* (New York: Columbia University Press, 1991); Kristeva and Cixous, in Tom Bishop and Raymond Federman, eds., *Cahier de L'Herne: Samuel Beckett* (Paris: Éditions de l'Herne, 1976).

10. Deleuze gave an interpretation of Beckett's *Film* in Gilles Deleuze, *Cinema 1* (London: Athlone Press, 1992); Nussbaum gave a reading of Beckett as an exercise in deconstructing emotions in Martha Nussbaum, "Narrative Emotions: Beckett's Genealogy of Love," *Ethics*, January 1988; Ricoeur referred to the example of Beckett in *Time and Narrative* (Chicago: University of Chicago Press, 1984–1988); Lyotard writes about Beckett in Jean-François Lyotard, "Scapeland," in *L'inhumain* (Paris: Galilée, 1988).

11. Beckett and Schopenhauer (Ulrich Pothast, *Die eigentlich metaphysische Tätigkeit. Über Schopenhauers Ästhetik und ihre Anwendung durch Samuel Beckett* [Frankfurt am Main: Suhrkamp, 1982]); Beckett and Nietzsche (Jacquart, 1983); Beckett and Heidegger (Lance St.-J Butler, *Samuel Beckett and the Meaning of Being* [London: Macmillan Press, 1984]); Beckett (Watt, 1998).

12. Alain Badiou, "L'écriture du générique: Samuel Beckett," in *Conditions* (Paris: Seuil, 1992); Alain Badiou, *Beckett: L'increvable désir* (Paris: Hachette, 1995); Deleuze, "L'épuisé," in Gilles Deleuze, *Critique et clinique* (Paris: Minuit, 1993); Maurice Blanchot, "Oh tout finir," *Critique* 46, nos. 519–20 (1990): 635–37; Marjorie Perloff, "Witt-Watt: The Language of Resistance/The Resistance of Language," in *Wittgenstein's Ladder* (Chicago: University of Chicago Press, 1996); Uhlmann, *Beckett and Post-structuralism* (Cambridge: Cambridge University Press, 1999); Richard Lane, ed., *Beckett and Philosophy* (Houndmills, Basingstoke, Hampshire, and New York: Palgrave, 2002).

13. Peter Hallward, *Badiou: A Subject to Truth* (Minneapolis, London: University of Minnesota Press, 2003), xxiv.

14. Alain Badiou, *Manifesto for Philosophy* (Albany, NY: SUNY Press, 1999), 66.

15. Ibid., 70.

16. Jacques Derrida, *Monolingualism of the Other; or, the Prosthesis of Origin* (Stanford, CA: Stanford University Press, 1998), 4. "[V]ous n'êtes pas un philosophe sérieux! Si vous continuez, on vous mettra dans un département . . . de littérature," Jacques Derrida, *Le monolinguisme de l'autre* (Paris: Galilée, 1996).

17. Contrary to what is often thought, Socrates' condemnation of poets reported in the dialogue does not hinge only on the argument that poetry is imitation "thrice removed from the truth" ("must we not infer that all those poetical individuals, beginning with Homer, are only imitators: they copy images of virtue and the like but the truth they never reach?") (*Republic*, X, 600e). Imitation can still be vindicated, provided it serves to display the exemplary ethos. The ultimate argu-

ment is pedagogic. Since the poet, in his role of an imitator, is moreover "concerned with an inferior part of the soul . . . , we shall be right in refusing to admit him [the poet] into a well-ordered State, because he awakens and nourishes and strengthens the feelings and impairs the reason." *Republic* X [605a–605b].

18. Plato "banish[ed] poetry from his republic—but not from his Republic, the city of words." Stanley Cavell, *Conditions Handsome and Unhandsome: The Constitution of Emersonian Perfectionism* (La Salle, IL: Open Court, 1990), 11.

19. Arthur C. Danto, *Philosophical Disenfranchisement of Art* (New York: Columbia University Press, 1986), 1–21.

20. Immanuel Kant, *Critique of Judgement*, trans. J. H. Bernard (New York: Hafner Press, 1951), 73.

21. Mark Edmundson, *Literature against Philosophy, Plato to Derrida* (Cambridge: Cambridge University Press, 1995), 8.

22. Philippe Lacoue-Labarthe and Jean-Luc Nancy, *The Literary Absolute: The Theory of Literature in German Romanticism* (Albany, NY: SUNY Press, 1988).

23. See Rodolphe Gasché, "Ideality in Fragmentation," in *Friedrich Schlegel: Philosophical Fragments* (Minneapolis, London: University of Minnesota Press, 1991), xxix.

24. Lacoue-Labarthe and Nancy, *The Literary Absolute*, 31.

25. See Daniela Vallega-Neu, "Poietic Saying," in *Companion to Heidegger's Contributions to Philosophy*, ed. Charles Scott, Susan Schoenbohm, Daniela Vallega-Neu, and Alejandro Vallega (Bloomington, IN: Indiana University Press, 2001).

26. Jacques Derrida and Maurizio Ferraris, *A Taste for the Secret* (Cambridge: Polity Press, 2001), 11.

27. Ibid., 11–12.

28. "[S]i la littérature garde ici quelque privilège à mes yeux, c'est d'une part en raison de ce qu'elle thématise de l'événement d'écriture et d'autre part de ce qui, dans son histoire politique, la lie à cette autorisation principielle de 'tout dire' qui la rapporte de façon unique à ce qu'on appelle la vérité, la fiction, le simulacre, la science, la philosophie, la loi, le droit, la démocratie." Jacques Derrida, "Une 'folie' doit veiller sur la pensée," *Magazine Littéraire* 286 (March 1991): 23. [Here and in what follows, where the English source is not provided, the translation is mine.]

29. Ibid., 23.

30. Jacques Derrida, "Ulysses Gramophone: Hear Say Yes in Joyce," in *Acts of Literature*, ed. Derek Attridge (London: Routledge, 1992), 262. Jacques Derrida, *Ulysse gramophone* (Paris: Galilée, 1987), 66.

31. Derrida, "This Strange Institution Called Literature," 42.

32. Kant, *Critique of Judgement*, 48–51.

33. "[L]e poème au fond, est dédié non pas tant au coucher de soleil en général qu'à ce coucher de soleil, non pas tant à la couleur de la tuile en général qu'à ce couleur de ces tuiles-là; il n'y parvient jamais absolument, mais c'est quand même sa visée." Alain Badiou, "La poésie en condition de la philosophie," *Europe: Revue littéraire mensuelle* 78, nos. 849–850 (2000): 65–75.

34. "[I]l y a mise de la philosophie sous condition du poème: accepter de se confronter aux formes successives de cette expérience de l'incandescence du visible telle que le poème tente de la capturer." Ibid., 72, my emphasis.

35. Iterability is a powerful concept in Derrida's philosophy. It is the condition of all experience. Timothy Clark gives a useful description of the working of iterability: "[T]he date, in idea, is unique and idiomatic. Yet, to be readable at all, a date must, so to speak, have effaced its putative singularity in its repeatability within the calendar. . . . A date necessarily emerges as the very negation of that which it names in its singularity. This is the structure of its readability. Without that, the date would be no more than an undecipherable mark, not a date at all in fact" (Clark, *Derrida, Heidegger, Blanchot*, 168).

36. Derrida, *Signéponge/Signsponge*, 116/117.

37. Lacoue-Labarthe and Nancy, *The Literary Absolute: The Theory of Literature in German Romanticism*, 77.

38. G.W.F. Hegel, *Phenomenology of Spirit* (Oxford: Oxford University Press, 1979), 66.

39. Derrida, "This Strange Institution Called Literature," 68.

40. Ibid., 68.

41. Hegel, *Phenomenology of Spirit*, § 143, p. 86.

42. "L'être développé par la Force (*Kraft*), c'est le phénomène (*Erscheinung*)." Alexandre Kojève, *Introduction à la lecture de Hegel* (Paris: Gallimard, 1947), 47. The abridged English edition (Alexandre Kojève, *Introduction to the Reading of Hegel: Lectures on the Phenomenology of Spirit*, assembled by Raymond Queneau, edited by Allan Bloom [Ithaca, NY: Cornell University Press, 1980]) omits the relevant fragment.

43. Jacques Derrida, *Writing and Difference* (London: Routledge, 1978), 26–27; Jacques Derrida, *L'écriture et la différence* (Paris: Seuil, 1967), 45.

44. Jacques Derrida, "Force of Law: The 'Mystical Foundation of Authority,'" in *Deconstruction and the Possibility of Justice*, ed. David Gray Carlson, Drucilla Cornell, and Michel Rosenfeld (London, New York: Routledge, 1992), 7; Jacques Derrida, *Force de loi* (Paris: Galilée, 1994), 20.

45. Ibid., 7/20–21.

46. Derrida, "This Strange Institution Called Literature," 41.

47. Gilles Deleuze, *Difference and Repetition*, trans. Paul Patton (London: Continuum, 1994), 119.

48. Jacques Derrida, *Limited Inc* (Evanston, IL: Northwestern University Press, 1988), 149.

49. Derrida, "This Strange Institution Called Literature," 42–43.

50. Jacques Derrida, "The Deaths of Roland Barthes," in *Philosophy and Non-philosophy since Merleau-Ponty*, ed. Hugh J. Silverman (London: Routledge, 1988), 286. French original, "Les morts de Roland Barthes," was published in Jacques Derrida, *Psyché: Inventions de l'autre* (Paris: Galillée, 1987), 296.

51. Derrida, "This Strange Institution Called Literature," 41–42.
52. And what Barthes (in opposition to Descartes' dream of *mathesis universalis*) calls the *mathesis singularis*.
53. Samuel Beckett, *Trilogy* (London: Calder, 1959), 380.
54. Badiou, *Beckett: L'increvable désir*, 29.
55. Samuel Beckett, *The Complete Dramatic Works* (London: Faber and Faber, 1986), 16.
56. Ibid., 15.
57. Ibid., 16.
58. Ibid., 61.
59. Portions of the French text of *Signsponge* were originally delivered as a lecture before the colloquium on Francis Ponge, held at Cerisy-la-Salle in July 1975, but the whole text was not published until 1984.
60. It seems advisable to use the term "tone" ("'tone,' *Stimmung* or *pathos*," 291), which Derrida uses with reference to the work of James Joyce, rather than the even less neutral-sounding "perfume of discourse" or "perfumative." Derrida, "Ulysses Gramophone: Hear Say Yes in Joyce," 297, 300.
61. Jürgen Habermas, "Philosophy and Science as Literature?" in *Postmetaphysical Thinking: Philosophical Essays* (Cambridge, MA: MIT Press, 1994), 209.
62. Derrida, "Ulysses Gramophone: Hear Say Yes in Joyce," 297.
63. Ibid., 290.
64. Ibid., 293, my emphasis.

1. THE QUESTION OF LITERATURE

1. Jacques Derrida, *Demeure: Fiction and Testimony*, trans. Elizabeth Rottenberg (Stanford, CA: Stanford University Press, 2000), 20.
2. Jacques Derrida, "The Law of Genre," in *Demeure: Fiction and Testimony*, 227.
3. Jacques Derrida, "Before the Law," in *Acts of Literature*, 187; Jacques Derrida, "Préjugés: Devant la loi," in *La faculté de juger* (Paris: Minuit, 1985), 104.
4. Samuel Beckett, "Company," *Nohow On* (New York: Grove Press, 1996), 46.
5. For the discussion of the difference between Derrida and the various strains of literary criticism, see Gasché, "Literature in Parentheses," in *The Tain of the Mirror* (Cambridge, MA: Harvard University Press, 1986); for the difference between Derrida's "literature" and Heidegger's *Dichtung*, see Joseph G. Kronick, *Derrida and the Future of Literature* (Albany, NY: SUNY Press, 1999), 6–9. In his *Tain of the Mirror*, Rodolphe Gasché gives a reading of Derrida's "literature" that places it within his debate with phenomenology and in particular with Husserl. On the other hand, Derrida himself considers his work on Husserl a detour in a more general pursuit of his interests in writing and literature. As he says, at the time he was about to translate and comment on Husserl, "une thématique obsédante organisait déjà tout un espace de questions et d'interprétations: celle de l'écriture, en-

198 Notes to Chapter 1

tre littérature, philosophie et science. . . . Le passage par Husserl n'a pas été seulement un détour. Mais il est vrai que, injustement, je le crois de plus en plus, je m'en suis aussi détourné." Derrida, "Une 'folie' doit veiller sur la pensée," 20–22.

6. Jacques Derrida, *Sur Parole: Instantanés Philosophiques* (Paris: Éditions de l'aube, 1999), 24.

7. Derrida, "This Strange Institution Called Literature," 39–40.

8. Derrida, "Mes chances," *Confrontation* 19 (1988): 27.

9. Derrida, "Before the Law," 186/103.

10. Samuel Beckett, "Le monde et le pantalon," *Cahiers d'art* 20–21 (1945).

11. Derrida, "This Strange Institution Called Literature," 42.

12. Ibid., 36. The translator emphasizes that "tout dire" means "both to 'say everything' with a sense of exhausting a totality, and to 'say anything,' i.e., to speak without constraints."

13. Derrida, "This Strange Institution Called Literature," 36, my emphasis.

14. Ibid., 35

15. The word "singular" is perhaps crucial here for distinguishing between the Hegelian totalizing and the literary one: whereas the first one gathers under a concept that in itself does not form a part of the gathered set, the latter gathers starting from a singular that always already belongs to the created set. Whereas the former gathers by subsumption (there is a hierarchy involved), the latter gathers by translating (cf., again: "to gather, by translating, all figures into one another, to totalize by formalizing" [ibid., 36]—there is no hierarchy here, since the subsumption is reciprocal). A singular totality is thus theorized, totalized, differently. Already here the immense importance of the singular for Derrida's thinking about literature becomes apparent.

16. Derrida, "This Strange Institution Called Literature," 41–42.

17. Ibid. The principle of iterability functions also for the singularity of the oeuvre: "Without the mark there is certainly no oeuvre. Each oeuvre, being absolutely singular in some respect, must have and admit the proper name. This is the condition of its iterability as such."

18. "Yes, everything has already happened to us with *Ulysses* and has been signed in advance by Joyce." Whatever we might invent on Joyce "finds itself already programmophoned in the Joycean corpus." Derrida, "Ulysses Gramophone: Hear Say Yes in Joyce," 281–83. Joyce, the "gathering" author par excellence, is not for nothing the only literary author to whose work Derrida goes to considerable pains to demonstrate a constant affiliation (see "Deux mots pour Joyce," the opening essay in Derrida, *Ulysse gramophone*), and Derrida even admits to feeling a sort of envious "ressentiment" toward Joyce's hypermnesic mastery.

19. This *secrétaire*-approach, the love for the hidden reserves of language, is incidentally the part of Derrida's approach to literature that is perhaps the most apt to come into conflict with the analytic approaches to Beckett that insist on the hidden (or plain) literality of Beckett's work, resisting the figurative reading of his texts (cf. Cavell and, more recently, Perloff; in fact, Perloff—by reading Beckett

through the situation of resistance where language abounds in enigmas and secret meanings—is already in complicity with Derrida and continental philosophy). Both approaches, however, fail to take the notorious Beckett statement "no symbols where none intended" seriously enough; Beckett's texts are not without figurative meaning altogether, but they are also not only that. This undecidability between the literal and the "metaphysical" is precisely what makes Beckett's texts so unpretentious and at the same time so captivating. But Derrida also problematizes the opposition between the figurative and the literal.

20. Derrida, "Before the Law," 197/115.

21. Samuel Beckett, "Dante . . . Bruno. Vico . . . Joyce," *Transition* 16–17 (1929).

22. Samuel Beckett, *Complete Dramatic Works* (London: Faber and Faber, 1986), 223.

23. Samuel Beckett, *How It Is* (New York: Grove Press, 1964), 35; Samuel Beckett, *Comment c'est* (Paris: Éditions de Minuit, 1961), 55.

24. Beckett, "Company," 86.

25. Derrida, *Signéponge/Signsponge*, 68/69.

26. Beckett, *How It Is*, 38; *Comment c'est*, 60.

27. Derrida, *Monolingualism of the Other; or, The Prosthesis of the Origin*, 51, translation modified. *Le monolinguisme de l'autre*, 85.

28. Again, it has to be kept in mind that in a recent interview, Derrida suggested that a "distinctive criteri[on]" of literature can be found in its "relation with natural language." Derrida, *A Taste for the Secret*, 11.

29. This text, in discussing idiom as a product of bilingualism, becomes relevant for consideration of the issue of bilingualism in Beckett's work. Derrida explores here the "juncture between the universal structure and its idiomatic witness" (Derrida, *Monolingualism of the Other; or, The Prosthesis of the Origin*, 59, translation modified. *Le monolinguisme de l'autre*, 116). The universal language is not the language of concepts but rather "la traduction absolue" (117), a transparency of meaning between languages (between mother tongue and foreign language, for example), without ultimate source. The idiomatic language of the witness, the private idiom of a writer, situates itself in the division between languages.

30. Gilles Deleuze and Felix Guattari, *A Thousand Plateaus: Capitalism and Schizophrenia* (Minneapolis: University of Minnesota Press, 1987), 320; Gilles Deleuze, *Mille plateaux* (Paris: Minuit, 1980), 393.

31. Beckett, *Complete Dramatic Works*, 473.

32. Derrida, "This Strange Institution Called Literature," 43.

33. "Let me tell you this, when social workers offer you, free, gratis and for nothing, something to hinder you from swooning, which with them is an obsession, it is useless to recoil, they will pursue you to the ends of the earth, the vomitory in their hands. . . . The liquid overflowed, the mug rocked with a noise of chattering teeth . . . Until, panic-stricken, I flung it all far from me." Beckett, *Trilogy*, 24. Could it be that the hermeneutic activity of a critic, his efforts to extract as

much as possible from the text, or add something of his own to the text ("gratis, free and for nothing"), is represented here by Beckett as a "vomitory," which Molloy rejects? Could Derrida's grafting, the most nonviolent approach to literature (just like the activity of a social worker), also be seen as such a vomitory?

34. Deleuze, *A Thousand Plateaus: Capitalism and Schizophrenia*, 333–34; *Mille plateaux*, 411–12.

35. Deleuze, *A Thousand Plateaus: Capitalism and Schizophrenia*, 521, n. 1. (Deleuze quotes from Roland Omnès, *L'univers et ses métamorphoses* [Paris: Hermann, 1973], 164.)

36. Beckett, *The Complete Short Prose*, (New York: Grove Press, 1995), 62.

37. Jacques Derrida, "The Double Session," in *Dissemination* (London: Athlone, 1981), 261.

38. In the works that came later, it is much more clear that this element of death (a necessary detour, loss of presence) promotes life (in the sense of preservation and multiplication of meaning).

39. Martin Heidegger, *Poetry, Language, Thought* (New York: Harper and Row, 1971), 23. "[O]der ist gar der so vorgestellte Bau des Dinges entworfen nach dem Gerüst des Satzes?" Martin Heidegger, "Der Ursprung des Kunstwerkes," in *Holzwege* (Frankfurt am Main: Vittorio Klostermann, 1950), 13.

40. Derrida, *Monolingualism of the Other; or, The Prosthesis of the Origin*, 33/60.

41. Derrida, *Demeure: Fiction and Testimony*, 60.

42. Derrida, "This Strange Institution Called Literature," 36.

43. Ibid., 39.

44. Derrida is quite ambiguous (or just eager to meet his interlocutor halfway) here: on the one hand he tells us that the idea of "suspension of reference" is a "stupid and uninformed rumor" and that "a work that was purely self-referential would immediately be annulled." This seems to be consistent with his understanding of the literary work as being capable of reflecting both on itself and on the external world (in contrast to the New Criticism theory of the autonomy of the literary work). Then, however, he goes on to say, "You'll say that that's maybe what's happening. In which case it is this experience of the nothing-ing of nothing that interests our desire under the name of literature" (Derrida, "This Strange Institution Called Literature," 47).

45. Derrida, "This Strange Institution Called Literature," 41. The "force" and "power" depend for Derrida on iterability: "The 'power' that language is capable of, the power that there is, as language or as writing, is that a singular mark should also be repeatable, iterable, as a mark" (42–43).

46. Jacques Derrida, *Dissemination* (London: Athlone, 1981), 324.

47. Rodolphe Gasché, *The Tain of the Mirror* (Cambridge, MA: Harvard University Press, 1986), 120. According to Gasché, Derrida's critical project begins with specularity: in the "first step of the deconstruction of reflection and speculation, the mirroring is made excessive in order that it may look through the look-

ing glass" (Gasché, *The Tain of the Mirror*, 238). In this way, Derrida's philosophy shows the limits of reflection by "reinscribing reflection and speculation into what exceeds it," namely into the "minimal constellations" of the "infrastructures" (101). These are the general textual effects explored by Derrida, such as *différance*, arche-trace, the supplement, and the "quasi-transcendental" in *Glas*. In the wake of Gasché's book, readers of Derrida (Derek Attridge, Richard Rand, Joseph Kronick) started to dissociate the work of the latter from the figures of the specular, mirror reflection and even from the *mise en abyme*.

48. Derrida, "This Strange Institution Called Literature," 70. Significantly, Derrida chooses not to follow Gasché's pluralized "infrastructures." This would seem to suggest that beyond all the "singular" applications, he himself sees a unity in the variety of traits of which Gasché provided a very precise quasi-taxonomy in his *Tain of the Mirror*. In what follows, I will often address those traits in their generality, in Gasché's own formulation: "différance is not a generalization of the ontico-ontological difference but rather the generalization of the set of traits to which this difference yields in spite of its recognized superiority to all regional differences." Gasché, "God, for Example," *Inventions of Difference*, (Cambridge, MA: Harvard University Press, 1994), 158.

49. This term, borrowed from ancient heraldry, designates a device whereby a shield has a smaller copy of itself represented on its surface that in turn has a smaller copy of itself on its surface, and so on. (Dutch native speakers know this as the "Droste effect.") "In literary parlance, the *mise en abyme*, or 'placement in abyss,' is meant to designate the way in which the operations of reading and writing are represented in the text, and *in advance*, as it were, of any other possible reading." From the translator's introduction to Derrida, *Signéponge/Signsponge*, ix. For the discussion of the interplay of *abîme, s'abîmer*, and *mise en abyme*, see the latter essay by Derrida. The first use of the term in the sense of a literary figure is attributed to Gide. For the discussion of the figure in literary theory, see Lucien Dällenbach, *The Mirror in the Text* (Chicago: University of Chicago Press, 1989), in particular pp. 41–116, and Mieke Bal, "Reprise de l'interruption ou la mise en abyme," in *Femmes imaginaires* (Paris: Nizet, 1986), 159–66.

50. Jacques Derrida, *Of Grammatology*, trans. Gayatri Spivak (Baltimore: Johns Hopkins University Press, 1976), 36. "Le reflet, l'image, le double dédouble ce qu'il redouble." *De la grammatologie*, 55.

51. Derrida, "This Strange Institution Called Literature," 72.

52. Jacques Derrida, ". . . That Dangerous Supplement . . . ," in *Acts of Literature*, ed. Derek Attridge (London: Routledge, 1992), 108.

53. Derrida, "This Strange Institution Called Literature," 72.

54. Rodolphe Gasché, *The Tain of the Mirror* (Cambridge, MA: Harvard University Press, 1986), 127.

55. Martin Heidegger, *Being and Time* (New York: Harper & Row, 1962), 320.

56. Jacques Derrida, "This Strange Institution Called Literature," 72.

57. Derrida, *Demeure: Fiction and Testimony*, 72.

58. The gesture of reflection makes it possible for us to address literature in terms of law rather than of anarchy. The *mise en abyme* on the other hand ensures that the reflection does not sublate differences but multiplies them.

59. There is no doubt that Deleuze and Guattari perceive Beckett's characters "in their trashcan or on their bench"—as they put it in *A Thousand Plateaus*—as exemplifying the nomadic. Not only because of their ambulant way of life and "fundamental indiscipline," which makes them resemble nomadic warriors, but also because of their anonymity and vicariousness, which makes them like the nameless stones in a game of Go. One should be wary, though, of reading a kind of ethos into the nomadic: it is as much an object of Beckett's irony as any other ethos.

60. Deleuze and Guattari, *A Thousand Plateaus: Capitalism and Schizophrenia*, 354; *Mille plateaux*, 437.

61. Beckett, *Trilogy*, 23.

62. Ibid., 24.

63. The opposition between the anonymous game of Go and the coded game of chess, which Deleuze uses to illustrate the difference between *nomos* and *polis*, can explain something about Derrida and Beckett. In contrast to the chess pieces that have intrinsic properties, Go pieces are "pellets, disks, simple arithmetic units, and have only an anonymous, collective, or third-person function: 'It' makes a move. 'It' could be a man, a woman, a louse, an elephant." (Deleuze, *A Thousand Plateaus*, 352–53; *Mille plateaux*, 436). Both this fundamental vicariousness of the Go pieces/characters and its corollary—what Deleuze and Guattari call "another justice": the justice of the reversibility of roles—are very characteristic of Beckett. (This setting of vicariousness could, for example, account for the puzzling reversibility of the master/slave positions in *How It Is*.) The Go pieces' way of dealing with space is thereby also different from that of chess pieces: whereas in chess "it is a question of occupying the maximum number of squares with the minimum number of pieces," Go is about "arraying oneself in an open space," perpetual movement "without aim or destination, without departure or arrival." Derrida tends to treat literature like (coded) chess pieces (the secret, the *secrétaire*, the enigma). Beckett's work resembles more a game of Go—for example, in the case of the permutations of identical and substitutable pebbles in *Molloy*.

64. Samuel Beckett, *Nohow On* (New York: Grove Press, 1996), 96.

65. In chess, the game of the state, "each [chess piece] is like a subject of the statement endowed with a relative power, and these relative powers combine in a subject of enunciation, that is, the chess player." This again seems to be an argument for a reading of Derrida's understanding of literature in terms of chess and state because it reflects the "spectral filiation" and a distribution of power between the author-player and the distinct characters of the different chess pieces. Moreover, since in Go the power is not distributed among the particular pieces but can

only be found in the configuration of the whole over which the player-author has total control, this kind of game could be used to express the hubris of the author who does not communicate with his characters or readers but treats them in a purely instrumental way. The relation of compassion that Derrida describes as proper to literature is not possible in this context.

66. "[T]his is not one institution among others or like the others." Derrida, "This Strange Institution Called Literature," 72.

67. Beckett, *Trilogy*, 302.

68. "That Time," in Beckett, *Complete Dramatic Works*, 389–91.

69. Beckett, *The Complete Short Prose*, 61, 63.

70. "[M]ettre . . . l'abîme en abyme." Derrida, *Signéponge/Signsponge*, 142/143.

71. Beckett, *Trilogy*, 307–8.

72. Beckett, "Company," 21–22. Samuel Beckett, *Compagnie* (Paris: Les Éditions de Minuit, 1985), 40–41.

73. The history of the hedgehog starts with the *Athenaeum* Fragment 206. See Friedrich Schlegel, *Philosophical Fragments* (Minneapolis: Minnesota University Press, 1991), 45. (In Peter Firchow's translation, the hedgehog becomes a porcupine.) The animal also appears in Nietzsche's *Ecce Homo*; in Heidegger's *Identität und Differenz*; in an extensive discussion of the fragmentary in Lacoue-Labarthe, *The Literary Absolute: The Theory of Literature in German Romanticism*; and in Derrida's two contributions ("*Istrice 2*" and "*Che cos'è la poesia?*" both in Jacques Derrida, *Points . . . : Interviews, 1974–1994*, trans. Peggy Kamuf and others [Stanford, CA: Stanford University Press, 1995]). The latter two contributions address all of the sources mentioned here.

74. Derrida wants to distinguish his understanding of the hedgehog from the "German" one (of, among others, Schlegel), which for him defines poetry in terms of a totalizing logic (according to the interpretation of Schlegel made by Lacoue-Labarthe and Nancy). Derrida's hedgehog is "older than logic" ("*Istrice 2*," 303/312) and hence must be presupposed by it.

75. Beckett, "Company," 22; *Compagnie*, 41.

76. There are arguments for an allegorical reading of this fragment. For example, the "provision des vers" in the French version finds its echo in *Comment c'est*, where "ver" stands for "imagination" ("si Bom ne venait pas si seulement ca mais alors comment finir cette fesse la main qui plonge tâtonnante de l'imagination donc et la suite et cette voix ses consolations ses promesses de l'imagination cher fruit cher ver"). Beckett, *Comment c'est*, 124–25.

77. Derrida, "This Strange Institution Called Literature," 72.

78. Paul Celan, *Gesammelte Werke* (Frankfurt am Main: Suhrkamp, 1983), 1:251–52; also in Jacques Derrida, "Shibboleth: For Paul Celan," in *Word Traces: Readings of Paul Celan*, ed. Aris Fioretos (Baltimore: Johns Hopkins University Press, 1994), 5–6.

79. Celan, *Gesammelte Werke*, 1:170.
80. Derrida, "Shibboleth: For Paul Celan," 48.
81. "Et te tournant et te retournant dans la chaleur des draps en attendant le sommeil tu éprouvais encore un petit chaud su cœur en pensant à *la chance* qu'avait eue ce hérisson-là de *croiser ton chemin* comme il l'avait fait. En *l'occurrence* un sentier de terre bordé de buis flétri. Comme tu te tenais là en t'interrogeant sur la meilleure façon de tuer le temps jusqu'à l'heure du coucher il fendit l'une des bordures et filait tout droit vers l'autre lorsque tu *entras dans sa vie*." Beckett, *Compagnie*, 39–40, my emphasis.
82. Beckett, "Company," 21; *Compagnie*, 38–39.
83. Derrida, "Before the Law," 183/100.
84. Ibid., 205/122.

2. A SINGULAR ODYSSEY

1. Jacques Derrida, "This Strange Institution Called Literature," 44.
2. Derrida, *A Taste for the Secret*, 11.
3. Rodolphe Gasché, *Of Minimal Things: Studies on the Notion of Relation* (Stanford, CA: Stanford University Press, 1999), 370, n. 6.
4. Gasché, *Of Minimal Things*, 291.
5. Derrida, "Before the Law," 213/131.
6. Ibid., 213.
7. This is another formulation of what I discussed as the "economical" and "juridical" gesture of literature in the previous chapter.
8. See Heimsoeth for an investigation of the development of the notion of individuality (das Einzelne) from Plato to Fichte. Heinz Heimsoeth, *Die sechs grossen Themen der Abendländischen Metaphysik* (Stuttgart: W. Kohlhammer Verlag, 1958), chap. 5: "Das Individuum," 172–203.
9. Jean-François Marquet, *Singularité et événement* (Grenoble: Editions Jérôme Millon, 1995), 44.
10. G.W.F. Hegel, *Logic: Being Part One of the Encyclopaedia of the Philosophical Sciences* (1830), trans. William Wallace (Oxford: Clarendon Press, 1975), 226. "[Die] Einzelheit [ist] [die] Reflexion in sich der Bestimmtheiten der Allgemeinheit und Besonderheit, welche negative Einheit mit sich das an und für sich bestimmte und zugleich mit sich identische oder allgemeine ist." Hegel, *Enzyklopädie der Philosophischen Wissenschaften im Grundrisse* (Hamburg: Felix Meiner, 1992), 179–182.
11. Alféri, *Guillaume d'Ockham: Le singulier*, 15–28.
12. Gilles Deleuze and Claire Parnet, "De la supériorité de la littérature anglaise-américaine," in *Dialogues* (Paris: Flammarion, 1996), 79. Badiou, *Manifesto for Philosophy*, 84.
13. Derrida, "Force of Law: The 'Mystical Foundation of Authority,'" 41/98.

An event may be an event of thought. For example, according to Derrida, the arrival of psychoanalytic discourse constitutes an event (Derrida, "My Chances/Mes Chances," in *Taking Chances,* ed. Joseph H. Smith and William Kerrigan [Baltimore: Johns Hopkins University Press, 1984], 27). So does speculative logic and philosophy in general: "[w]hat one cannot predict is what upholds philosophy and makes possible speculative logic." Derrida, *Demeure: Fiction and Testimony.* And so is literature: "Psychoanalysis" and "Literature . . . name events or a series of events." Jacques Derrida, "My Chances," 1. (Literature's event is "the oeuvre." Ibid., 28.) In other texts, Derrida works with the following examples, or "names," of singular events: death ("arrivant," Jacques Derrida, *Aporias* [Stanford, CA: Stanford University Press, 1993], 22); date (Jacques Derrida, *Schibboleth: Pour Paul Celan* [Paris: Galilée, 1986], passim); decision and reference (both in Jacques Derrida, "The Deaths of Roland Barthes," in *Philosophy and Non-philosophy since Merleau-Ponty,* ed. Hugh J. Silverman [London: Routledge, 1988], 259); the work of literature (Attridge, ed., *Acts of Literature*); shibboleth (Derrida, *Schibboleth: Pour Paul Celan*); and one language among others (Derrida, *Le monolinguisme de l'autre*).

14. "Par le mot par commence donc ce texte." Attridge, ed., *Acts of Literature,* 319. The term "re-presentation," discussed previously, stems from Jacques Derrida, *Speech and Phenomena* (Evanston, IL: Northwestern University Press, 1973), 7/5, and is a translation of Husserl's *Vergegenwärtigung.*

15. Roland Barthes, *Camera Lucida: Reflections on Photography,* trans. Richard Howard (London: Vintage, 1982). Singularity is for Barthes as close as we can come to the "essence" of photography: "photography is . . . only contingency, singularity, risk" (20).

16. Derrida, "The Deaths of Roland Barthes," 279. "Les morts de Roland Barthes" in Derrida, *Psyché: Inventions de l'autre,* 290.

17. Maurice Blanchot, *La part du Feu* (Paris: Gallimard, 1949), 325–26.

18. Barthes, *Camera Lucida: Reflections on Photography,* 75.

19. Derrida, "The Deaths of Roland Barthes," 287/297.

20. Beckett, *Complete Dramatic Works,* 219–20.

21. Ibid., 220.

22. Jacques Derrida, "Economimesis," *Diacritics* 11, no. 2 (Summer 1981): 22. Barthes, *Camera Lucida,* passim; Derrida, "The Deaths of Roland Barthes," 277/289.

23. Derrida, "The Deaths of Roland Barthes," 295/304.

24. Barthes, *Camera Lucida,* 8, 71.

25. Derrida, "The Deaths of Roland Barthes," 286/296.

26. Barthes, *Camera Lucida,* 20, 38.

27. Ibid., 26.

28. Ibid., 49.

29. Derrida, "The Deaths of Roland Barthes," 264–65/278.

206 Notes to Chapter 3

30. Ibid., 285/296: "As the place of the irreplaceable singularity . . . the *punctum* irradiates and, what is most surprising, lends itself to metonymy. As soon as it allows itself to be drawn into a system of substitutions, it can invade everything, objects as well as affects. This singularity which is nowhere in the field mobilizes everything everywhere; it pluralizes itself."

31. Ibid., 267/280.

32. Ibid., 262/276.

33. Ibid., 274/286.

34. For equivalence of the mother, the punctum, and the "Law," see Ibid., 269/281–82.

35. Ibid., 272/284.

36. Ibid., 287.

37. Attridge, ed., *Acts of Literature*, 42–43.

38. Jacques Derrida, "Sauf le nom," in *On the Name* (Stanford, CA: Stanford University Press, 1995), 56. Jacques Derrida, *Sauf le nom* (Paris: Galilée, 1993), 56.

39. Nancy, "Surprise de l'événement," 193. "La surprise—l'événement—n'appartient pas à l'ordre de la representation" (199).

40. Jacques Derrida and Geoffrey Bennington, *"Circumfession": Jacques Derrida* (Chicago: University of Chicago Press, 1993), 32; French translation (Paris: Seuil, 1991), 33.

41. Jacques Derrida, "Paul Celan: La langue n'appartient pas (entretien)," *Europe: Revue littéraire mensuelle* 79, nos. 861–62 (2001): 83.

42. Beckett, *How It Is*, 13, 18.

43. Ibid., 146. Beckett, *Comment c'est*, 227.

44. See Deleuze's appraisal of structuralism in Gilles Deleuze, *The Logic of Sense* (New York: Columbia University Press, 1990), 71–73, and Alain Badiou, *Deleuze: The Clamor of Being*, trans. Louise Burchill (Minneapolis: University of Minnesota Press, 2000), 36–39.

45. Beckett, *How It Is*.

46. Ibid., 94; Beckett's French version is quite different: *Comment c'est*, 146.

47. Derrida, "Ulysses Gramophone: Hear Say Yes in Joyce," 293. Derrida shows that next to the hubris of the Demiurg who collects all, we hear in Joyce's laughter a self-deprecating irony that reflects his awareness of the limits of his enterprise.

3. BECKETT, DERRIDA, AND THE ORDINARY

1. In his afterword to *Limited Inc*, Derrida insists that it is rather his opponent Searle who has "inherited numerous gestures and a logic . . . from a certain Continental tradition . . . I try to deconstruct." Derrida describes himself as "paradoxically, more foreign to that tradition" (130–31). If I occasionally resort to this term, it is for the sake of convenience, especially when discussing the repercussions of

the so-called continental-analytic debate—for example, in Perloff's book. Conversely, the "analytic tradition" must also be seen as a coat of many colors: even distinct currents within that tradition, such as ordinary-language philosophy, show some significant degree of diversity (e.g., Austin engages in systematic theorizing, an approach that Wittgenstein criticizes; and Davidson endorses literal meaning, where Wittgenstein does not).

2. Samuel C. Wheeler III, "Wittgenstein as Conservative Deconstructor," *New Literary History* 19, no. 2 (1988): 239–58, 239.

3. Samuel C. Wheeler III, *Deconstruction as Analytic Philosophy* (Stanford, CA: Stanford University Press, 2000), 37–44.

4. Stanley Cavell, *A Pitch of Philosophy* (Cambridge, MA: Harvard University Press, 1996), 73.

5. Such a conjecture would require further exploration, which does not fall in the scope of the present study.

6. Stanley Cavell, *Emerson's Transcendental Etudes,* ed. David Justin Hodge (Stanford, CA: Stanford University Press, 2003), 103–4.

7. Stanley Cavell, *A Pitch of Philosophy,* 62–63.

8. Ludwig Wittgenstein, *Culture and Value,* ed. Georg Henrik von Wright in collaboration with Heikki Nyman, rev. ed. of the text by Alois Pichler, trans. Peter Winch (Oxford: Blackwell, 1998), 48: "Someone is *imprisoned* in a room if the door is unlocked, opens inwards; but it doesn't occur to him to *pull,* rather than push against it."

9. Perloff, "Witt-Watt: The Language of Resistance/The Resistance of Language," 53.

10. Ibid., 117; Beckett, *Watt* (New York: Calder, 1998), 87+.

11. Perloff understands the determining context as exclusively syntagmatic ("large sequences"), ignoring the paradigmatic context (i.e., those where the "context" of "yellow" is "red" and "blue").

12. Perloff, "Witt-Watt: The Language of Resistance/The Resistance of Language," 140.

13. Ibid.

14. Beckett, *Watt,* 95. (Many critics have pointed out that, intentionally or not, the real mathematical precision in Beckett's work was often flawed.)

15. Perloff, "Witt-Watt: The Language of Resistance/The Resistance of Language," 53–54.

16. Ibid., 142–43.

17. Jacques Derrida, "Signature, Event, Context," in *Limited Inc* (Evanston, IL: Northwestern University Press, 1988).

18. Derrida, *Limited Inc.* This book, which records the discussion, consists of Derrida's critique of speech-act theory (the 1971 article "Signature, Event, Context"), a summary of the response to it by prominent speech-act theorist John Searle

Notes to Chapter 3

(since Searle did not wish to contribute to the abortive enterprise into which he thought the discussion had degenerated), and Derrida's response to it in turn.

19. J. L. Austin, *How to Do Things with Words* (Oxford: Clarendon Press, 1965).

20. Derrida, "Signature, Event, Context," 9. "[U]n signe écrit comporte une force de rupture avec son contexte." "Signature événement contexte," in Jacques Derrida, *Marges de la philosophie* (Paris: Minuit, 1972), 377.

21. Donald Davidson, "A Nice Derangement of Epitaphs," in *Philosophical Grounds of Rationality*, ed. Richard Grandy (Oxford: Clarendon Press, 1986), 157+.

22. Jacques Derrida, "My Chances/Mes Chances: A Rendezvous with Some Epicurean Stereophonies," in *Taking Chances: Derrida, Psychoanalysis and Literature*, ed. Joseph H. Smith and William Kerrigan (Baltimore: Johns Hopkins University Press, 1984), 16.

23. Derrida, *Limited Inc*, 53, 48.

24. Derrida, *Signéponge/Signsponge*, 30/31, 64/65.

25. Derrida, "The Deaths of Roland Barthes," 291/300. In other words, the significance of a date is "testimonial": a date is marked by the witness who says, "I was there."

26. Derrida, "The Deaths of Roland Barthes," 279.

27. "What Did Derrida Want of Austin," in Stanley Cavell, *Philosophical Passages: Wittgenstein, Emerson, Austin, Derrida* (Oxford, England and Cambridge, MA: Blackwell, 1995), 42–65; see also Cavell, *A Pitch of Philosophy*, 55–125.

28. I will not address in this chapter the distinction made by Cavell between what he takes to be two different theories in Austin: the theory of excuses and the theory of seriousness. This distinction is of course vital to Cavell because it allows him to redefine the debate in such a way that it fits into his own field of interests (tragedy and skepticism as opposed to comedy). My reading of Cavell's account of the discussion between Derrida and Austin is in this sense biased.

29. Austin, *How to Do Things with Words*, 10.

30. Euripides, "Hippolytus," in *The Complete Greek Tragedies: Euripides I*, ed. David Grene and Richmond Lattimore (Chicago: University of Chicago Press, 1955), 612.

31. Cavell, *Philosophical Passages: Wittgenstein, Emerson, Austin, Derrida*, 65.

32. Cavell, *A Pitch of Philosophy*, viii.

33. Ibid.

34. J. L. Austin, "A Plea for Excuses: The Presidential Address," *Proceedings of the Aristotelian Society* 57 (1957).

35. For a description of the paradigmatic relations that exist between literature and truth, see Alain Badiou, *Petit manuel d'inesthétique* (Paris: Seuil, 1998), 10–15.

36. Ludwig Wittgenstein, *Zettel* (Oxford: Basil Blackwell, 1967), 160.

37. James Joyce, *Finnegans Wake* (London: Penguin, 1992), 403.

38. Ludwig Wittgenstein, *Philosophical Investigations,* trans. G.E.M. Anscombe, 3rd ed. (Oxford: Blackwell, 1967), 116.

39. Derrida, "Signature, Event, Context," 16/386.

40. "[L]a voix simule la garde de la presence." Derrida, *Speech and Phenomena,* 15/15. Husserl's gesture might only be interpreted as essentialist if we understand ideas in the Kantian sense as "essentialist." Husserl himself insists that the ideality in an "authentic" mode should not be confused with Platonism.

41. Cavell, "Ending the Waiting Game: A Reading of Beckett's *Endgame,*" 119.

42. Stanley Cavell, *The Claim of Reason: Wittgenstein, Skepticism, Morality and Tragedy* (Oxford: Oxford University Press, 1979), 183: "what will *count* as a legitimate projection is deeply controlled." And later on: "What is essential to the projection of a word is that it proceeds, or can be made to proceed, *naturally;* what is essential to a functioning metaphor is that its 'transfer' is *unnatural*—it breaks up the established, normal directions of projection" (190).

43. Derrida, "Ulysses Gramophone: Hear Say Yes in Joyce," 294.

44. Heidegger also calls our attention to Plato's daring use of "ordinary" language: "We, late born, are no longer in a position to appreciate the significance of Plato's daring to use the word *eidos* for that which in everything and in each particular thing endures as present. For *eidos,* in the common speech, meant the outward aspect that a visible thing offers to the physical eye. Plato exacts of this word, however, something utterly extraordinary: that it names what precisely is not and never will be perceivable with physical eyes." Martin Heidegger, "The Question Concerning Technology," in *Philosophical and Political Writings* (New York: Continuum, 2003), 290.

45. Perloff, "Witt-Watt: The Language of Resistance/The Resistance of Language," 118+. See also Kenneth Dauber and Walter Jost, eds., *Ordinary Language Criticism* (Evanston, IL: Northwestern University Press, 2003), including contributions by Martha Nussbaum, Marjorie Perloff, and an afterword by Stanley Cavell.

46. Marek Kedzierski, translator's comments to the Polish edition of *Watt* (Bydgoszcz: Pomorze, 1993), 225.

47. In order to see whether ordinary language philosophy can account for what is understood by an "event," one might explore whether jokes could function as events—by breaking a certain continuum and establishing their own law. One "ordinary language philosopher"—Hilary Putnam—has used jokes to illustrate the possibility of such "going on without rules." Hilary Putnam, "Rules, Attunement and 'Applying Rules to the World,'" in *The Legacy of Wittgenstein: Pragmatism and Deconstruction,* ed. Ludwig Nagl and Chantal Mouffe (New York: Peter Lang, 2001), 13, 19.

48. Again, Davidson's essay on malapropisms, "A Nice Derangement of Epitaphs," seems to offer a good solution. Furthermore, Davidson's account of "normality," in which he argues *against* conventions, is very different from that of either

Austin or Searle. Samuel C. Wheeler III demonstrates that Davidson cannot be plausibly seen as defending the literal meaning of metaphors in the "factual" sense. In light of this reading, we must come to the conclusion that the only possible difference between what we take to be ordinary or literal and what we take to be metaphorical is a difference of degree and not of kind. Every explication presupposes a detour, which sometimes happens to be longer than in (what we perceive to be) "ordinary" situations. "The contrast between metaphorical and literal cannot be sustained." Wheeler, *Deconstruction as Analytic Philosophy*, 49. See also Donald Davidson, "What Metaphors Mean," in *Inquiries into Truth and Interpretation* (Oxford: Clarendon Press, 1984), 245–64, and Donald Davidson, "Locating Literary Language," in *Literary Theory after Davidson*, ed. Reed Way Dasenbrock (University Park: Pennsylvania State University Press, 1993).

4. BECKETT'S "EXHAUSTED" ARCHIVES

1. Samuel Beckett, *Murphy* (London: Calder, 1963), 12.
2. C. J. Ackerley, "Demented Particulars: Annotated Murphy," *Journal of Beckett Studies* 7, nos. 1–2 (1998).
3. "The German Diaries," 15 January 1937, quoted in James Knowlson, *Damned to Fame* (London: Bloomsbury, 1996), 748, n. 3.
4. Beckett, *Murphy*, 57.
5. Gilles Deleuze, "The Exhausted," in *Essays Critical and Clinical* (London and New York: Verso, 1998), 154; Gilles Deleuze, "L'Épuisé," in *Quad et autres pièces pour la télévision*, ed. Edith Fournier (Paris: Minuit, 1992), 62.
6. Ludovic Janvier, "Beckett était obsédé par la voix" (interview), *Magazine Littéraire* (January 1999): 36.
7. Jacques Derrida, *Edmund Husserl's "Origin of Geometry": An Introduction*, trans. John P. Leavey Jr. (Lincoln: University of Nebraska Press, 1989), 104/106, my emphasis.
8. Ibid., 102/104.
9. Derrida, *Ulysse gramophone*, 27–34.
10. Gilles Deleuze, "Le plus grand film irlandais (en hommage à Samuel Beckett)," *Revue d'esthétique* (1986): 381–82; and Deleuze, "The Exhausted."
11. Filmed interview, quoted by Mary Bryden in *Beckett and Philosophy*, ed. Richard Lane (New York: Palgrave, 2002), 80, and transcripts online, Gilles Deleuze, "L'Abécédaire de Gilles Deleuze," 1996, http://www.langlab.wayne.edu/CStivale/D-G/ABC2.html (accessed November 2005).
12. Badiou, *Deleuze: The Clamor of Being*, 70.
13. Jacques Derrida, "I'm Going to Have to Wander All Alone," in *Philosophy Today* (Spring 1998): 3–5.
14. Mary Bryden gives two readings of this text: "Deleuze: Reading Beckett," in *Beckett and Philosophy*; and "The Schizoid Space: Beckett, Deleuze and *L'Epuisé*,"

Samuel Beckett Today/Aujourd'hui 5 (1996): 85–95. However, though very thoroughly dealing with the Beckettian resonances in Deleuze, these essays fail to address the more systematic issues in Deleuze's argument. These would include the relations that hold between the particular steps of exhausting, the identity of the exhausted self, or the objective of the whole enterprise of exhausting.

15. Beckett discusses this Bergsonian motif with respect to the painting of Tal Coat in Samuel Beckett, "Three Dialogues with Georges Duthuit," in *Proust and Three Dialogues* (London: Calder, 1965), 103.

16. Beckett, "Three Dialogues with Georges Duthuit," 103.

17. Beckett speaks there about the objective of leaving the "field of the possible" or the "plane of the feasible." To Duthuit's question, "What other plane can there be for a maker?" Beckett answers, "Logically none."

18. Badiou, *Beckett: L'increvable désir*, 38.

19. Christopher Ricks, *Beckett's Dying Words* (Oxford: Clarendon Press, 1993), 152–203.

20. Badiou, *Beckett: L'increvable désir*, 13.

21. Deleuze, "The Exhausted," 152/58.

22. Beckett, *Murphy*, 57.

23. It might seem that the hierarchy of exhaustion presented by Deleuze—three levels of exhaustion: words, voices, and images/spaces—suggests a temporal antecedence of the act of exhausting or exhausted objects with respect to the self that exhausts. However, we should rather see it as a circular movement without an end or beginning: exhausting can only be an act of an exhausted self that exhausts itself in the act of exhausting.

24. Deleuze, "The Exhausted," 152/57.

25. Deleuze, "L'Abécédaire de Gilles Deleuze."

26. Friedrich Nietzsche, *Thus Spoke Zarathustra* (London: Penguin, 1974), 250.

27. Deleuze, "The Exhausted," 154/62.

28. Derrida, *A Taste for the Secret*, 14.

29. Benedict de Spinoza, *Ethics,* trans. G.H.R. Parkinson (Oxford: Oxford University Press, 2000), 92. "[I]f he were to create everything that he understands, then he would . . . exhaust his omnipotence and make himself imperfect." Similarly, in Curley's translation, Benedict de Spinoza, *Ethics* (London: Penguin, 1994), 14: "[I]f he created everything he understood [to be creatable] he would . . . exhaust his omnipotence and render himself imperfect."

30. Deleuze and Parnet, *Dialogues II,* 50.

31. Ibid.

32. The online transcripts of Gilles Deleuze, "Spinoza," 1981, http://www.webdeleuze.com/html/index2.html (accessed March 2004).

33. Gilles Deleuze, *Spinoza et le problème d'expression* (Paris: Minuit, 1968), 78.

34. Spinoza, *Ethics*, 24–25.

35. Deleuze, "The Exhausted," 152/57.
36. Beckett, *Murphy*, 22.
37. The NS insertions are based on the so-called *Nagelate Schriften*, a Dutch translation of Spinoza's works published after his death. Their status is controversial, but in the present case, the phrase "understanding to be creatable" is perhaps illuminating for the discussion of the possible.
38. Spinoza, *Ethics*, 14, my emphasis.
39. Deleuze, "The Exhausted," 152/58.
40. Exhaustion seen in this way seems to be the telos of all "minoritarian becomings" in Deleuze. Those becomings (that produce nothing but other becomings) end up becoming invisible, becoming "everybody." See Paola Marrati's reading of "becoming" in Deleuze: Paola Marrati, "L'animal qui sait fuir," in *L'animal autobiographique: Autour de Jacques Derrida* (Paris: Galilée, 1999), 197–214. In another contribution (Paola Marrati, "Against the Doxa: Politics of Immanence and Becoming-Minoritarian," in *Micropolitics of Media Culture: Reading the Rhizomes of Deleuze and Guattari* [Amsterdam: Amsterdam University Press, 2001]) she explains: "[B]ecoming-everybody (*devenir tout le monde*) is not just a matter of being unrecognisable, of being like 'everybody else.' Deleuze and Guattari are playing here with the different possible meanings allowed by the French expression 'tout le monde.' Thus *devenir tout le monde* also entails . . . a *becoming of the world itself*" (213–14). The Spinozistic character of Deleuze's "becoming" is here quite clear. In the first of the mentioned essays, Marrati points out the radical Spinozism in Deleuze's central thesis of the "univocity of Being": "un spinozisme qui ne tolérerait même plus l'indépendance de la substance par rapport aux modes" (208).
41. Gottfried Wilhelm Leibniz, *Discourse on Metaphysics* (Buffalo, NY: Prometheus Books, 1992), 4.
42. Derrida, "Deux mots pour Joyce," in *Ulysse gramophone*, 22.
43. Deleuze, "The Exhausted," 154/62.
44. "Amor intellectualis quo Murphy se ipsum amat." Beckett, *Murphy*, 63, parodies "Proposition 35" of Spinoza's *Ethics*: "God loves himself with an infinite intellectual love" (176). The citation is usually interpreted as Beckett's attempt to subvert Spinoza's God as the only substance by introducing Murphy as a "competition."
45. Samuel Beckett, *Nohow On: Company, Ill Seen Ill Said, Worstward Ho* (New York: Grove Press, 1996), 96.
46. Beckett, *Watt*, 73–74.
47. Beckett, *Trilogy*, 63–64.
48. Deleuze, "The Exhausted," 156/66.
49. Ibid.
50. Ibid., 157/68.
51. Ibid., 157/69.
52. Ibid., 162/79.

53. The essay was first published as a postface to Samuel Beckett, *Quad et autres pièces pour la télévision* (Paris: Minuit, 1992).
54. Beckett, *Complete Dramatic Works*, 320–34. *Film* was written in English in 1963, filmed in 1964, and first shown publicly in 1965 (at the New York Film Festival).
55. Deleuze, *Cinema 1*, 61–66.
56. Henri Bergson, *Creative Evolution* (Mineola, NY: Dover Publications, 1998), 179.
57. Deleuze, *Cinema 1*, 68.
58. Deleuze, "The Exhausted," 153/60.
59. Beckett, *Murphy*, 61, 62. Another example is the "spatial ritornello" of the "Quad."
60. Deleuze, *Cinema 1*, 110.
61. See the chapter on "Faciality" in Deleuze and Guattari, *A Thousand Plateaus*, 167–91; *Mille plateaux*, 205–34.
62. Deleuze, *Cinema 1*, 100.
63. Deleuze always italicizes the indefinite article that announces a pure image: *a* woman, *a* hand, *a* mouth, *some* eyes, *a* quadrilateral, *a* square, *a* young girl dies; regarding space, he says that it must become "disused, unmodified." Apparently, at stake is the stripping down of space or of the object to its bare essentials.
64. It is not easy to pinpoint a place of dispute between Deleuze and Derrida; as Deleuze himself says, "Les philosophes ne se contredisent pas. Jamais un philosophe n'a contredit un autre philosophe." Gilles Deleuze, "Lectures on Bergson," 1981, www.webdeleuze.com. Yet Deleuze's steadfast conviction that the redundancy of memory has to be overcome presents us with a very concrete case of dissent.
65. "[L]a grande erreur, la seule erreur, serait de croire qu'une ligne de fuite consiste à fuir la vie; la fuite dans l'imaginaire, ou dans l'art. Mais fuir au contraire, c'est produire du réel, créer la vie, trouver une arme." Gilles Deleuze and Claire Parnet, *Dialogues* (Paris: Flammarion, 1996), 47 (English translation, p. 49).
66. Again, for the analysis of the notion of "becoming" in Deleuze, see the two contributions by Marrati mentioned in note 43.
67. Derrida, "This Strange Institution Called Literature," 36.
68. Derrida, *Limited Inc*, 150.
69. Deleuze and Parnet, *Dialogues*, 60. Deleuze, "Experiment, Never Interpret," in *Dialogues II*, 48.
70. Deleuze and Parnet, *Dialogues II*, 47.
71. Deleuze and Parnet, *Dialogues*, 58–60.
72. Deleuze and Parnet, *Dialogues II*, 37.
73. The notion of "interpretation," insofar as it applies to Derrida (who would probably prefer to call it "translation" or "substitution"), is defined differently: not only is it nonhierarchical and not absolute (against Hegel) but it also (against

214 Notes to Chapter 4

Gadamer, who would agree with Derrida that every interpretation is finite) never presupposes a unitary horizon of meaning.

74. Deleuze and Parnet, *Dialogues*, 78.

75. Ibid.

76. On the other hand, in *Différence et répétition* we encounter a perception of literature that is very similar to Derrida's: "il s'agit toujours de rassembler un maximum de séries disparates (à la limite, toutes les séries divergentes constitutives du cosmos), en faisant fonctionner des précurseurs sombres linguistiques (ici mots ésotériques, mots-valises)" (159). The aforementioned "mots-valises" are used to gather (*rassembler*) all the series of the cosmos—in which case, are they not functioning according to an economy of means? The answer might be that the notion of the "mots-valises" dates from a period when, as Badiou puts it, Deleuze was "delighted with the [structuralist] approach." Badiou, *Deleuze: The Clamor of Being*, 37. See also Deleuze, *The Logic of Sense*, 71–73. In *A Thousand Plateaus*, written in the seventies, Deleuze and Guattari still state that "structuralism represents a great revolution" but also that it "does not account for ... becomings." Deleuze and Guattari consequently conclude that "none [of it] satisfies us." Deleuze and Guattari, *A Thousand Plateaus: Capitalism and Schizophrenia*, 237; Deleuze, *Mille plateaux*, 290.

77. Deleuze and Parnet, *Dialogues*, 60. The English translation has, less appropriately, "garish light" (49).

78. Derrida, "Before the Law," 197/115, my emphasis.

79. Deleuze, *Difference and Repetition*, 35/52. "There has only ever been one ontological proposition: Being is univocal."

80. Badiou, *Deleuze: The Clamor of Being*, 32.

81. Ibid., 36.

82. Deleuze, *Difference and Repetition*, 36/53.

83. Gilles Deleuze, *Foucault*, trans. Seán Hand (Minneapolis: University of Minnesota Press, 1988), 111.

84. Badiou, *Deleuze: The Clamor of Being*, 23.

85. Even though Derrida has distanced himself from Heidegger's gesture of hermeneutic gathering, he is nonetheless vulnerable to the same critique if we adopt Gasché's view that "[t]he Derridean word *text* is a translation ... of the Heideggerian word *Being*." "Heidegger's notion of Being and Derrida's notion of text are akin.... Being and text appear to be words that can be exchanged and substituted for one another." Gasché, *Of Minimal Things: Studies on the Notion of Relation*, 226.

86. Derrida's radicalization would be that Lévi-Strauss's "internal homologies" (Claude Lévi-Strauss, *Totemism*, trans. Rodney Needham [Boston: Beacon Press, 1963], 78) are not strictly necessary to posit a link between two terms; a chance relationship or encounter would be sufficient.

87. Deleuze and Guattari, *A Thousand Plateaus*, 237–38.

88. Gilles Deleuze and Félix Guattari, *What Is Philosophy?* (New York: Columbia University Press, 1994), 172.
89. Ibid., 169, 167.
90. Ibid., 167.
91. Derrida, *A Taste for the Secret*, 31.
92. Ibid., 30–32.
93. Deleuze and Guattari, *A Thousand Plateaus*, 187; *Mille plateaux*, 229, my emphasis.
94. Ibid., 265/324.
95. It seems possible that the two sorts of the singular in Ockham that I addressed in Chapter 2 might shed some light on any difference between Deleuze and Derrida. Deleuze's singular is one that has a numerical unity (the ontological singular, the one that is "extra animam"—beyond mind). Derrida's singular is one that has a unity of signification (the sign for the singular thing allowing the singular thing to enter into a series). For Ockham, these two types of the singular are irreducibly different, and the major difference is that the "ontological" singular is "before" all particularity. This distinction seems in any case to be relevant for Deleuze's thinking of the singular; for example, to address the singular with words, Beckett has to overcome "the adhesions that keep them (the words) bound to the general or the particular." Deleuze, "The Exhausted," 173/104.
96. Deleuze and Guattari, *A Thousand Plateaus*, 186; *Mille plateaux*, 228.
97. Deleuze and Guattari, *What Is Philosophy?* 170.
98. Deleuze and Guattari, *A Thousand Plateaus*, 185–87; *Mille plateaux*, 227–29.
99. Ibid., 294; *Mille plateaux*, 360.
100. Ibid., 296–97/364.
101. Deleuze, "The Exhausted," 155/63.
102. Ibid., 155/64.
103. Ibid., 173/103.
104. Ibid., 172–73.
105. In Derrida, *Edmund Husserl's "Origin of Geometry": An Introduction*—one of his early considerations of singularity—Derrida shows that it is impossible to think a singular object in its univocity (since univocity requires a name that is iterable, able to be shared and thus exposed to equivocity) (102/104). The name enters "a culture, . . . a network of linguistic relations and oppositions, which would load the word with intentions or with virtual reminiscences" (103/105). This is the reason for Beckett's difficulty with the language of words.
106. Deleuze and Parnet, *Dialogues II*, 50.
107. Deleuze and Guattari, *A Thousand Plateaus*, 191/233.
108. Writing must always be "related purely to a consciousness," be "haunted by a virtual intentionality." Cf. Derrida, *Edmund Husserl's "Origin of Geometry": An Introduction*, 88/85; and Leonard Lawlor, *Derrida and Husserl: The Basic Problem of Phenomenology* (Bloomington, IN: Indiana UP, 2002), 117. Writing presupposes the

necessary possibility of its freeing itself from all actual subjects, but "without any factual subjects, writing would be deprived of its transcendental function." Lawlor, *Derrida and Husserl*, 118.

109. Deleuze, "The Exhausted," 154–55/61–62.
110. Ibid., 158/71.
111. Knowlson, *Damned to Fame*, 29.
112. Deleuze, "The Exhausted," 158/71.

5. SINGULAR POINTS OF TRANSACTION (I): THE SUBJECT

1. Jacques Derrida, "The Time of a Thesis: Punctuations," in *Philosophy in France Today*, ed. A. Montefiori (Cambridge: Cambridge University Press, 1982), 36–37.

2. Attridge, ed., *Acts of Literature*, 44–45. By insisting that next to the noetic (intentional) aspect there is also a noematic aspect of literarity, Derrida in fact returned to his thesis-project on the ideality of the literary object. Derrida's questioning of what is "in" the text that "call(s) for the literary reading" and of what "recall(s) the convention, institution or history of literature" (before it puts phenomenology "in crisis") addresses the noetic content of the literary work.

3. "On the French philosophical scene, the moment when a certain central hegemony of the subject was being put into question again in the 1960's was also the moment when, phenomenology still being very present, people began to become interested in those places in Husserl's discourse where the egological and more generally the subjective form of the transcendental experience appeared to be more *constituted* than *constitutive*." Jacques Derrida, "'Eating Well,' or the Calculation of the Subject," in *Points . . . : Interviews, 1974–1994*, ed. Elisabeth Weber (Stanford, CA: Stanford University Press, 1995), 263; "Il faut bien manger," 277–78.

4. Derrida, *Speech and Phenomena*, 45; *La voix et le phénomène* (Paris: Presses Universitaires de France, 1967), 50.

5. On the "experience of unity of presentation and representation," see Lawlor, *Derrida and Husserl*, in particular p. 174.

6. Derrida, *Speech and Phenomena*, 45; *La voix et le phénomène*, 50.

7. Ibid., 14, my emphasis; *La voix et le phénomène*, 14.

8. Derrida, "'Eating Well,'" 259/273.

9. Jacques Derrida, "Structure, Sign and Play in the Discourse of the Human Sciences," in *The Languages of Criticism and the Sciences of Man*, ed. Richard Macksey and Eugenio Donato (Baltimore and London: Johns Hopkins University Press 1970), 271 (quote from memory).

10. Derrida, *A Taste for the Secret*, 40–41. "The autobiographical" does not refer to what we know as a genre of autobiography. "In literature what . . . interests me is essentially the autobiographical—not what is called the 'autobiographical genre,' but rather the autobiographicity that greatly overflows the 'genre' of autobiography. Indeed, I find the vast majority of autobiographical novels not nearly

autobiographical enough" (41). "The autobiographical" in the sense Derrida proposes is that which explores the "singularity of experience and existence and its link to language" (41).

11. "Sous le nom de circoncision, je me demande souvent . . . s'il y a un événement 'réel' que je peux tenter, non pas de me rappeler, bien sûr, mais de réélaborer, de réactiver dans une sorte de mémoire sans représentation—ou si c'est un leurre, un simulacre (mais alors d'où viendrait son privilège?), un écran destiné à la projection figurée de tant d'autre événements du même type, pour m'égarer autant que pour me guider. La circoncision signifie, entre autres choses, une certaine marque qui, venue des autres, et subie dans la passivité absolue, reste dans le corps, et visible, indissociable sans doute du nom propre alors également reçu de l'autre. C'est aussi le moment de la signature (de l'autre autant que de soi) par laquelle on se laisse inscrire dans une communauté ou dans une alliance ineffaçable: *naissance du sujet.*" Derrida, "Une 'folie' doit veiller sur la pensée," 18, my emphasis.

12. Derrida and Ferraris, "This Strange Institution Called Literature," 34, 41.

13. Ibid., 35.

14. Derrida and Ferraris, *A Taste for the Secret*, 40–41.

15. Derrida, *Signéponge/Signsponge*, 64/65.

16. As I mentioned before, this book deals with the English part of the bilingual, self-translated oeuvre of Beckett.

17. Beckett felt that the demand to confer identities is conditioned by language: we want to know who or what it is that acts, speaks, or is "acted upon" or "spoken about" because every proposition of our language requires a subject or the specification of "what it is about." It is almost impossible to think anything without giving a provisional name to the subject matter. How difficult and idiosyncratic such a language would be can be seen in *Worstward Ho* (1983), in which Beckett experimented with operating the English language without a grammatical subject. The text consists almost entirely of phrases in the imperative mood, elliptical sentences, or sentence-words: "On. Say on. Be said on. Somehow on. Till nohow on. Said nohow on." Beckett, *Nohow On: Company, Ill Seen Ill Said, Worstward Ho* (New York: Grove Press, 1996) 89.

18. The result of Derrida's claim that the subject is "constituted" rather than "constitutive" is that the notions of subjectivity and authorship overlap. Just like the subject, the author is not understood here as the creator "before" the text but as "someone who is himself determined by the text." Raoul Mortley, *French Philosophers in Conversation: Levinas, Schneider, Serres, Irigaray, Le Doeuff, Derrida* (London and New York: Routledge, 1991).

19. Beckett, *Trilogy*, 418.

20. Derrida, "This Strange Institution Called Literature," 36.

21. Ulrich Pothast argues that in Beckett's case, the "subject" is equivalent to the "thing told." ("[D]as 'Subjekt' setzt nicht die erzählte Sache wie einen intentionalen

Gegenstand aus sich heraus in die Welt des Werkes; sonder es *ist* sie.") Pothast, *Die eigentlich metaphysische Tätigkeit: Über Schopenhauers Ästhetik und ihre Anwendung durch Samuel Beckett*, 305.

22. Beckett, *Trilogy*, 305.

23. For "ventriloquism," see Steven Connor, *Dumbstruck: A Cultural History of Ventriloquism* (Oxford: Oxford University Press, 2002), 392.

24. Beckett, *Trilogy*, 309.

25. Variations of this gesture of exhausting the possible are for the "I" to "tell the truth," to pronounce a secret formula, to praise its "master" (on the hypothesis that there is one) in order to obtain forgiveness, or in general to discharge an unknown to itself *pensum* so as to be released from the duty to speak. Yet even if one of these actions were to bring relief, this would not solve the "I"'s problems, since the "I" does not know what these things—"all," "truth," "the formula," "the master"—are, nor what the "pensum" could consist in.

26. Derrida, *Speech and Phenomena*, 45; *La voix et le phénomène*, 50.

27. Edmund Husserl, *Logical Investigations* (London: Routledge, 1970), 190–91.

28. Ibid., 183.

29. Edmund Husserl, *Formal and Transcendental Logic*, trans. Dorion Cairns (The Hague: Martinus Nijhoff, 1965), 316.

30. Gasché, *The Tain of the Mirror*, 231.

31. Derrida paraphrases the functioning of the phenomenon of speech in Husserl's work in the following way: "Phonic signs ... are heard ... by the subject who proffers them in the absolute proximity of their present. The subject does not have to pass forth beyond himself to be immediately affected by his expressive activity. My words are 'alive' because they seem not to leave me: not to fall outside me, ... not to cease to belong to me." Derrida, *Speech and Phenomena*, 76; *La voix et le phénomène*, 85.

32. In his thesis of 1954—*Le problème de la genèse dans la philosophie de Husserl*—Derrida shows that the temporal experience posited by Husserl as the absolute constituting source contains an aporia. Since retention (the constituted) is a part of the temporal experience (the constitutive source), the constituted precedes the constitutive that constitutes it.

33. Derrida has demonstrated in *Speech and Phenomena* that this "hearing-oneself-speak" is never pure, but always built on a more fundamental difference. The relation to the other and the relation to self are two inseparable aspects of the same moment, two poles between which the "I" is suspended in endless movement. This functions just as does a mirror reflection when two mirrors are facing each other, involving not only the movement outside to the reflecting surface and back but also the other way around. I reflect myself in the other, yet at the same time I am the mirror in which the other, in whom I am reflected, is reflected in

me. No constitution of the self is possible without this endless movement, but with it, no constitution of the self is absolutely originary or complete.

34. Beckett, *Trilogy*, 341–42.

35. This is not based on the empirical observation that the sound waves take time to reach my own ear, for I can imagine that I "hear" the words that I only think about saying. (I can imagine that the words are present in my mind while spoken.)

36. This would mean the exclusion of the mediating effect of the signs and consequently the exclusion of my alter ego, leading to paradoxes in Husserl, who did not want this exclusion.

37. Beckett, *Trilogy*, 350.

38. Ibid., 54. At another place: "What can one do but speculate, speculate, until one hits on the happy speculation?" (372).

39. Badiou, *Beckett: L'increvable desir*, 36.

40. Beckett, *Trilogy*, 352, my emphasis.

41. Jacques Derrida, "Psyche: Inventions of the Other," in *Reading de Man Reading*, ed. L. Waters and W. Godzich (Minneapolis: University of Minnesota Press, 1989).

42. Jacques Derrida, "Maddening the Subjectile," *Yale French Studies* 84 (1994): 154–71; "Forcener le subjectile," 55–105.

43. See also Wilma Siccama, *Het waarnemend lichaam: Zintuiglijkheid en representatie bij Beckett en Artaud* (Nijmegen: Vantilt, 2000), where the author approaches the issues of the sensory experience in Beckett and Artaud to a large extent through Derrida's insights.

44. Derrida, "Maddening the Subjectile," 169–70, emphasis in the original; "Forcener," 65.

45. Derrida, "Maddening the Subjectile," 164, emphasis in the original; "Forcener," 60.

46. "The subjectile . . . becomes a membrane." Derrida, "Maddening the Subjectile," 168; "Forcener," 63.

47. "[T]he notion ['subjectile'] belongs to the code of painting and designates what is in some way lying below (*sub-jectum*) as a substance, a subject. . . . [A] surface, that of the wall or of wood, but already also that of paper, of textiles and of the panel. A sort of skin with holes for pores." Derrida, "Maddening the Subjectile," 158/56.

48. Cf. Derrida, "Maddening the Subjectile," and Beckett's much-cited letter to Axel Kaun in Samuel Beckett, *Disjecta* (New York: Grove Press, 1984).

49. Derrida, "Maddening the Subjectile," 170/63.

50. Ibid., 168/63.

51. "A violent obstetrics gives passage to the words through which however it passes. With all the music, painting, drawing, it is operating with a forceps." Derrida, "Maddening the Subjectile," 167/63.

52. Even in *Waiting for Godot*: "Astride of a grave and a difficult birth. Down in the hole, lingeringly, the gravedigger puts on the forceps." Beckett, *Complete Dramatic Works*, 84.

53. Beckett, *Trilogy*, 387.

54. "They love each other, marry, in order to love each other better...". Beckett, *Trilogy*, 410–11. By projecting the analogy with doors below (doors between names and images), what Beckett is describing here as the story of the unintentional bigamy and its sad consequences is the metaphoric rendering of the instability of "marriages" (again, the marriage is the "hymen") between words and images, and the referential instability of language.

55. Beckett, *Disjecta*, 171–73.

56. Derrida, *A Taste for the Secret*, 41.

57. Derrida, *Sur Parole: Instantanés Philosophiques*, 25–26.

58. "La littérature peut appeler à la plus grande responsabilité mais elle est aussi la possibilité de la pire trahison . . . et la dépossession. . . . Au fond, ce n'est pas moi qui signe, dès que c'est lancé sur le marché littéraire, ça ne vient plus de moi." Derrida, *Sur Parole: Instantanés Philosophiques*, 25–26, translation mine.

59. Paul Ricoeur, *Time and Narrative* (Chicago: University of Chicago Press, 1984–1988), 2:10.

60. Ricoeur, *Time and Narrative*, 2:26; and Frank Kermode, *The Sense of an Ending: Studies in the Theory of Fiction* (New York: Oxford University Press, 1967), 115–16.

61. For the distinction between *ipseité* and *mêmeté* in Ricoeur, see also Rudolf Bernet, "The Other in Myself," in *Deconstructive Subjectivities*, ed. Simon Critchley (Albany: SUNY Press, 1996), 170–73.

62. Ricoeur, *Time and Narrative*, 3:247.

63. Beckett, *Trilogy*, 380–81.

64. Ricoeur, *Time and Narrative*, 3:248.

65. Paul Ricoeur, *Oneself as Another* (Chicago: University of Chicago Press, 1992), 2.

66. Ricoeur, *Time and Narrative*, 3:249.

67. The question is whether this moment of impetus, this singular moment of decision, indeed arises within the narrative experience or whether it is not something which is incorporated into it only afterwards. Is it really so that when faced with a decision, we first summarize our life to ourselves, the outcome becoming our "identity," and that the act of our decision will be in continuity with respect to that which has been summarized?

68. Derrida, *A Taste for the Secret*, 85.

69. "J'insiste en général sur la possibilité de 'tout dire' comme droit reconnu en principe à la littérature, pour marquer non pas l'irresponsabilité de l'écrivain, de quiconque signe de la littérature, mais son *hyper-responsabilité*, c'est-à-dire le

fait que sa responsabilité ne répond pas devant les instances déjà constituées." Derrida, *Sur Parole: Instantanés Philosophiques*, 24. My translation and emphasis.

70. Derrida, "This Strange Institution Called Literature," 37.

71. Beckett, *Trilogy*, 418.

72. Derrida, "Maddening the Subjectile," 169.

6. SINGULAR POINTS OF TRANSACTION (II): "WHAT ARE POETS FOR?"
THE AUTHORITY OF LITERATURE

1. Derrida, "Force of Law: The 'Mystical Foundation of Authority,'" 41; *Force de loi*, 98–99. Walter Benjamin, *Selected Writings Volume 1* (Cambridge, MA: Harvard University Press, 1996), 236–52.

2. For the discussion of "Gewalt" in Derrida, see also Giovanna Borradori, *Philosophy in a Time of Terror* (Chicago and London: University of Chicago Press, 2003), 165.

3. Derrida, "Force of Law: The 'Mystical Foundation of Authority,'" 7, 12/21, 30. The expression "legitimate fictions," also from Montaigne, is used by Derrida to refer both to literature (as the incipit to Kafka's "Before the Law," 183/87) and to the law of a revolutionary instant ("Force of Law," 12/30). See also "legal fiction" in Jacques Derrida and James Trilling, "La Veilleuse," *James Joyce ou l'écriture matricide* (Belfort: Éditions Circé, 2001), 21.

4. Derrida, "Force of Law: The 'Mystical Foundation of Authority,'" 44/105.

5. Ibid., 11. I am leaving out of the scope of this discussion what Derrida, in his examination of Benjamin, calls "the *other* mystical foundation of authority," God.

6. See, for example, "mystical" in *Merriam-Webster's Collegiate Dictionary*, 11th ed.

7. Derrida, "Force of Law: The 'Mystical Foundation of Authority,'" 14.

8. Derrida, "This Strange Institution Called Literature," 60.

9. Derrida, "Force of Law: The 'Mystical Foundation of Authority,'" 7/20.

10. See the Introduction.

11. Derrida, *Writing and Difference*, 27/45.

12. Derrida, *Sur Parole: Instantanés Philosophiques*, 25.

13. Ibid., 24.

14. Beckett, *Trilogy*, 72.

15. Maurice Blanchot, *The Space of Literature*, trans. Ann Smock (Lincoln: University of Nebraska Press, 1982), 25.

16. Nussbaum, "Narrative Emotions: Beckett's Genealogy of Love." See also Simon Critchley, *Very Little . . . Almost Nothing: Death, Philosophy, Literature* (London and New York: Routledge, 1997), 143.

17. Beckett, *Trilogy*, 115, my emphasis.

18. "[J]e ne cesse recommencer la même histoire différemment. . . . [J]e prends chacque fois la responsabilité que je peux. L'arrêt de cette . . . injonction

ne peut être qu'un arrêt de mort.... c'est ça qui fait écrire: c'est ce qui à la fois rend possible et menace tout." Derrida, *Sur Parole: Instantanés Philosophiques*, 27, translation mine.

19. For, as Moran says, "each agent had his own particular messenger, and ... each messenger had his own particular agent" (Beckett, *Trilogy*, 107). The relationship between death and responsibility in Beckett resembles strongly one that we encounter in Kafka and Heidegger. Contrary to Kafka's doorkeeper, instead of preventing the man from entering the law, Gaber delivers the order himself. However, his position as an intermediary who both hides and reflects the top of the hierarchy of power is the same as that of Kafka's doorkeeper.

20. Totally in harmony with what we would expect from Beckett, this "conception through the ear" (which, in Derrida's vocabulary, can immediately be placed together with *voice as breath, as life and as presence*: la "parole soufflée") is brought about by Gaber's "corpsed transmissions."

21. Beckett, *Trilogy*, 137.

22. Blanchot uses the term "tyrannical prehension" to refer to a type of compulsive behavior that makes the writing person squeeze the pencil instead of letting it go, a phenomenon explained by a drive to mastery that governs the hand in its vain effort to remain in control of something that is beyond control. The hand cannot release the pencil "because what it holds it doesn't really hold; what it holds belongs to the realm of shadows and is itself a shade." The real mastery characterizes the other hand: "the one that doesn't write and is capable of intervening at the right moment to seize the pencil and put it aside." Blanchot, *The Space of Literature*, 25.

23. In his essay *Survivre*, Derrida gives a similarly allegorical reading of Blanchot's novel *L'arrêt de mort*. There characters function as agencies, or "events," involved in the process of writing. Jacques Derrida, "Living On: Border Lines," in *Deconstruction and Criticism*, ed. Harold Bloom (London: Routledge, 1979).

24. Beckett, *Trilogy*, 109, 152.

25. In Derrida's essay, the "gift of death" stands for the paradox of responsible decision that is always irresponsible at the same time. This counts for every decision: "there can be no ethical generality that is not always already subject to the Abrahamic paradox" (Hent de Vries, *Religion and Violence: Philosophical Perspectives from Kant to Derrida* [Baltimore and London: Johns Hopkins University Press, 2001], 176). Abraham's decision and its paradox becomes a singular point in time that reinstantiates itself in all other singular decisions and thereby gathers all other decisions, becoming exemplary and universal. The same interaction of the singular and the universal takes place in the literary work.

26. Tom Cousineau, "The Lost Father in Beckett's Novels," in *Beckett and la psychanalyse and Psychoanalysis*, ed. Sjef Houppermans (Amsterdam and Atlanta, GA: Rodopi, 1996), 79.

27. Beckett, *Trilogy*, 92.
28. Ibid.
29. The iteration of the sacrificial story of Abraham and Isaac is quite striking in Beckett, especially when Hamm recounts how he forced a father to let his son die. "I finally offered to take him into my service. . . . In the end he asked me would I consent to take in the child as well . . . I can see him still, down on his knees . . . It was the moment I was waiting for . . . I put him before his responsibilities." Beckett, *Complete Dramatic Works*, 118, 133.
30. Derrida, "The Deaths of Roland Barthes," 295/304.
31. Derrida, "This Strange Institution Called Literature," 46.
32. Ludovic Janvier, "Beckett était obsédé par la voix" (interview), *Magazine Littéraire*, January 1999, 36.
33. Edmund Husserl, *Cartesian Meditations: An Introduction to Phenomenology*, trans. Dorion Cairns (Dordrecht: Kluwer Academic Publishers, 1999), 2.
34. Alain Badiou, "Être, existence, pensée: Prose et concept," in *Petit manuel d'inesthétique* (Paris: Seuil, 1998), 137–38 and 180. English translation: "Being, Existence, Thought," in Alain Badiou and Alberto Toscano, eds., *On Beckett* (Manchester, England: Clinamen Press, 2004), 79–80, 107–8.
35. Ibid. "Au fond, la méthode de Beckett est comme l'épochè de Husserl mise à l'envers. L'épochè de Husserl consiste à soustraire la thèse du monde, à soustraire le 'il y a' pour se retourner vers le mouvement ou le flux pur de l'intériorité qui vise ce 'il y a.' Husserl est dans la filiation du doute cartésien. . . . La méthode de Beckett est exactement le contraire: il s'agit de soustraire le sujet, de le suspendre, pour voir ce qui alors advient à l'être." Badiou, "Être, existence, pensée: Prose et concept," 180. Such a reading of Beckett would embrace a whole strain of Beckett critique that reads Beckett's work as a subtracting, chiselling work that, in the long run, aims at revealing a truth.
36. Derrida, *Edmund Husserl's "Origin of Geometry": An Introduction*, 144/159.
37. Beckett, *Trilogy*, 293.
38. Beckett, *How It Is*; Beckett, *Nohow On*; and "What Where," in Beckett, *Complete Dramatic Works*, 470–76.
39. Badiou, *Beckett: L'increvable désir*, 38.
40. Ibid.
41. Badiou does not give up the distinction between poetry and prose, but for him it is poetry that is the "condition of philosophy." Badiou, "La poésie en condition de la philosophie," 68.
42. Badiou, *Manifesto for Philosophy*, 70.
43. "La singularité dont le poème doit rendre compte est finalement la singularité du poème lui-même! C'est cet élément de torsion sur soi-même de la vocation de la langue à la singularité absolue qui va être pris comme la singularité dont le poème s'alimente et se nourrit: d'où la thèse mallarméenne d'un sonnet qui ne

renvoie à rien d'autre que lui-même, qui est elle-même en écho d'une thèse flaubertienne sur le roman sur rien; ça, c'est la modernité. Mais ce rien, ce vide, c'est simplement le vide entouré par une torsion de l'objet artistique sur lui-même, une auto-référence du poème à lui-même." Badiou, "La poésie en condition de la philosophie," 73, translation mine.

44. Badiou, *Manifesto for Philosophy*, 69.
45. Ibid., 69.
46. Ibid., 61.
47. Ibid., 86.
48. Ibid.
49. Ibid., 86–87.
50. "[P]our le philosophe, un certain type de poème guide ou oriente la speculation." Badiou, "La poésie en condition de la philosophie," 68.
51. Ibid., 69.
52. Badiou, *Beckett: L'increvable désir*, 12.
53. An example of this reception can be found in an essay by Emmanuel Jacquart: "Whereas Dante's objective is to 'uproot those who live in this life in a state of misery and lead them to a state of happiness' . . . , Beckett's objective runs in the opposite direction. The aspiration to happiness, whose legitimacy and depth he recognizes, is nevertheless an illusion denied by horrid reality. *Story over, only misery exists and subsists*." Emmanuel Jacquart, "*Endgame*, Master Game," in "Beckett in France," special issue, *Journal of Beckett Studies* 4, no. 1 (1994): 85. (It was to this edition that Derrida turned down the invitation to contribute, excusing himself with his inability to comment on Beckett.)
54. Alain Badiou, "Beckett's Generic Writing," in "Beckett in France," special issue, *Journal of Beckett Studies* 4, no. 1 (1994): 13–21.
55. Jennifer Birkett and Kate Ince, eds., *Samuel Beckett* (London: Longman Critical Readers, 2000), 9.
56. Wolfgang Iser, "When Is the End Not the End? The Idea of Fiction in Beckett," in *The Implied Reader* (London: Johns Hopkins University Press, 1974).
57. Badiou, *Beckett: L'increvable desir*, 22.
58. Ibid., 42.
59. Ibid., 46.
60. Iser, "When Is the End Not the End?" 257.
61. Ibid., 258.
62. Beckett, *Trilogy*, 64.
63. Ibid., 134.
64. Badiou, *Beckett: L'increvable desir*, 13.
65. Ibid., 7.
66. Badiou, "La poésie en condition de la philosophie," 73.
67. Ibid., 74.
68. Quoted in Jacquart, "*Endgame*, Master Game," 78.

69. "On se tourne vers l'événement." "Peu à peu, non sans hésitations ni repentirs, l'œuvre de Beckett va s'ouvrir au hasard, aux incidents, à de brusques modifications du donné." Badiou, *Beckett: L'increvable désir*, 39.

70. Badiou, "La poésie en condition de la philosophie."

71. Samuel Beckett, *Ill Seen Ill Said*, in *Nohow On* (New York: Grove Press, 1996), 83.

72. Badiou, *Manifesto for Philosophy*, 146, n. 12.

73. Badiou, "La poésie en condition de la philosophie," 73.

74. "La poésie est ce qui, dans le langage—d'autres arts le feront autrement que dans le langage—convoque a l'absolu de la singularité." Badiou, "La poésie en condition de la philosophie," 73, translation mine. The distinction in the procedures of disobjectivation (described in the introduction to part 2 as the distinction between the implementing of lack and of excess) seems to apply to Beckett's work. Beckett can then, on Badiou's terms, be approached as a "Poet of a lack," and his work as aiming at self-dissolution, self-consummation, disappearance.

75. Badiou, "L'écriture du générique: Samuel Beckett," 329–65.

76. Badiou, *Manifesto for Philosophy*, 35. The function of generic (or truth) procedures is to name the unnameable, that whereof one cannot speak "in the sense of 'there is nothing to say about it that specifies it and grants it separating properties.'" Badiou, *Manifesto for Philosophy*, 95. The reference to—and critique of—Wittgenstein is explicit.

77. Badiou, "La poésie en condition de la philosophie," 72.

78. Birkett and Ince, eds., *Samuel Beckett*, 9.

79. Badiou, *Manifesto for Philosophy*, 109.

80. Badiou, *On Beckett*, 80.

81. The latter charge is leveled at Wittgenstein and Derrida, among others.

82. Jean-Marie Magnan, "Les chaines et relais du néant," in Bishop and Federman, eds., *Cahier de L'Herne: Samuel Beckett*, 288.

7. SINGULAR POINTS OF TRANSACTION (III): "WANTING IN INANITY." NEGATIVITY, LANGUAGE, AND "GOD" IN BECKETT

1. What Marlène Zarader argues with respect to Blanchot applies just as well to Beckett: he wanted to be the "guardian of Nothing" rather than the "shepherd of Being." Marlène Zarader, *L'être et le neutre: A partir de Maurice Blanchot* (Lagrasse, France: Verdier, 2001).

2. Beckett, *Disjecta*, 171–73.

3. Leslie Hill, *Beckett's Fiction: In Different Words* (Cambridge: Cambridge University Press, 1990), 163, my emphasis.

4. In a presentation held at the Beckett Against the Grain conference, York, England, May 1999.

5. Jacques Derrida, "How to Avoid Speaking: Denials," in *Derrida and Negative Theology*, ed. H. Coward and T. Foshay (Albany: State University of New York Press, 1992), 76–77. Originally appeared as "Comment ne pas parler: Dénégations," in *Psyché: Inventions de l'autre* (Paris: Galilée, 1987), 535–95.

6. Rico Sneller, *Het Woord is schrift geworden: Derrida en de negatieve theologie* (Kampen: Kok Agora, 1998), 52.

7. For example, by Mikel Dufrenne in "Pour une philosophie non théologique." See also Derrida, "How to Avoid Speaking: Denials," 73–77/535–39. For an extensive discussion of the misunderstandings surrounding this issue (in particular, those of Mikel Dufrenne and Jean-Luc Marion), see "Revealing Revelations" in Hent de Vries, *Philosophy and the Turn to Religion* (Baltimore and London: Johns Hopkins University Press, 1999), 40–95. Rodolphe Gasché's "God, for Example," also contains a recapitulation of the discussion around this issue (pp. 150–70).

8. Among others, "How to Avoid Speaking: Denials" and "Sauf le nom."

9. See, for example, John D. Caputo, *The Prayers and Tears of Jacques Derrida: Religion without Religion* (Bloomington: Indiana University Press, 1997); and de Vries, *Philosophy and the Turn to Religion*.

10. J. Quint, ed., *Meister Eckhart: Die Deutschen Werke* (Zürich: Diogenes Verlag AG, 1979), III, 431.

11. Pseudo-Dionysius, *The Complete Works* (New York: Paulist Press, 1987), 139.

12. Derrida, "How to Avoid Speaking: Denials," 74; Derrida, *Psyché: Inventions de l'autre*, 536.

13. Cited in Knowlson, *Damned to Fame*, 352.

14. The meaning of "unsaying" in Beckett evolves: from the neat reversal of the order of what is said (*Watt*), through the bringing of language into turmoil or "undoing" of it (Lucky's monologue in *Waiting for Godot*), to the retraction of what has been said (*The Unnamable*).

15. Shira Wolosky, *Language Mysticism: The Negative Way of Language in Eliot, Beckett and Celan* (Stanford: Stanford University Press, 1995), 90, 97.

16. Beckett, *Watt*, 165.

17. Beckett, *Trilogy*, 326.

18. Wolosky, *Language Mysticism*, 93.

19. Quoted in Mary Bryden, *Samuel Beckett and the Idea of God* (Basingstoke: Macmillan, 1998).

20. Derrida also invokes his "religion about which no one understands anything." Derrida, *Circonfession*, 146; Derrida, *Circumfession*, 155; on the "forms of atheism," cf. Derrida, "Sauf le nom," 36/18.

21. "(I)l faille libérer 'Dieu' de la question sur/de l'Être." Jean-Luc Marion, *Dieu sans l'être* (Paris: Fayard, 1982), 91. This is also how Heidegger may be said to have attempted to speak about God: by crossing out or erasing the notion of being.

22. Beckett, *Complete Dramatic Works*, 119, my emphasis.

23. Beckett, *Watt*, 64, my emphasis.
24. Derrida, "How to Avoid Speaking: Denials," 96/558.
25. Angelus (Johannes Scheffler) Silesius, *The Cherubinic Wanderer*, trans. Maria Shrady (New York: Paulist, 1986), 1:205.
26. "Place" is a "site of gathering [that accommodates] Being and beings"—hence a site that accommodates ontological difference. Language is not the only thing that can do this, but perhaps the most prominently appearing to us as such. Hent de Vries, "Winke," in *The Solid Letter*, ed. Aris Fioretos (Stanford, CA: Stanford University Press, 1999), 97. Cf. also Hent de Vries, "Theotopographies: Nancy, Hölderlin, Heidegger," *Modern Language Notes* 109 (1994).
27. Beckett, *Watt*, 73.
28. Anatole France, *Le jardin d'Epicure* (Paris: Calmann-Levy, 1895).
29. Beckett, *Watt*, 74, my emphasis.
30. Beckett, *Complete Dramatic Works*, 108.
31. Rodolphe Gasché, "God, for Example," in *Inventions of Difference: On Jacques Derrida* (Cambridge, Massachusetts: Harvard University Press, 1994), 152.
32. Gasché, "God, for Example," 154.
33. Derrida, *Of Grammatology*, 71/104.
34. Derrida, *Writing and Difference*, 115–16/170.
35. Jacques Derrida, *Margins of Philosophy*, trans. Allan Bass (Chicago: University of Chicago Press, 1982), 67; *Marges de la philosophie*, 77.
36. Ibid.
37. Charles Krance, "*Worstward Ho* and On Words: Writing to(wards) the Point," in *Rethinking Beckett: A Collection of Critical Essays*, ed. Lance St.-J. Butler and R. Davis (London: Macmillan, 1990), 130–31.
38. Heidegger, *Being and Time*, 22; *Sein und Zeit* (Tübingen: Max Niemeyer Verlag, 1993), 3.
39. Ernst Tugendhat, "'Die Seinsfrage und ihre sprachliche Grundlage, in *Philosophische Rundschau* (Frankfurt am Main: Suhrkamp, 1992), 24/3–4; Charles K. Kahn, *The Verb "Be" in Ancient Greek* (Dordrecht: Reidel, 1973).
40. Heidegger, *Being and Time*, 26; Heidegger, *Sein und Zeit*, 6.
41. "S'il m'arrivait encore d'avoir à mettre par écrit une théologie—ce à quoi je me sens parfois incité—alors le terme d'être ne saurait en aucun cas y intervenir. La foi n'a pas besoin de la pensée de l'être." Quoted in Marion, *Dieu sans l'être*, 5.
42. Derrida, "How to Avoid Speaking: Denials," 128/592.
43. Ibid.
44. Derrida, *Margins of Philosophy*, 27.
45. Beckett, "Intercessions by Denis Devlin," in *Disjecta*, 91.
46. Locatelli, *Unwording the World: Samuel Beckett's Fiction After the Nobel Prize*, 228.
47. Beckett, *Nohow On: Company, Ill Seen Ill Said, Worstward Ho* (New York: Grove Press, 1996), 99.

48. See Kevin Hart's reading of canto XXVI, *Paradiso*, in Hart, *The Trespass of the Sign: Deconstruction, Theology and Philosophy* (Cambridge and New York: Cambridge University Press, 1989).
49. Ibid., 3–4.
50. Beckett, *Nohow On*, 89.
51. Locatelli, *Unwording the World*, 230.
52. Hart, *The Trespass of the Sign*.
53. Beckett, *Disjecta*, 172.
54. John D. Caputo, ed. *God, the Gift, and Postmodernism* (Bloomington: Indiana University Press, 1999), 188.
55. Beckett, *Nohow On*, 96.
56. Henri Bergson, *The Two Sources of Morality and Religion* (Notre Dame: University of Notre Dame Press, 1977), 47.
57. See Jacques Derrida, *Of Spirit: Heidegger and the Question* (Chicago: University of Chicago Press, 1989), 129–36. (Jacques Derrida, *Heidegger et la question: De l'esprit et autres essais* [Paris: Flammarion, 1990], 114–21.) In the much-discussed footnote 5, Derrida addresses the privileging of the question in Heidegger. Derrida writes: The "infinite legitimacy of questioning . . . tips over into the memory of a language, of an experience of language 'older' than it, always anterior and presupposed. . . . Language is *already* there, in advance. . . . This advance is, before any contract, a sort of promise of originary alliance to which we must have in some sense already acquiesced, already said *yes*, given a pledge" (129/115).
58. Derrida, "Ulysses Gramophone: Hear Say Yes in Joyce," 270. See also Samuel Weber, "The Debts of Deconstruction and Other, Related Assumptions," in *Institution and Interpretation,* ed. Wlad Godzich (Minneapolis: University of Minnesota Press, 1987).
59. Derrida, *Of Spirit: Heidegger and the Question*, 93/118.
60. Paul de Man, *Allegories of Reading* (New Haven: Yale University Press, 1979), 277.
61. Derrida, *Of Spirit*, 93–94/114.
62. Beckett, *Trilogy*, 301.
63. Beckett, *Nohow On*, 105.
64. Beckett, *Disjecta*, 139.
65. Beckett, *Watt*, 74.
66. Beckett, "Three Dialogues with Georges Duthuit," 139.
67. Silesius, *The Cherubinic Wanderer*, 1:199.
68. Beckett, *Disjecta*, 142.
69. Beckett, *Nohow On*, 108.
70. Martin Heidegger, "What Are Poets For?" in *Poetry, Language, Thought* (New York: Harper, 1975), 129.
71. Locatelli, *Unwording the World*, 233.

72. Octavio Paz, ed., *Anthology of Mexican Poetry*, trans. Samuel Beckett (London: Thames and Hudson, 1957), 135–37.
73. Beckett, *Nohow On*, 99.
74. Heidegger, *Being and Time*, 318; *Sein und Zeit*, 273.
75. Derrida, "How to Avoid Speaking: Denials," 99/561.
76. Beckett, *Nohow On*, 98.
77. Heidegger, *Being and Time*, 318/274.
78. Caputo, *The Prayers and Tears of Jacques Derrida*, 3.
79. Ibid., 9.
80. Ibid., 13.
81. Beckett, *Nohow On*, 89.
82. Ibid., 104.
83. Derrida, "How to Avoid Speaking: Denials," 95/557.
84. Jacques Derrida and Maurizio Ferraris, *A Taste for the Secret* (Cambridge, England: Polity Press, 2001).
85. Samuel Beckett, *Proust* (New York: Grove Press, 1931), 51.
86. Derrida, *Speech and Phenomena*, 54/60.
87. de Vries, *Philosophy and the Turn to Religion*, 314.
88. Derrida, "Sauf le nom," 55–56/56.
89. Ricks, *Beckett's Dying Words*, 55. Also, Charles Julliet recounts: "We discuss religion, and I ask whether he has been able to free himself from its influence. SB: 'Perhaps in my external behaviour, but as for the rest . . .' " Charles Julliet, "Meeting Beckett," *TriQuarterly* 77 (1990): 27.

CONCLUDING REMARKS

1. Badiou, *Manifesto for Philosophy*, 66.
2. Cavell, "Ending the Waiting Game: A Reading of Beckett's *Endgame*," passim.
3. Ibid., 117. See also the discussion of Cavell's reading of Beckett in Critchley, *Very Little . . . Almost Nothing: Death, Philosophy, Literature*, 179–80.
4. Beckett, *Complete Dramatic Works*, 59, 68.
5. Ibid., 36.
6. Badiou, *On Beckett*, 90, my emphasis.
7. Cavell, "Ending the Waiting Game," 161.
8. Thus, in Cavell: "[I]n modernist arts the achievement of the autonomy of the object is a problem—the artistic problem. Autonomy is no longer provided by the conventions of an art . . . nor is it furthered by any position the artist can adopt, towards anything but his art." Cavell, "Ending the Waiting Game," 116.
9. In his essay under the same title (*Aporias*), Derrida devotes a substantial passage to link the rhetoric of partitions to the question of the aporia. Derrida, *Aporias*, 15. The rhetoric of partitions includes the singular ("the birth date that only happens by effacing itself," discussed in *The Shibboleth*).

10. Derrida, *Aporias*, 78–79.
11. Ibid., 15; and Derrida, *Psyché: Inventions de l'autre*, 27.
12. Beckett, *How It Is*, 53.
13. Beckett, *The Complete Short Prose*, 64.
14. Beckett, "Company," 46.
15. Derrida, "La Veilleuse," 7–32.
16. "[L]écriture rêve de souveraineté, l'écriture est *cruelle*, meurtrière. . . . Le crime contre l'humanité, le génocide même commencent là, et le crime contre la génération." Derrida, "La Veilleuse," 31.
17. "[C]ommencer enfin à aimer la vie, à savoir sa naissance. Entre autres la mienne. . . . Nouvelle règle de vie: respirer sans écriture, désormais, souffler au-delà de l'écriture. . . . Sans écriture, sans phrase, sans meurtre. . . . Au-delà de la pulsion de mort, de toute pulsion de pouvoir et de maîtrise. Écriture sans écriture. L'autre écriture, l'autre de l'écriture aussi, l'écriture altérée, celle qui a toujours travaillé la mienne en silence." Derrida, "La Veilleuse," 31–32.
18. Derrida, "La Veilleuse," 31.
19. Beckett, *Trilogy*, 92.
20. Jacques Derrida, *Glas* (Paris: Éditions Galilée, 1974), 231/258.

Bibliography

Ackerley, C. J. "Demented Particulars: Annotated Murphy." *Journal of Beckett Studies* 7, nos. 1–2 (1998).
Adorno, Theodor. "Trying to Understand *Endgame*." In *Notes to Literature*. New York: Columbia University Press, 1991, 241–75.
Alféri, Pierre. *Guillaume d'Ockham: Le singulier*. Paris: Minuit, 1989.
Attridge, Derek, ed. *Acts of Literature*. London: Routledge, 1992.
Austin, J. L. *How to Do Things with Words*. Oxford: Clarendon Press, 1965.
Badiou, Alain. *Beckett: L'increvable désir*. Paris: Hachette, 1995.
———. "Beckett's Generic Writing." In "Beckett in France." Special issue, *Journal of Beckett Studies* 4, no. 1 (1994): 13–21.
———. *Deleuze: The Clamor of Being*. Minneapolis: University of Minnesota Press, 2000.
———. "L'écriture du générique: Samuel Beckett." In *Conditions*. Paris: Seuil, 1992.
———. "Être, existence, pensée: Prose et concept." In *Petit manuel d'inesthétique*, 137–87. Paris: Seuil, 1998.
———. *Manifesto for Philosophy*. Albany, NY: SUNY Press, 1999.
———. *Petit manuel d'inesthétique*. Paris: Seuil, 1998.
———. "La poésie en condition de la philosophie." *Europe: Revue littéraire mensuelle* 78, nos. 849–50 (2000): 65–75.
Bal, Mieke. "Reprise de l'interruption ou la mise en abyme." In *Femmes imaginaires*, 159–66. Paris: Nizet, 1986.
Barthes, Roland. *Camera Lucida: Reflections on Photography*. London: Vintage, 1982. Originally published as *La Chambre Claire* (Paris: Éditions du Seuil, 1980).
Bataille, Georges. "Le Silence de Molloy." *Critique* 7 (1951): 387–96.
Beckett, Samuel. *Comment c'est*. Paris: Éditions de Minuit, 1961.
———. *Compagnie*. Paris: Les Éditions de Minuit, 1985.
———. *Complete Dramatic Works*. London: Faber and Faber, 1986.
———. *The Complete Short Prose*. New York: Grove Press, 1995.

———. "Dante . . . Bruno. Vico . . . Joyce." *Transition* 16–17 (1929).
———. *Disjecta*. New York: Grove Press, 1984.
———. *How It Is*. New York: Grove Press, 1964.
———. *Mercier and Camier*. London: Calder, 1974.
———. "Le monde et le pantalon." *Cahiers d'art* 20–21 (1945).
———. *Murphy*. London: Calder, 1963.
———. *Nohow On: Company, Ill Seen Ill Said, Worstward Ho*. New York: Grove Press, 1996.
———. *Proust*. New York: Grove Press, 1931.
———. "Three Dialogues with Georges Duthuit." In *Proust and Three Dialogues*. London: Calder, 1965.
———. *Trilogy: Molloy, Malone Dies, The Unnamable*. London: Calder, 1959.
———. *Watt*. New York: Calder, 1998.
Birkett, Jennifer, and Kate Ince, eds. *Samuel Beckett*. London: Longman Critical Readers, 2000.
Bishop, Tom, and Raymond Federman, eds. *Cahier de L'Herne: Samuel Beckett*. Paris: Éditions de l'Herne, 1976.
Blanchot, Maurice. "Enigma." *Yale French Studies* 79 (1991): 8.
———. "Oh tout finir." *Critique* 46, nos. 519–20 (1990): 635–37.
———. "Où maintenant? Qui maintenant?" *Nouvelle Revue Française* 2 (1953): 678–86.
———. *La part du Feu*. Paris: Gallimard, 1949.
Bryden, Mary. "Deleuze Reading Beckett." In *Beckett and Philosophy*, edited by Richard Lane. Houndmills, Basingstoke, Hampshire, and New York: Palgrave, 2002.
———. *Samuel Beckett and the Idea of God*. Basingstoke: Macmillan, 1998.
———. "The Schizoid Space: Beckett, Deleuze and *L'Epuisé*." *Samuel Beckett Today/Aujourd'hui* 5 (1996): 85–95.
Butler, Lance St. John. *Samuel Beckett and the Meaning of Being*. London: Macmillan Press, 1984.
Caputo, John D. *The Prayers and Tears of Jacques Derrida: Religion without Religion*. Bloomington: Indiana University Press, 1997.
Cavell, Stanley. *The Claim of Reason: Wittgenstein, Skepticism, Morality and Tragedy*. Oxford: Oxford University Press, 1979.
———. "Ending the Waiting Game: A Reading of Beckett's *Endgame*." In *Must We Mean What We Say?* Cambridge: Cambridge University Press, 1976.
———. *Philosophical Passages: Wittgenstein, Emerson, Austin, Derrida*. Oxford, England, and Cambridge, MA: Blackwell, 1995.
———. *A Pitch of Philosophy*. Cambridge, MA: Harvard University Press, 1996.
Celan, Paul. *Gesammelte Werke*. Frankfurt am Main: Suhrkamp, 1983.

Clark, Timothy. *Derrida, Heidegger, Blanchot: Sources of Derrida's Notion and Practice of Literature.* Cambridge: Cambridge University Press, 1992.
Connor, Steven. *A Cultural History of Ventriloquism.* Oxford: Oxford University Press, 2002.
Cousineau, Tom. "The Lost Father in Beckett's Novels." In *Beckett and la psychanalyse and Psychoanalysis,* edited by Sjef Houppermans, 73–85. Amsterdam and Atlanta: Rodopi, 1996.
Dällenbach, Lucien. *The Mirror in the Text.* Chicago: University of Chicago Press, 1989.
Danto, Arthur C. *Philosophical Disenfranchisement of Art.* New York: Columbia University Press, 1986.
Dauber, Kenneth, and Walter Jost, eds. *Ordinary Language Criticism.* Evanston, IL: Northwestern University Press, 2003.
Davidson, Donald. "Locating Literary Language." In *Literary Theory after Davidson,* edited by Reed Way Dasenbrock. University Park: Pennsylvania State University Press, 1993.
———. "A Nice Derangement of Epitaphs." In *Philosophical Grounds of Rationality,* edited by Richard Grandy. Oxford: Clarendon Press, 1986.
———. "What Metaphors Mean." In *Inquiries into Truth and Interpretation,* 245–64. Oxford: Clarendon Press, 1984.
Deleuze, Gilles. "L'Abécédaire de Gilles Deleuze" (transcript), 1996, http://www.langlab.wayne.edu/CStivale/D-G/ABC2.html.
———. *Cinema 1.* London: Athlone Press, 1992.
———. *Critique et clinique.* Paris: Minuit, 1993.
———. *Difference and Repetition.* London: Continuum, 1994. Originally published as *Différence et répétition* (Paris: Presses Universitaires de France, 1968).
———. "The Exhausted." In *Essays Critical and Clinical.* London and New York: Verso, 1998.
———. *Foucault.* Minneapolis: University of Minnesota Press, 1988. Originally published in French (Paris: Les Éditions de Minuit, 1986).
———. "Lectures on Bergson," 1981, www.webdeleuze.com.
———. *The Logic of Sense.* New York: Columbia University Press, 1990.
———. "Le plus grand film irlandais (en hommage à Samuel Beckett)." *Revue d'esthétique* (1986): 381–82.
———. "Spinoza," 1981, http://www.webdeleuze.com/html/index2.html.
———. *Spinoza et le problème d'expression.* Paris: Minuit, 1968.
Deleuze, Gilles, and Felix Guattari. *A Thousand Plateaus: Capitalism and Schizophrenia.* Minneapolis: University of Minnesota Press, 1987.
———. *What Is Philosophy?* New York: Columbia University Press, 1994. Originally published as *Qu'est-ce que la philosophie?* (Paris: Minuit, 1991).

Bibliography

Deleuze, Gilles, and Claire Parnet. "De la supériorité de la littérature anglaise-américaine." In *Dialogues*. Paris: Flammarion, 1996.
———. *Dialogues*. Paris: Flammarion, 1996.
———. *Dialogues II*. New York: Columbia, 2002.
Derrida, Jacques. *Aporias*. Stanford, CA: Stanford University Press, 1993.
———. "Before the Law." In *Acts of Literature*, edited by Derek Attridge, 181–220. London and New York: Routledge, 1992.
———. *Circumfession*. Chicago: University of Chicago Press, 1993.
———. "The Deaths of Roland Barthes." In *Philosophy and Non-philosophy since Merleau-Ponty*, edited by Hugh J. Silverman. London: Routledge, 1988.
———. *Demeure: Fiction and Testimony*. Translated by Elizabeth Rottenberg. Stanford, CA: Stanford University Press, 2000.
———. *Dissemination*. London: Athlone, 1981.
———. "The Double Session." *Dissemination*. London: Athlone, 1981.
———. "'Eating Well' or the Calculation of the Subject." In *Points . . . : Interviews, 1974–1994*, edited by Elisabeth Weber. Stanford, CA: Stanford University Press, 1995.
———. "Economimesis." *Diacritics* 11, no. 2 (summer 1981): 3–25.
———. *Edmund Husserl's "Origin of Geometry": An Introduction*. Translated by John P. Leavey Jr. Lincoln: University of Nebraska Press, 1989. Originally published as *Introduction à "L'Origine de la géométrie" de Husserl* (Paris: Presses Universitaires de France, 1962).
———. "Force of Law: The 'Mystical Foundation of Authority.'" In *Deconstruction and the Possibility of Justice*, edited by David G. Carlson, Drucilla Cornell, and M. Rosenfeld. London and New York: Routledge, 1992.
———. *The Gift of Death*. Chicago: University of Chicago Press, 1995. Originally published as "Donner la mort" in *L'éthique du don, Jacques Derrida et la pensée du don* (Paris: Métailié-Transition, 1992).
———. "How to Avoid Speaking: Denials." In *Derrida and Negative Theology*, edited by H. Coward and T. Foshay. Albany: State University of New York Press, 1992.
———. "The Law of Genre." In *Acts of Literature*, edited by Derek Attridge. London and New York: Routledge, 1992.
———. *Limited Inc*. Evanston, IL: Northwestern University Press, 1988.
———. "Living On: Border Lines." In *Deconstruction and Criticism*, edited by Harold Bloom. London: Routledge, 1979.
———. "Maddening the Subjectile." *Yale French Studies* 84 (1994): 154–71.
———. *Le monolinguisme de l'autre*. Paris: Galilée, 1996.
———. "My Chances/Mes Chances: A Rendezvous with Some Epicurean Stereophonies." In *Taking Chances: Derrida, Psychoanalysis and Literature*, edited by Joseph H. Smith and William Kerrigan. Baltimore: Johns Hopkins University Press, 1984.

———. *Of Grammatology*. Baltimore: Johns Hopkins University Press, 1976. Originally published as *De la Grammatologie* (Paris: Minuit, 1967).
———. "Paul Celan: La langue n'appartient pas (entretien)." *Europe: Revue littéraire mensuelle* 79, nos. 861–62 (2001): 81–91.
———. *Points . . . : Interviews, 1974–1994*. Edited by Elisabeth Weber. Stanford, CA: Stanford University Press, 1995.
———. "Psyché: Invention de l'autre." In *Psyché: Inventions de l'autre*. Paris: Galilée, 1987.
———. "Psyche: Inventions of the Other." In *Reading de Man Reading*, edited by L. Waters and W. Godzich. Minneapolis: University of Minnesota Press, 1989.
———. "Sauf le nom." In *On the Name*. Stanford, CA: Stanford University Press, 1995.
———. *Schibboleth: Pour Paul Celan*. Paris: Galilée, 1986.
———. "Shibboleth: For Paul Celan." In *Word Traces: Readings of Paul Celan*, edited by Aris Fioretos. Baltimore: Johns Hopkins University Press, 1994.
———. "Signature, Event, Context." In *Limited Inc*. Evanston, IL: Northwestern University Press, 1988.
———. *Signéponge/Signsponge*. New York: Columbia University Press, 1984.
———. *Speech and Phenomena*. Evanston, IL: Northwestern University Press, 1973.
———. "Structure, Sign and Play in the Discourse of the Human Sciences." In *The Languages of Criticism and the Sciences of Man*, edited by Richard Macksey and Eugenio Donato. Baltimore and London: Johns Hopkins University Press, 1970.
———. *Sur Parole: Instantanés Philosophiques*. Paris: Éditions de l'aube, 1999.
———. "This Strange Institution Called Literature." In *Acts of Literature*, edited by Derek Attridge, 33–76. New York and London: Routledge, 1992.
———. "The Time of a Thesis: Punctuations." In *Philosophy in France Today*, edited by A. Montefiori. Cambridge: Cambridge University Press, 1982.
———. *Ulysse gramophone*. Paris: Galilée, 1987.
———. "Ulysses Gramophone: Hear Say Yes in Joyce." In *Acts of Literature*, edited by Derek Attridge. London: Routledge, 1992.
———. "Une 'folie' doit veiller sur la pensée." *Magazine Littéraire* 286 (March 1991): 18–26.
———. *Writing and Difference*. London: Routledge, 1978.
Derrida, Jacques, and Maurizio Ferraris. *A Taste for the Secret*. Cambridge: Polity Press, 2001.
Derrida, Jacques, and Elisabeth Roudinesco. *De quoi demain . . .* Paris: Fayard/Galilée, 2001.
Edmundson, Mark. *Literature against Philosophy, Plato to Derrida*. Cambridge: Cambridge University Press, 1995.
Euripides. "Hyppolytus." In *The Complete Greek Tragedies*, edited by David Grene and Richmond Lattimore. Chicago: University of Chicago Press, 1995.

France, Anatole. *Le jardin d'Epicure*. Paris: Calmann-Levy, 1895.
Gadamer, Hans-Georg. "Plato and the Poets." In *Dialogue and Dialectic: Eight Hermeneutical Studies on Plato*, 39–72. New Haven and London: Yale University Press, 1980.
Gasché, Rodolphe. "God, for Example." *Inventions of Difference*. Cambridge, MA: Harvard University Press, 1994.
———. "Ideality in Fragmentation." In *Friedrich Schlegel: Philosophical Fragments*, vii–xxxi. Minneapolis and London: University of Minnesota Press, 1991.
———. *Of Minimal Things: Studies on the Notion of Relation*. Stanford, CA: Stanford University Press, 1999.
———. *The Tain of the Mirror*. Cambridge, MA: Harvard University Press, 1986.
Gibson, John, and Wolfgang Huemer, eds. *The Literary Wittgenstein*. London: Routledge, 2004.
Habermas, Jürgen. "Philosophy and Science as Literature?" In *Postmetaphysical Thinking: Philosophical Essays*, 205–29. Cambridge, MA: MIT Press.
Hallward, Peter. *Badiou: A Subject to Truth*. Minneapolis and London: University of Minnesota Press, 2003.
Hart, K. *The Trespass of the Sign: Deconstruction, Theology and Philosophy*. Cambridge and New York: Cambridge University Press, 1991.
Hegel, G.W.F. *Enzyklopädie der Philosophischen Wissenschaften im Grundrisse*. Hamburg: Felix Meiner, 1992 (1830).
———. *Phenomenology of Spirit*. Oxford: Oxford University Press, 1979.
Heidegger, Martin. *Being and Time*. New York: Harper & Row, 1962.
———. "Der Ursprung des Kunstwerkes." In *Holzwege*. Frankfurt am Main: Vittorio Klostermann, 1950.
———. *Nietzsche II: The Eternal Recurrence of the Same*. San Francisco: Harper and Row, 1984.
———. "The Question Concerning Technology." In *Philosophical and Political Writings*, 279–303. New York: Continuum, 2003.
———. *Sein und Zeit*. Tübingen: Max Niemeyer Verlag, 1993.
Heimsoeth, Heinz. *Die sechs grossen Themen der Abendländischen Metaphysik*. Stuttgart: W. Kohlhammer Verlag, 1958.
Hill, Leslie. *Beckett's Fiction: In Different Words*. Cambridge: Cambridge University Press, 1990.
Husserl, Edmund. *Formal and Transcendental Logic*. The Hague: Martinus Nijhoff, 1965.
———. *Logical Investigations*. London: Routledge, 1970.
Iser, Wolfgang. "When Is the End Not the End? The Idea of Fiction in Beckett." In *The Implied Reader*. London: Johns Hopkins University Press, 1974.
Jacquart, Emmanuel. "*Endgame*, Master Game." In "Beckett in France." Special issue, *Journal of Beckett Studies* 4, no. 1 (1994): 85.

Janvier, Ludovic. "Beckett était obsédé par la voix" (interview). *Magazine Littéraire* (January 1999): 34–37.
Joyce, James. *Finnegans Wake*. London: Penguin Books, 1992.
Julliet, Charles. "Meeting Beckett." *TriQuarterly* 77 (1990).
Kahn, Charles K. *The Verb "Be" in Ancient Greek*. Dordrecht: Reidel, 1973.
Kant, Immanuel. *Critique of Judgement*. New York: Hafner Press, 1951.
Kermode, Frank. *The Sense of an Ending: Studies in the Theory of Fiction*. New York: Oxford University Press, 1967.
Knowlson, James. *Damned to Fame*. London: Bloomsbury, 1996.
Kojève, Alexandre. *Introduction à la lecture de Hegel*. Paris: Gallimard, 1947.
———. *Introduction to the Reading of Hegel: Lectures on the Phenomenology of Spirit*. Assembled by Raymond Queneau. Edited by Allan Bloom. Ithaca, NY: Cornell University Press, 1980.
Krance, Charles. "*Worstward Ho* and On Words: Writing to(wards) the Point." In *Rethinking Beckett: A Collection of Critical Essays*, edited by Robert Davis and Lance St. John Butler. London: Macmillan, 1990.
Kronick, Joseph G. *Derrida and the Future of Literature*. Albany, NY: SUNY Press, 1999.
Lacoue-Labarthe, Philippe, and Jean-Luc Nancy. *The Literary Absolute: The Theory of Literature in German Romanticism*. Albany, NY: SUNY Press, 1988.
Lane, Richard, ed. *Beckett and Philosophy*. Houndmills, Basingstoke, Hampshire, and New York: Palgrave, 2002.
Lawlor, Leonard. *Derrida and Husserl: The Basic Problem of Phenomenology*. Bloomington, IN: Indiana University Press, 2002.
Leibniz, Gottfried Wilhelm. *Discourse on Metaphysics*. Buffalo, NY: Prometheus Books, 1992.
Lévi-Strauss, Claude. *Totemism*. Boston: Beacon Press, 1963.
Locatelli, Carla. *Unwording the World*. Philadelphia: University of Pennsylvania Press, 1990.
Lyotard, Jean-François. *L'inhumain*. Paris: Galilée, 1988.
Marion, Jean-Luc. *Dieu sans l'être*. Paris: Fayard, 1982.
Marquet, Jean-François. *Singularité et événement*. Grenoble: Editions Jérôme Millon, 1995.
Marrati, Paola. "Against the Doxa: Politics of Immanence and Becoming-Minoritarian." In *Micropolitics of Media Culture: Reading the Rhizomes of Deleuze and Guattari*. Amsterdam: Amsterdam University Press, 2001.
———. "L'animal qui sait fuir." In *L'animal autobiographique: Autour de Jacques Derrida*. Paris: Galilée, 1999.
———. *La genèse et la trace: Derrida lecteur de Husserl et Heidegger*. Dordrecht: Kluwer Academic Publishers, 1998.
———. *Gilles Deleuze: Cinéma et philosophe*. Paris: Presses Universitaires de France, 2003.

Mortley, Raoul. *French Philosophers in Conversation: Levinas, Schneider, Serres, Irigaray, Le Doeuff, Derrida*. London and New York: Routledge, 1991.
Murphy, Peter. "At Beckett's Grave (or Why Jacques Derrida Has Given Up on Writing in the Direction of Beckett—for the Moment)." *Textual Studies in Canada/Études Textuelles au Canada* 6 (1995): 55–58.
Nancy, Jean-Luc. "Surprise de l'événement." In *Être singulier pluriel*, 185–202. Paris: Galilée, 1996.
Nietzsche, Friedrich. *Thus Spoke Zarathustra*. London: Penguin, 1974.
Nussbaum, Martha. "Narrative Emotions: Beckett's Genealogy of Love." *Ethics* (January 1988): 225–54.
Paz, Octavio, ed. *Anthology of Mexican Poetry*. Translated by Samuel Beckett. London: Thames and Hudson, 1957.
Perloff, Marjorie. "Witt-Watt: The Language of Resistance/The Resistance of Language." In *Wittgenstein's Ladder: Poetic Language and the Strangeness of the Ordinary*, 115–45. Chicago: University of Chicago Press, 1996.
Pilling, John, ed. *The Cambridge Companion to Beckett*. Cambridge: Cambridge University Press, 1994.
Pothast, Ulrich. *Die eigentlich metaphysische Tätigkeit: Über Schopenhauers Ästhetik und ihre Anwendung durch Samuel Beckett*. Frankfurt am Main: Suhrkamp, 1982.
Putnam, Hilary. "Rules, Attunement and 'Applying Rules to the World.'" In *The Legacy of Wittgenstein: Pragmatism and Deconstruction*, edited by Ludwig Nagl and Chantal Mouffe. New York: Peter Lang, 2001.
Quint, J., ed. *Meister Eckhart: Die Deutschen Werke*. Zürich: Diogenes Verlag AG, 1979.
Ricks, Christopher. *Beckett's Dying Words*. Oxford: Clarendon Press, 1993.
Ricoeur, Paul. *Oneself as Another*. Chicago: University of Chicago Press, 1992.
———. *Time and Narrative*. Chicago: University of Chicago Press, 1984–1988.
Schlegel, Friedrich. *Philosophical Fragments*. Minneapolis: Minnesota University Press, 1991.
Schulte Nordholt, Anne-Lise. *Maurice Blanchot: L'écriture comme expérience du dehors*. Genève: Librarie Droz, 1995.
Siccama, Wilma. *Het waarnemend lichaam: Zintuiglijkheid en representatie bij Beckett en Artaud*. Nijmegen: Vantilt, 2000.
Silesius, Angelus (Johannes Scheffler). *The Cherubinic Wanderer*. New York: Paulist, 1986.
Sneller, Rico. *Het Woord is schrift geworden: Derrida en de negatieve theologie*. Kampen: Kok Agora, 1998.
Spinoza, Benedict de. *Ethics*. London: Penguin, 1994.
Tugendhat, Ernst. "Die Seinsfrage und ihre sprachliche Grundlage." In *Philosophische Rundschau* 24, nos. 3–4 (1977): 161–76.
Uhlmann, Anthony. *Beckett and Post-structuralism*. Cambridge: Cambridge University Press, 1999.

Vallega-Neu, Daniela. "Poietic Saying." In *Companion to Heidegger's Contributions to Philosophy*, edited by Charles E. Scott, Susan M. Schoenbohm, Daniela Vallega-Neu, and Alejandro Vallega, 66–80. Bloomington, IN: Indiana University Press, 2001.

Vries, Hent de. *Philosophy and the Turn to Religion*. Baltimore and London: Johns Hopkins University Press, 1999.

———. *Religion and Violence: Philosophical Perspectives from Kant to Derrida*. Baltimore and London: Johns Hopkins University Press, 2001.

Wheeler, Samuel C. "Wittgenstein as Conservative Deconstructor." *New Literary History* 19, no. 2 (1988): 239–58.

Wittgenstein, Ludwig. *Culture and Value*. Edited by George Henrik von Wright in collaboration with Heikki Nyman. Revised edition of the text by Alois Pichler. Translated by Peter Winch. Oxford: Blackwell, 1998.

———. *Philosophical Investigations*. Oxford: Blackwell, 1967.

———. *Zettel*. Oxford: Basil Blackwell, 1967.

Wolosky, Shira. *Language Mysticism: The Negative Way of Language in Eliot, Beckett and Celan*. Stanford, CA: Stanford University Press, 1995.

Index

Adorno, Theodor, 5, 6, 194n9
Affirmation, in Beckett, 153–55
Age of Poets, 149–52
Alferi, Pierre, 58
Anonymity, Derrida's move from, 37
Archiving, 31–33, 39, 114–15
Artaud, 2–3, 130
"At Beckett's Grave," 5–6
Attridge, Derek, 1–5
Austin, J. L., 78–80, 84–86
Author, voice of, 46, 54
Authority, 140–60, 177–82
Auto-affection, 125

Badiou, Alain: on Beckett, 7–8, 148–60, 186, 187, 188–89, 225n74; on Deleuze, 95, 111; on events, 59; on philosophy and literature, 183; on poetry, 14–15, 21, 149–52, 223n41; on the task of art, 25
Barthes, Roland, 23–24, 59–65, 184
Bataille, Georges, 6, 13, 153, 193n9
Baudrillard, Jean, 7
Beckett, Samuel: archiving and recording, 32–35; authority of characters, 147; and author's voice, 46; Badiou on, 148–60; and bilingualism, 199n29; characters of, 46–48; Deleuze on, 94–117; and Derrida, 2–3, 21, 24–25, 118–91, 139, 183; and exhaustion, 94–117, 186–87; faith of, 181–82; and gathering, 92–96, 184; on God, 169; on happiness, 224n53; and homonyms, 129; and hyper-totalizing, 55; on identity, 217n17; impoverishment of language in, 93; Joyce, differences from, 108; Kaun, letter to, 161, 173–74; language and God in, 173–74; and memory, 116; and *mise en abyme*, 45–47, 48–50; and *Molloy*, 140–48; on music, 114; and mysticism, 165–66; on negativity, 161–68; as nihilist, 152–54; and obligation to express, 53; and ordinary language, 84–91; Perloff on, 73–78; and permutation, 98; and philosophy, 6–8; Ricouer on, 133–39; and singularity, 62, 70; Spinozism of, 99–102; and subject identity, 125; on subtraction, 172–73; television plays of, 105; and *The Unnamable*, 122–29; work as odyssey, 68–70; writing in French, 93
Beckett's Fiction: In Different Words, 162
Becoming, 100, 115
Before the Law, 32, 43–45
Being, 111, 113, 171–72, 214n85
Being and Time, 11
Belaqua, 102
Bergson, 105, 174–75
Bernold, Andre, 2–3
Bilingualism, in Beckett, 199n29
Birth imagery, 131, 219n51, 220n52
Black holes, 35
Blanchot, Maurice, 3, 6, 7, 145, 222n22

Calmative, 49
Camera Lucida, 59–60, 63–64
Capturing, act of, 51–52

Caputo, John D., 179
Cartesian Meditations, 148
Cavell, Stanley: on Austin, 208n28; on autonomy, 229n8; on Beckett, 6, 184, 186; on Derrida, 84–91; on philosophy and literature, 11; on poetry, 9; on projection of words, 209n42; on Wittgenstein, 71–73
Celan, Paul, 3, 51, 150–51
Chess, game of, 202n63, 202n65
Cinema I, 105–6
Cixous, Helene, 6, 194n9
Combinatory, art of, 98
Company, 50, 189
Conditions, 156–57
Contre-abyme, 43, 45
Creative exigency, 174–75
Critique, 31–32

Davidson, Donald, 209–10n48
Death: of the author, 6, 116–17; Derrida's views on, 36, 222n25; in *Molloy*, 144–46; and responsibility, 222n19; and singularity, 60–62
Deaths of Roland Barthes, 59–65, 83
Decomposition, in Beckett's work, 47
Deconstruction, 72
Deleuze, Gilles: on Beckett, 7, 94–117; and becoming vs. gathering, 111–12; and black holes, 35; definition of event, 59; vs. Derrida, 108–17, 213n64, 215n95; Derrida on, 112; on differential force, 18; on exhausting, 210–11n14; influence of Spinoza on, 99–102; on music, 114; and *nomos* vs. *polis*, 47, 202n63
Demented particulars, in Beckett, 92–93
Demeure, 27, 46
Denkerisch-dichterisch, 10, 13
Der Ort ist dass Wort, 168–69
Derrida, Jacques: and affirmation of meaning, 175; and analytic tradition, 206–7n1; on aporia, 188, 218n32, 229n9; on Artaud, 2–4, 130–31; and Attridge interview, 1–5; and Austin, 78–83, 84–86; and author's signature, 54; and Badiou, 148–49, 158–59; on Barthes, 59–65; and Beckett, 1–6, 21, 24–25, 118–19, 139, 180, 183, 190–91; on Benjamin, 140–42; Cavell critique of, 84–86; on death, 36, 222n25; definition of event, 58–59; and Deleuze, 95–96, 108–17, 112, 213n64, 215n95; on force in literature, 17–20; on gathering, 31–34, 60, 83, 108, 110–11; hearing/seeing difference, 41; on Heidegger, Martin and theology, 172; on Husserl, 125–27, 190, 216n3, 218n31–232; on the "I," 125–27, 130; and idiom in language, 34; and interpretation, 213–14n73; and iterability, 78–83; on Joyce, 25, 31, 190, 198n18, 206n47; and juridical aspects of literature, 46; on language, 72–78, 228n57; *Before the Law*, reading on, 43–45; and literary character, 56; literature, views on, 27–54; vs. other literary criticism, 197n5; and phenomenology, 119–20; on philosophy and literature, 8, 12–14, 183; on presence, 17, 36, 41–42, 45, 119, 127, 170, 190; and Ricoeur, 137; on the secret, 180; shift in emphasis of, 35–38; and singularity, 15–21, 184; and singular literary work, 53; and specular reflection motif, 39–43; on theology and negativity, 162–65, 168, 170–71, 179; and *The Unnamable*, 122–23; on writing, 189–90, 215–16n108
Différance, 26, 142, 165, 201n48
Dissemination, 40
Dream of Fair to Middling Women, 165
Duthuit, Georges, 176

Eckhart, Meister, 163–65, 182
Economico-juridical character, of literary work, 31–32, 68, 111
Economy, of literary work, 4, 32–35
Egoyan, Atom, 63
Endgame, 47, 88, 176
Enigma, literature as, 27
Entrance, as structure in literature, 43–44
Estragon, 22–23, 185

Event: and archives, 112; in Beckett, 155; Beckett/Derrida differences, 21; connected to a mark, 67; Derrida's definition of, 58–59; of thought, 204–5n13
"Exhausted, The," 94–97
Exhausting, exhaustion: Beckett using, 96–97, 101–2; and becoming, 212n40; defined, 106–7; vs. gathering, 94–96, 107–17; and the "I," 218n25; levels of, 211n23; as parallel to archiving, 114–15; the possible, 97–99; three stadia of, 103–7; as variation of becoming, 100

Fiction, as literature, 29
Film, 105–7
Finnegan's Wake, 87
Force, in literature: differential, 17–19; economic, juridical, 31–32; formalizing, 18–20; and gathering, 142; and hyper-totalization, 30
"Force of Law," 140–42
Formalizing, literary, 39
Foucault, Michel, 6, 7, 144

Gaber, 144–46, 157
Gasché, Rodolphe, 40, 56, 200–201n47, 201n48
Gathering: vs. exhausting, 94–96, 107–17; as figure of power, 34–35; function, in literature, 31–35; and law, 31–32; resistance in Beckett, 92–96; and responsibility, 133–39; signature of, 82–83
Gift of Death, 146
God: Beckett on, 173–74; Deleuze on, 102–3; as language, 168–72, 178–79; and negativity, 161–65
Grammatology, 100
Guillaume d'Ockham: le singulier, 58

Habermas, Jurgen, 25
Hamm, 169
"Hearing-oneself-speak," 125–27, 218–19n33
Hearing/seeing difference, 41
Hedgehog, as imagery, 50–53, 203n73–274

Hegel, G.W.F.: and law of the force, 19; and reflection, speculation, 41; on the relationship between art and philosophy, 9; on singularity, 16–17, 57–58
Heidegger, Martin: on art, 36; and Beckett, 6, 7; on Being, 171–72; vs. Celan, 151; on philosophy and literature, 10–11; and reflexivity, 178
Hermeneutics, 109, 110
Hill, Leslie, 162
How It Is, 34, 37, 68–69, 147
"How to Avoid Speaking: Denials," 171–72
How to Do Things with Words, 78–79
Humor, 154, 209n47
Husserl, Edmund: Derrida on, 88, 119–20, 125–27, 190, 216n3, 218n31–232; on ideality, 209n40; on poverty, 148; and subject identity, 125; on univocity, 93
Hyper-responsibility, 137–38, 143
Hyper-totalization, in literature: Beckett's recalcitrance to, 55; Derrida and, 30–31, 108–9; and gathering, 137–38; vs. philosophical discourse, 41

"Ideality of the Literary Object, The," 119–22
Identity, narrative, 136–37, 217n17
Idiom, 34, 37
"I" in literature, 69–70, 123–31, 218–19n33, 218n25
Ill Seen Ill Said, 155
Image, 107
Instant, 59, 60, 116, 140, 221n3
Interpretation, as gathering instrument, 110–11, 213–14n73
Iser, Wolfgang, 153
Iteration, iterability: defined, 81–82, 196n35; excess, in literary work, 31–32; and law, 38, 81; of a mark, 67–68; in *Molloy*, 140–48; and *punctum*, 66; and re-presentation, 120–21; and self-reflection, 41–42; and the singular, 21, 61, 65–70, 198n17

244 Index

Janvier, Ludovic, 93, 94–95
Jena romanticism, 10, 50, 51
Joyce, James: and Barthes, 23–24, 66–67, 70; Beckett, differences from, 108; Derrida on, 25, 31, 190, 198n18, 206n47; hyper-totalizing enterprise of, 95; literary project of, 60; and use of language, 87, 89

Kafka, read by Derrida, 43–45
Kant, Immanuel, 9–10, 15
Kaun, Axel, 161, 173–74
Knowlson, James, 116, 182
Krapp's Last Tape (book), 33–34, 50, 62
Krapp's Last Tape (film), 63
Kristeva, Julia, 6

Lane, Richard, 7, 194n12, 210n11
Lacoue-Labarthe, Philippe, 149, 150, 151
Language: backwards speaking, 166–67; compared to "the mother," 37; Derrida on, 228n57; and literature, 36; games, in Beckett, 185–86; as gathering site, 227n26; and God, 168–72, 173–74; idiom in, 34; impoverished, in Beckett, 93; legitimate, illegitimate projections in, 88–90; and "limits that tremble," 27; non-serious uses of, 78–79; ordinary, 72–78, 84–91, 209n44, 209n47
Law: abyssal structure of, 43–45; in Beckett's work, 46–47; constitutional, 45–46; and gathering, 31–32; and reflexivity, 44; relation of a work to, 38–45; and singularity, 184
Le secret: motif et moteur de la litterature, 31
Levinas, Emmanuel, 24–25
Literary Absolute, The, 10
Literary work, 31–32
Literature: abyssal structure of, 42–43; as autobiography, 121–22, 216–17n10; competing definitions of, 78; continental approach to, 71–72; Derrida's views on, 27–31; exceeding its context, 25; as an institution, 12–14; noematic aspect of, 216n2; and ordinary language, 72–73, 86, 88–89; and philosophy, 8–21, 56–59; as reservoir of language, 88; as self-reflexive structure, 43; as Western institution, 28
Locatelli, Carla, 172
Logical Investigations, 125–26
Lyotard, Jean-Françoise, 7, 194n10

Mahood, 128–29, 136
Marion, Jean-Luc, 168
Mark, 67–68, 81
Marquet, Jean-Francois, 57
Mathesis singularis, 23–24, 25–26, 59–65
Matricide, 190
Membrane, as literary structure, 131
Memory, 50–51, 60, 112–13, 116
Metonymic expansion, 61–62, 64, 65, 66
Mirror image, reflection, 40–46, 48–49, 146, 200–201n47
Mise en abyme: in Beckett, 48–50, 146; defined, 201n49, 202n58; as law, 38, 44–46; meanings of, 49; and self-recognition, 41–43
Molloy: capturing events in, 157–58; iterated authority in, 140–48; and the law, 47; and naming, 104; as parable, 147; as personification of the sensible, 144; and symbol of power, 34
Monolingualism of the Other, 8, 20–21, 34
Moran, Jacques, 143–48, 157–58, 222n19
Mots valises, 214n76
Movement-image, 105–6
Murphy, 93, 102, 107
Music, Beckett and Deleuze on, 114
Must We Mean What We Say?, 88
Mystical foundation, of authority, 141–42
Mysticism, and Beckett, 165–66

Nancy, Jean-Luc, 67, 150
Narrative identity, 136–37
Narrativity, in philosophy, 56
Negative theology, 26, 161–65, 174, 181
Negativity, and God, 161–65

New Criticism, 6, 25
Nietzsche, Friedrich, 7, 99, 149, 194n11, 211n26
Nihilism, in Beckett, 152–54
Nomads, in Beckett, 202n59
Nomination, 151–52, 155–56
Nomos vs. *polis*, 47–48, 202n63
Nussbaum, Martha, 7, 144, 194n10, 209n45, 221n16

Obligation to express, 53, 174–77, 181
Ockham, William of, 58, 215n95
Odyssey, of iterable singular, 68–70
Of Grammatology, 84
Oneself as Another, 136
Ordinary language philosophy, 72–78, 84–91, 209n44, 209n47
Origin of Geometry, The, 56, 93

Partition, as literary structure, 131
Perloff, Marjorie: approach to literature, 7, 71–78; on Beckett, 7, 24, 184, 186
Permutation, in Beckett's work, 98
Phenomenon, phenomenality, 142–43, 147–49, 187
Phenomenology, and Derrida, 119–20, 125–26, 147–48
Phenomenology of Spirit, 19, 128
Philosophy: Badiou on, 149–52, 159; and literature, 8–21, 56–59; narrativity in, 56; of ordinary language, 72–78, 84–91
Photograph, as symbolic death, 60–61, 63
Pitch of Philosophy, A, 84
Poetry, 7–8, 14–15, 149–52, 194–95n17
Points of transaction, Beckett/Derrida: authority of literature, 140–60; negativity, language, and God, 161–91; the singular, 24–25; the subject, 118–39; the subjectile, 130–31, 138–39, 187–88
Power: differences from force, 42; and gathering, 34–35, 142; and iterability, 200n45; and singularity, 19
Pozzo, 185
Prayers and Tears of Jacques Derrida, The, 179

Proust and the Signs, 113
Punctum, in *Camera Lucida*: as metaphor of singularity, 23, 206n30; metonymy of, 61; singularity of, 19, 64–66, 83

Recording, 32
Reflection, reflexive, 38–39
Re-presentation, 120–21
Responsibility, and gathering, 133–39
Ricks, Christopher, 182
Ricoeur, Paul, 7, 133–39
Romanticism, origin of, 150

Sauf le nom, 67
Schlegel, Friedrich, 50
Second Trilogy, 47–48
Secretaire, as gathering receptacle, 31, 198–99n19
Sein und Zeit, 44
Self-referential text, failures of, 39
Self-reflection, literary, 13–14, 51, 58
Signature, 37, 38, 82–83
"Signature, Event, Context," 78, 84
Signsponge, 6, 16, 193n7, 197n59
Silesius, Angelus, 168, 176
Singular work, singularity: archiving gesture of, 31; Beckett/Derrida differences on, 21, 139; coexistence with law, 66; critique gesture of, 31; Deleuze/Derrida differences on, 215n95; Derrida on Barthes, 59–65; gathering, condensing properties of, 31–32, 57; Hegelian vs. literary totalizing, 198n15; inevitable loss of, 52; and iterability, 65–70, 78, 198n17; later Derrida's interest in, 37; and law, 184; as odyssey, 68–70; origins of, 57–58; points of transaction, 118–39, 140–60, 161–91; preserving, 32, 61; and production of law, 39; totalizing, 30–31, 35; uniqueness of, 63; and universality of the literary work, 14–21; and univocity, 215n105; validity and context of, 80; works-events, 55

Skepticism, 72
Socrates, 194–95n17
Solitary mental life, 125
Solitary speech, 126–28
Space, 107
Speculation, speculative, 39–40
Speech-act theory, 78–81, 207–8n18
Speech and Phenomena, 125
Spinoza, Benedict de, 6, 99–102, 211n29, 212n37, 212n44
Sponging, 33, 122
Structuralism, 69, 214n76
Studium, in *Camera Lucida*, 65–66
Subject, 119–22, 125, 217n18
Subjectile, 118, 130–33, 219n47
Substitution, 109
Subtraction, in Beckett, 172–73

Tain of the Mirror, The, 40, 200–201n47, 201n48
Television plays, of Beckett, 105
That Time, 49
Thousand Plateaus, A, 47, 113
"Three Dialogues," 175–76
Time and Narrative, 133–39
Totalization, in literature, 30, 35
Transformation, 32
The Trial, 43
Trilogy, 155, 157, 199–200n33
Two Sources of Morality and Religion, 174–75
"Tyrannical Prehension," 145

Ulysses, 31, 70, 89, 175
Univocity, 93–94, 111, 215n105
Unnamable: and alter ego, 127–28; and impossibility, 135–36; and negative theology, 167–68; as penetrator, 131; as "the between," 130; and words as doors, 132
Unnamable, The: autobiographic quality of, 122–23; Badiou on, 148–49; and Derrida's issues, 122–23; discourse of, 123–29; failure of, 133; imagery of ball in, 50, 62; locating of, 129; Ricoeur on, 135–39; self-reflection in, 49; the subjectile in, 188
Unsaying, 166–67, 187, 226n14
Unwording the World: Samuel Beckett's Fiction after the Nobel Prize, 172

Via negativa, 60–61, 161, 164–68
Violence, 69, 140–42
Vladimir, 22–23

Waiting for Godot, 22–23, 167–68, 185
Watt: abstract ideas in, 169–70; backwards speaking in, 166–67; exhaustion in, 104; and obligation to express, 175–76; Perloff's reading of, 73–78; piano-tuning incident in, 155
"What Did Derrida Want of Austin?," 84
What Where, archiving in, 33
William of Ockham, 58, 215n95
Winter Garden photograph, 60–61
Wittgenstein, Ludwig, 6, 71–78
Wittgenstein's Ladder: Poetic Language and the Strangeness of the Ordinary, 7, 71
Wolosky, Shira, 166
Words: exhausting, 103–4; flow of, in *The Unnamable*, 123–29; meanings of, 75–76, 80–81; repeatability of, 90
Work-event, archiving and recording in, 32
Worm, 128–129
Worstward Ho: archiving in, 33; Badiou on, 148; Being in, 171; God in, 170; ill-saying in, 186; impasse in, 176; imperative mode of, 177–78; language in, 37, 173–74, 178–79; religious aspects of, 180–81; secrecy in, 179–80; subtraction in, 172–73; "unsaying" of, 48
Writing, 189–90, 215–16n108, 222n22–223

Yeses, of Joyce, 70, 206n47
Youdi, 143–48

Zabus, Chantal, 31
Zur Kritik der Gewalt, 140–42

Cultural Memory in the Present

Bella Brodzki, *"Can These Bones Live?" Translation, Survival, and Cultural Memory*

Sara Guyer, *Romanticism after Auschwitz*

Gerhard Richter, *Thought-Images: Frankfurt School Writers' Reflections from Damaged Life*

Alison Ross, *The Aesthetic Steering of Philosophy*

Rodolphe Gasché, *The Honor of Thinking: Critique, Theory, Philosophy*

Brigitte Peucker, *The Material Image: Art and the Real in Film*

Natalie Melas, *All the Difference in the World*

Jonathan Culler, *The Literary in Theory*

Michael G. Levine, *The Belated Witness*

Jennifer A. Jordan, *Structures of Memory*

Christoph Menke, *Reflections of Equality*

Marlène Zarader, *The Unthought Debt: Heidegger and the Hebraic Heritage*

Jan Assmann, *Religion and Cultural Memory: Ten Studies*

David Scott and Charles Hirschkind, *Powers of the Secular Modern: Talal Asad and His Interlocutors*

Gyanendra Pandey, *Routine Violence: Nations, Fragments, Histories*

James Siegel, *Naming the Witch*

J. M. Bernstein, *Against Voluptuous Bodies: Late Modernism and the Meaning of Painting*

Theodore W. Jennings, Jr., *Reading Derrida/Thinking Paul: On Justice*

Richard Rorty and Eduardo Mendieta, *Take Care of Freedom and Truth Will Take Care of Itself: Interviews with Richard Rorty*

Jacques Derrida, *Paper Machine*

Renaud Barbaras, *Desire and Distance: Introduction to a Phenomenology of Perception*

Jill Bennett, *Empathic Vision: Affect, Trauma, and Contemporary Art*

Ban Wang, *Illuminations from the Past: Trauma, Memory, and History in Modern China*

James Phillips, *Heidegger's* Volk: *Between National Socialism and Poetry*

Frank Ankersmit, *Sublime Historical Experience*

István Rév, *Retroactive Justice: Prehistory of Post-Communism*

Paola Marrati, *Genesis and Trace: Derrida Reading Husserl and Heidegger*

Krzysztof Ziarek, *The Force of Art*

Marie-José Mondzain, *Image, Icon, Economy: The Byzantine Origins of the Contemporary Imaginary*

Cecilia Sjöholm, *The Antigone Complex: Ethics and the Invention of Feminine Desire*

Jacques Derrida and Elisabeth Roudinesco, *For What Tomorrow . . . : A Dialogue*

Elisabeth Weber, *Questioning Judaism: Interviews by Elisabeth Weber*

Jacques Derrida and Catherine Malabou, *Counterpath: Traveling with Jacques Derrida*

Martin Seel, *Aesthetics of Appearing*

Nanette Salomon, *Shifting Priorities: Gender and Genre in Seventeenth-Century Dutch Painting*

Jacob Taubes, *The Political Theology of Paul*

Jean-Luc Marion, *The Crossing of the Visible*

Eric Michaud, *The Cult of Art in Nazi Germany*

Anne Freadman, *The Machinery of Talk: Charles Peirce and the Sign Hypothesis*

Stanley Cavell, *Emerson's Transcendental Etudes*

Stuart McLean, *The Event and Its Terrors: Ireland, Famine, Modernity*

Beate Rössler, ed., *Privacies: Philosophical Evaluations*

Bernard Faure, *Double Exposure: Cutting Across Buddhist and Western Discourses*

Alessia Ricciardi, *The Ends of Mourning: Psychoanalysis, Literature, Film*

Alain Badiou, *Saint Paul: The Foundation of Universalism*

Gil Anidjar, *The Jew, the Arab: A History of the Enemy*

Jonathan Culler and Kevin Lamb, eds., *Just Being Difficult? Academic Writing in the Public Arena*

Jean-Luc Nancy, *A Finite Thinking*, ed. Simon Sparks

Theodor W. Adorno, *Can One Live after Auschwitz? A Philosophical Reader*, ed. Rolf Tiedemann

Patricia Pisters, *The Matrix of Visual Culture: Working with Deleuze in Film Theory*

Andreas Huyssen, *Present Pasts: Urban Palimpsests and the Politics of Memory*

Talal Asad, *Formations of the Secular: Christianity, Islam, Modernity*

Dorothea von Mücke, *The Rise of the Fantastic Tale*

Marc Redfield, *The Politics of Aesthetics: Nationalism, Gender, Romanticism*

Emmanuel Levinas, *On Escape*

Dan Zahavi, *Husserl's Phenomenology*

Rodolphe Gasché, *The Idea of Form: Rethinking Kant's Aesthetics*

Michael Naas, *Taking on the Tradition: Jacques Derrida and the Legacies of Deconstruction*

Herlinde Pauer-Studer, ed., *Constructions of Practical Reason: Interviews on Moral and Political Philosophy*

Jean-Luc Marion, *Being Given That: Toward a Phenomenology of Givenness*

Theodor W. Adorno and Max Horkheimer, *Dialectic of Enlightenment*

Ian Balfour, *The Rhetoric of Romantic Prophecy*

Martin Stokhof, *World and Life as One: Ethics and Ontology in Wittgenstein's Early Thought*

Gianni Vattimo, *Nietzsche: An Introduction*

Jacques Derrida, *Negotiations: Interventions and Interviews, 1971–1998*, ed. Elizabeth Rottenberg

Brett Levinson, *The Ends of Literature: The Latin American "Boom" in the Neoliberal Marketplace*

Timothy J. Reiss, *Against Autonomy: Cultural Instruments, Mutualities, and the Fictive Imagination*

Hent de Vries and Samuel Weber, eds., *Religion and Media*

Niklas Luhmann, *Theories of Distinction: Re-describing the Descriptions of Modernity*, ed. William Rasch

Johannes Fabian, *Anthropology with an Attitude: Critical Essays*

Michel Henry, *I Am the Truth: Toward a Philosophy of Christianity*

Gil Anidjar, *"Our Place in Al-Andalus": Kabbalah, Philosophy, Literature in Arab-Jewish Letters*

Hélène Cixous and Jacques Derrida, *Veils*

F. R. Ankersmit, *Historical Representation*

F. R. Ankersmit, *Political Representation*

Elissa Marder, *Dead Time: Temporal Disorders in the Wake of Modernity (Baudelaire and Flaubert)*

Reinhart Koselleck, *The Practice of Conceptual History: Timing History, Spacing Concepts*

Niklas Luhmann, *The Reality of the Mass Media*

Hubert Damisch, *A Childhood Memory by Piero della Francesca*

Hubert Damisch, *A Theory of /Cloud/: Toward a History of Painting*

Jean-Luc Nancy, *The Speculative Remark: (One of Hegel's Bon Mots)*

Jean-François Lyotard, *Soundproof Room: Malraux's Anti-aesthetics*

Jan Patočka, *Plato and Europe*

Hubert Damisch, *Skyline: The Narcissistic City*

Isabel Hoving, *In Praise of New Travelers: Reading Caribbean Migrant Women Writers*

Richard Rand, ed., *Futures: Of Jacques Derrida*

William Rasch, *Niklas Luhmann's Modernity: The Paradoxes of Differentiation*

Jacques Derrida and Anne Dufourmantelle, *Of Hospitality*

Jean-François Lyotard, *The Confession of Augustine*

Kaja Silverman, *World Spectators*

Samuel Weber, *Institution and Interpretation* (Expanded Edition)

Jeffrey S. Librett, *The Rhetoric of Cultural Dialogue: Jews and Germans in the Epoch of Emancipation*

Ulrich Baer, *Remnants of Song: Trauma and the Experience of Modernity in Charles Baudelaire and Paul Celan*

Samuel C. Wheeler III, *Deconstruction as Analytic Philosophy*

David S. Ferris, *Silent Urns: Romanticism, Hellenism, Modernity*

Rodolphe Gasché, *Of Minimal Things: Studies on the Notion of Relation*

Sarah Winter, *Freud and the Institution of Psychoanalytic Knowledge*

Samuel Weber, *The Legend of Freud* (Expanded Edition)

Aris Fioretos, ed., *The Solid Letter: Readings of Friedrich Hölderlin*

J. Hillis Miller and Manuel Asensi, *Black Holes: J. Hillis Miller; or, Boustrophedonic Reading*

Miryam Sas, *Fault Lines: Cultural Memory and Japanese Surrealism*

Peter Schwenger, *Fantasm and Fiction: On Textual Envisioning*

Didier Maleuvre, *Museum Memories: History, Technology, Art*

Jacques Derrida, *Monolingualism of the Other; or, The Prosthesis of Origin*

Andrew Baruch Wachtel, *Making a Nation, Breaking a Nation: Literature and Cultural Politics in Yugoslavia*

Niklas Luhmann, *Love as Passion: The Codification of Intimacy*

Mieke Bal, ed., *The Practice of Cultural Analysis: Exposing Interdisciplinary Interpretation*

Jacques Derrida and Gianni Vattimo, eds., *Religion*

The authorized representative in the EU for product safety and compliance is:
Mare Nostrum Group
B.V Doelen 72
4831 GR Breda
The Netherlands

www.ingramcontent.com/pod-product-compliance
Lightning Source LLC
Chambersburg PA
CBHW030535230426
43665CB00010B/906